Current perspectives in nursing
Social issues and trends

VOLUME ONE

Current perspectives in nursing
Social issues and trends

MICHAEL H. MILLER, Ph.D.

Associate Professor, School of Nursing and
Department of Sociology,
Vanderbilt University,
Nashville, Tennessee

BEVERLY C. FLYNN, R.N., Ph.D.

Associate Professor, School of Nursing,
Indiana University,
Indianapolis, Indiana

The C. V. Mosby Company

Saint Louis   1977

The C. V. Mosby Company
11830 Westline Industrial Drive, St. Louis, Missouri 63141

Library of Congress Cataloging in Publication Data

Main entry under title:

Social issues and trends.

  (Current perspectives in nursing)
  Bibliography: p.
  1. Nursing—Social aspects. I. Miller, Michael H.,
1942-   II. Flynn, Beverly, 1935-
RT86.5.S63   362.1'0425   76-57746
ISBN 0-8016-3464-4

VH/VH/VH 9 8 7 6 5 4 3 2 1

Contributors

MYRTLE K. AYDELOTTE, R.N., Ph.D.

Professor, College of Nursing, University of Iowa,
Iowa City, Iowa

DORIS BLOCH, R.N., Dr. P.H.

Chief, Research Grant Section, Nursing Research Branch,
Department of Health, Education, and Welfare,
Bethesda, Maryland

GLORIA CALHOUN, R.N., M.S.N.

Lecturer in Psychiatric Nursing, School of Nursing,
Vanderbilt University,
Nashville, Tennessee

BARRY D. COHEN, M.A.

Program for Human Development Specialists,
George Peabody College,
Nashville, Tennessee

LEE DODSON, M.A.

Department of Sociology, Vanderbilt University,
Nashville, Tennessee

BEVERLY C. FLYNN, R.N., Ph.D.

Associate Professor, School of Nursing,
Indiana University,
Indianapolis, Indiana

LOIS W. GAGE, R.N., Ph.D.

Associate Director, Primary Care/Community Medicine and Professor,
School of Nursing, University of Michigan,
Ann Arbor, Michigan

v

SUSAN R. GORTNER, R.N., Ph.D.

Chief, Nursing Research, Nursing Research Branch,
Division of Nursing, Bureau of Health Manpower,
Department of Health, Education, and Welfare,
Bethesda, Maryland

STANLEY K. HENSHAW, Ph.D.

Cornell University Medical College and Cornell University—New York,
Hospital School of Nursing,
New York, New York

RICHARD M. HESSLER, Ph.D.

Associate Professor,
Department of Family and Community Medicine,
School of Medicine and Department of Sociology,
University of Missouri,
Columbia, Missouri

WILFRED E. HOLTON, Ph.D.

Assistant Professor, Department of Sociology,
Northeastern University,
Boston, Massachusetts

IDA M. MARTINSON, R.N., Ph.D.

Associate Professor and Director of Research,
School of Nursing,
University of Minnesota,
Minneapolis, Minnesota

JUDE THOMAS MAY, Ph.D.

Assistant Professor,
Department of Human Ecology and Environmental Health,
College of Health, University of Oklahoma,
Norman, Oklahoma

MICHAEL H. MILLER, Ph.D.

Associate Professor, School of Nursing and
Department of Sociology, Vanderbilt University,
Nashville, Tennessee

PETER KONG-MING NEW, Ph.D.

Professor, Department of Behavioral Science,
Faculty of Medicine and Department of Sociology,
University of Toronto,
Toronto, Ontario, Canada

VIRGINIA OHLSON, R.N., Ph.D.

Professor and Head, Public Health Nursing,
College of Nursing, University of Illinois,
Chicago, Illinois

JOYCE Y. PASSOS, R.N., Ph.D.

Professor of Nursing, Boston State College, and
Adjunct Professor, School of Nursing,
Boston University,
Boston, Massachusetts

THOMAS P. PHILLIPS, R.N., Ph.D.

Chief, Advanced Nurse Training Program,
Division of Nursing, Bureau of Health Manpower,
Department of Health, Education, and Welfare,
Bethesda, Maryland

KENNETH A. WALLSTON, Ph.D.

Associate Professor, School of Nursing and
Department of Psychology, Vanderbilt University,
Nashville, Tennessee

CAROLYN A. WILLIAMS, R.N., Ph.D.

Associate Professor, School of Nursing, and
Assistant Professor of Epidemiology,
School of Public Health,
University of North Carolina at Chapel Hill,
Chapel Hill, North Carolina

FRANK C. WILLIAMS, Ph.D.

Associate Professor, Department of Philosophy,
Eastern Kentucky University,
Richmond, Kentucky

JEAN WOOD, R.N., Ph.D.

Associate Professor, Public Health Nursing,
College of Nursing, University of Illinois,
Chicago, Illinois

Preface

This book focuses on social issues in five major topical areas of nursing: ethics, research, health care delivery, organization, and education. These areas are delineated not only because they are strategic to a thorough understanding of the nursing profession, but also because they constitute areas in which the most changes are occurring.

As a text examining the social issues and trends in nursing, the perspective is decidedly one that seeks knowledge about nurses as social beings. It focuses, for example, on nurses in groups and on their relationship to one another, as well as on their relationship to other groups (for example, patients, physicians, housekeeping personnel, administration). It attempts to make known how these particular relationships arise, why they persist, dissolve, and/or change; and it examines the nature of nurses' customs and values and their institutions (for example, professional associations, schools, places of employment) and the patterns of stability and changes they undergo.

The organizing philosophy of this text is that health care is a social system that may be studied on varying levels. On one level, the patient interacts with the health care provider, who may be the nurse, physician, social worker, occupational therapist, and so forth. On another level, the health care agency or organization may be studied. Such an analysis may include the interaction between and within professional disciplines and the personnel hierarchy that exists in the provision of health care. Still another level is the community's health, which is conceived as the neighborhood, city, region, or state. On a final level is the nation's health. As the unit of analysis broadens, the issues involved in the delivery of health care become more complex. However, on every level there are physical, psychological, sociological, professional, and legal factors that are influencing the delivery of care to the people.

As these forces interact and compete with one another, changes occur not only within health care but also within nursing. These changes are manifested in the following examples: the establishment of the nurse practitioner role, the establishment of nursing unions as a political force in obtaining improved personnel benefits, the establishment of ethical standards, the focused efforts of nurses to create professional organizations sensitive to their needs, attempts to evaluate educational programs, changes in the issues the American Nurses' Association is addressing, recognition of the new needs of nurses in caring for special kinds of patients and clients, and the establishment of a joint practice commission between nursing and medicine.

This volume has the advantage of including many authors who have expertise in the analysis of the various forces influencing innovations and change in nursing. Their experiences and thoughts range across the numerous levels of the health care system, as conceptualized by the editors. The framework of health care as a social system integrates the various sections of this book. Key to this framework is its interdisciplinary focus. The complexity of change in nursing requires the exploration of issues by authors who view nursing from both outside and within the profession.

The topics and issues discussed in this book are timely and should be relevant not only to practicing nurses but also to consumers and providers of health care, educators, researchers, administrators, legislators, and others. Students in the health field, particularly nursing, should find this volume stimulating and thought provoking as they engage in living the future of nursing.

Michael H. Miller
Beverly C. Flynn

Contents

Current perspectives in nursing
Social issues and trends

part I
ETHICAL ISSUES

In recent years, the federal government has dramatically increased its involvement in ensuring the safety and well-being of all human subjects on whom research is to be conducted. In addition to developing ethical standards regarding the use of human subjects in research, the government has established a review procedure designed to evaluate whether or not research meets the accepted ethical standards. All grant and contract proposals seeking federal funds for both research and training must pass the scrutiny of an ethics committee at the institution (for example, the hospital, university, state or local government agency, or professional association) sponsoring the proposal. The federal government itself has ethics committees that also review research proposals to assess the effectiveness of the institutional committees in upholding the ethical standards.

Chapters 1 and 2 address numerous ethical issues that arise in nursing research. The issues discussed, on both the macro- and microlevel, are ones that are of central concern to all persons involved in research on human subjects.

Bloch and associates discuss, from a historical perspective, the controversy concerning the protection of human subjects in research investigations. They focus on the ethical responsibility of the researcher, the federal funding body, the institutional review groups, and the federal regulatory bodies. To minimize risks and maximize benefits in research, the authors propose that researchers select only indisputable research questions, prepare strong research designs, implement pilot studies with appropriate revisions in the research protocol, and publish problems of risk uncovered in research experiences.

The authors argue that studies posing controversial research questions should be discouraged. There appears to be some danger, however, in condemning the research value of studies offering a controversial ethical perspective. Since considerable ambiguity still exists regarding the ethical standards used to assess the risk level for human subjects as well as the implications of these standards for health care research, caution should be used in correlating ethical standards and quality of research. The problem is that many so-called ethically disputed research questions may not be posed, or those that are posed will not receive research funding. The history of health care in the United States is replete with research that was at one time controversial; however, much of it was also highly important.

Most discussions of biomedical ethical problems concentrate on ethical decisions made in the context of providing care for individual patients. As more health care is provided on the aggregate level, such as in health maintenance organizations, attention is warranted for examining the ethical issues in decision making at the group (aggregate) or program level. Drs. Frank and Carolyn Williams, in Chapter 1, focus on the various biomedical principles relevant to such decision making.

We do not see group and individual ethical principles as mutually exclusive. In fact, decisions made at the group level can influence the "degrees of freedom" available for decision making at the individual level. Until effective aggregate-level decision-making policy can be developed, the Williamses propose that consideration be given to maximization of benefits (greatest good for the greatest number) and distributive justice (fairness in allocation of resources, opportunities, and benefits).

1 Ethical issues in health care policy

FRANK C. WILLIAMS
CAROLYN A. WILLIAMS

To date, most discussions of biomedical ethical problems have focused on ethical decisions made in the context of providing care for individual patients. In this context, a number of general ethical principles have been identified and examined (Campbell, 1971; Frankena, 1975). Much less attention, however, has been given to considering ethical principles relevant to decision making at the group (aggregate) or program level. Indeed, there seems to be much less awareness that group-level decisions are an appropriate focus for ethical examination.

Despite the fact that some of the same ethical principles that provide guidance in individual patient decisions are also useful in group-level decision making, their application at the group level is fraught with additional complexities. Therefore, such application cannot be considered as a simple extension of the principles relevant for the one-to-one clinical approach. The discussion below begins with a brief exposition of the distinction between decisions made at the individual level and those involving aggregates, in order to support the importance of giving serious thought to the ethical issues related to group-level decision making. The next section surveys the major approaches to policy decisions emphasized by ethicists. Here the discussion centers on the ways in which the bases for action in individual-level decisions overlap with and differ from the bases appropriate for group-level decisions. We conclude that explicit attention to ethical considerations should be a necessary component of health policy decision making.

Basic professional education in nursing and medicine has focused primarily on preparing professionals to make decisions at the individual patient level. That is, the emphasis of the educational process has been to develop graduates who are competent in the use of various techniques of assessing the health status of individuals defined as patients (or clients), in making appropriate decisions regarding the care that the patient should receive, and in seeing that such care is provided by themselves or by others. The transition to defining problems and proposing solutions at the group level appears to be difficult for many health professionals. Although the integration of community health concepts into basic nursing programs might be expected to facilitate such thinking, in many curricula integration of these concepts has focused on individualistic approaches as opposed to aggregate levels of defining problems and means of assessing impact. Thus, the problem of shifting from one level of anlysis to the other remains. To put it bluntly, those responsible for undergraduate programs in nursing (unfortunately, this is also true for many Master's level programs in community nursing) have conceptualized the provision of direct care services to individuals and families in the extrahospital situation as community health practice. Moreover, in so doing they have either completely neglected or deemphasized the crux of community health practice: the focus on the health of subgroups in the population (aggregates), such as individuals who have common characteristics, whether or not they reside in a defined community. The practical result is that graduates are not familiar with group-level decision making, nor are they explicitly aware of the relationship between decisions made at the aggregate level and those made at the level of the patient-provider encounter.

Before the contemporary relevance of considering decision making at the group level is noted, it may be useful to elaborate further what is meant by the term *group*. A *group* is not here defined sociologically, as an interacting entity (although in some cases it may be); to avoid confusion with socially functioning groups, use of the term "aggregate" may be more appropriate. A group or aggregate consists of individuals who hold in common one or more personal or environmental characteristics. Some characteristics may place those possessing them at an increased risk of developing given health problems (for example, hypertension in relation to the incidence of subsequent stroke and coronary heart disease) or at risk of having a lower potential for dealing effectively with a variety of circumstances (for example, individuals living alone who are discharged from an institution to home). In prevalence surveys, other characteristics may be found to be positively associated with the actual presence of specified problems (for example, hypertension is more prevalent in black males than in white males).

As one takes a closer look at the health care sector, it is obvious that people who share common characteristics can be aggregated at many levels. For certain health-related decisions (for example, those associated with Medicare) individuals throughout the country are grouped. For other decisions aggregation may occur at local levels of government. Within institutions such as hospitals or agencies such as a health department or visiting nursing service, aggregate decisions are made when criteria are established delineating the people who can be admitted to service and, on occasion, the specific types of care that can be provided. Individual health care providers who work in the context of such programs may be tacitly aware that aggregate-level decisions represent a framework within which their own individual client-oriented decisions are made. In other words, the individual provider may realize that his "degrees of freedom" in individual clinical decision making are influenced by agency or institutional policy.

From an epidemiological perspective, it can be argued that health care delivery might be more effective in prevention, early identification, and solution of health problems if more serious attention were given to a more effective integration of aggregate and clinically oriented decision making. The need to give more thought to aggregate approaches and how they interface with the practice of clinicians is evident in view of the currently increased emphasis on new strategies for planning care (National Health Planning and Resources Development Act of 1974, Public Law 93-641), delivering and financing care (Health Maintenance Organizations and National Health Insurance), and evaluating care (Professional Standards Review Organizations).

Although not completely independent, the skills and biomedical data base needed at the two levels of decision making are different. This has led in recent years to an increasing recognition of the contribution that those competent in disciplines such as biostatistics and epidemiology can make in providing information for decision making. But if we are to have clinically viable programs directed to the most appropriate subgroups of the population, the need for close communication and collaborative efforts between clinicians and those disciplines concerned with aggregates is essential.

As the pressure to organize health care delivery mounts, the practice of clinicians will doubtless be increasingly influenced by aggregate-level decisions. In order for these aggregate decisions to be made in the light of the soundest clinical information available, it is necessary that clinicians have some input. Therefore, it seems timely to suggest that more attention be given to the ethical issues related to group-level decision making so that clinicians might have an appreciation of the context in which their own practice occurs and can contribute more knowledgeably to the process of policy decision making. For those charged with primary responsibility for group-level decisions, the appropriateness of considering ethical issues related to such decision making is obvious. The competing interests, rights, and well-being of large numbers of people are involved, and deciding among them is a difficult and complex task. Thus, some explicit consideration of ethical guidelines that are relevant to such decisions may be useful both to the administrators and policy makers who utlimately must make the decisions and to the clinicians who must practice within the limits set by them.

INDIVIDUAL-LEVEL PRINCIPLES

Health providers, when treating patients on a one-to-one basis, unavoidably encounter issues of right and wrong, good and bad. Since the ethical aspects of group-level decisions are often less obvious (or less easily appreciated), it is instructive to first take note of some of the major ethical principles or guidelines that apply at the individual level and that can be extended to the group level.

When a health provider deals with patients on a one-to-one basis, the *maximization of benefits* principle is an ethical guideline of major importance; that is, the provider is obligated to do what is best—what will be most beneficial, or least detrimental—for the patient. Following this principle in particular cases is, of course, no easy matter. The risks and benefits of alternative treatments must be weighed, and decisions must be made in the face of uncertain outcomes. But the point to be emphasized is simply that the principle of maximizing benefits for the patient is an obviously relevant and important ethical guideline. To neglect it and to treat patients merely on the basis of what is most convenient or profitable for the provider would be clearly unethical and a violation of professional responsibility.

In recent years another ethical guideline has come into prominence: *respect for patients' rights.* The rights receiving attention include the right to give informed consent to medical procedures (which includes the right to refuse treatment) and the right to confidentiality. Again, determination of precisely what actions by providers are required in order to avoid violating patients' rights is frequently a complex task; but what is important here is that a provider who acts without due concern for patient rights is violating a fundamental ethical guideline.

These two principles—maximization of benefits and respect for patient rights—can occasionally come into conflict. A provider might decide, for instance, that it is for a patient's maximum benefit that his family be fully informed of his medical condition, yet the patient may refuse to approve of their being informed. In such a case, the provider can respect the patient's right to confidentiality only at the expense of not doing what, in his or her best judgment, will maximally benefit the patient. There is also the possibility that if a patient is adequately informed of the nature of certain procedures that the provider believes he desperately requires, he will refuse to consent to them. In this situation, a judgment must be made as to which of the two principles is the more binding. The two principles mutually limit each other. Sometimes one will take priority, sometimes the other. Legal restrictions that make certain medications available only by prescription do, in fact, infringe on patients' rights to freedom of choice (at the risk of their own health); here the considerable benefits gained (or harm prevented) by such legislation are sufficient to justify the limitation placed on the right of free choice. But in cases of surgical procedures recommended for competent adults, the patients' right to refuse treatment takes priority even though it is clear that the surgery would be the most beneficial treatment. Here, the maximization of benefits is limited by respect for patients' rights. There seem to be no procedures that are guaranteed to resolve cases of conflict. This fact, though sobering, is no cause for despair. Moral judgments made after careful, although inconclusive, reflection on the relevant ethical guidelines are more likely to be correct than those made in the absence of such reflection.

We do not claim that the two ethical guidelines just mentioned are the only ones of importance in making moral judgments at the individual level; nor do we pretend that this brief discussion has adequately explored and elaborated them. Rather, we have pointed out two obvious and important ethical guidelines for those health providers who wish to make responsible decisions in caring for individual patients. To act without due regard for them is to act irresponsibly. The reason for emphasizing them here is that they have important applications to aggregate-level decisions, yet their relevance and importance at the aggregate level is less easily noticed and appreciated.

AGGREGATE-LEVEL PRINCIPLES

The application of these principles at the group level is admittedly more complex than at the one-to-one level, since the interests and rights of many people must be considered; thus, the possibilities for conflict are multiplied. Not only is conflict between the principle of maximization of benefits and that of respect for rights still possible; but now, in addition, each principle can in a sense conflict with itself. In other words, it may be impossible to maximize benefits for some people except by reducing the benefits to, or even inflicting harm upon, other people. And, in order to avoid infringing upon the rights of some, it may be necessary to restrict or deny the rights of others. In these situations, some sort of "balancing" of the rights and interests of the various persons involved is required.

Maximization of benefits

In a health context, the maximization of benefits at the group level requires that groups as wholes be considered as "patients." The proper "treatment," then, is that course of action which will yield the greatest benefits for the group as a whole. It is this approach (often called "utilitarianism") that lies behind the currently prominent cost/benefit approaches to health policy and that is the basis for the demand that careful pilot studies be conducted prior to the widespread introduction of new medical practices (Hiatt, 1975). When consistently followed, this approach sometimes leads to decisions that are at odds with established practices. For instance, in a developing country maximization of benefits might well dictate that available health funding be devoted to improving nutrition and sanitation, instead of to building and staffing hospitals, for given almost any reasonable way of measuring benefits (morbidity, mortality, or economic gains), the former approach would produce the greater benefits. To take another example, in the United States the strikingly low maternal and neonatal mortality rates found in an isolated, rural, high-risk population served by the Frontier Nursing Service suggest that for similar populations, greater benefits might result from an emphasis on mobile nurse midwives, rather than on the more common physician-oriented, hospital-centered approach to care (Browne and Isaacs, 1976). In addition, if intervention trials confirm preliminary indications that community-based antihypertensive therapy is effective in reducing not only blood pressure but also the morbidity and mortality associated with it (Borhani and others, 1974), then greater benefits might be gained by shifting funds toward such programs and away from curative approaches such as the development of implantable artificial hearts, which even if successful would benefit far fewer people.

An objection often raised to the maximization of benefits approach to ethical choice is that human life, health, and illness cannot be quantified and compared. That is, monetary costs may be measured and benefits in terms of discounted future earnings may be estimated, but moral costs and benefits are of a different order and hence incommensurable. There is a point to this objection. For example, genuine misgivings arise when one is asked to assign quantitative values to a shorter but healthier life as compared with a longer one plagued by chronic illness (although even here the economist's measure of discounted future earnings may have some use as a rough indicator) (Fuchs, 1974). It is similarly impossible to quantify human pain, joy, suffering, and happiness; and it is perhaps pointless to attempt to make fine distinctions between the "amounts" of harms and benefits to which various policies would lead. But the objection is overstated. In many cases it is possible to make reasonable comparative judgments. No estimate of the value—financial or otherwise—of a human life is needed in order to conclude that a program that will lead to a greater reduction in mortality rates is morally preferable to one that will lead to a lesser reduction. Likewise, if thorough pilot studies indicate that the only significant difference in two different medical procedures for treating the same disease is that one procedure is far more expensive than the other, one need not hesitate to conclude that the more expensive treatment should be discouraged, and the money and resources saved put to better use in other ways. It should be noted that comparison of the costs and benefits of differing procedures and programs involves examining the characteristics of defined aggregates, for example, the mean survival time for cancer patients receiving a certain type of treatment and the cost per year for each patient treated.

Respect for patient rights

At the group level the principle of respect for patient rights is complicated by the fact that there are two significantly different kinds of rights—negative and positive rights. Many individual rights that come readily to mind—the right of free speech, or the right to do as one wishes with one's property, or the right to privacy —are rights that require that other persons *refrain* from interfering in various ways with the one who has the right. In order to respect someone's right to privacy, no positive action need be taken. Instead, only the "negative" action of refraining from snooping or revealing confidential information is required. Hence, rights of this sort are categorized as negative. However, other rights require positive action on the part of some other person or persons if the one who has the right is to exercise it. For example, if a patient is to exercise his right to informed consent to some experimental procedure, investigators or health providers must take the positive action of giving him sufficient information about the procedure for him to make an intelligent choice. If a handicapped child is to exercise her right to receive appropriate special treatment, then some person or agency must take the positive step of making the special treatment facilities available. Thus, those rights whose exercise requires definite action by persons other than the one who has the right are categorized as positive.

In recent times increasing attention has been focused on positive rights—the right to education, to certain social services, to some minimal level of financial security, and especially the right to health care. When health care is viewed as a right, it is clear that in order for a person to exercise this right, there must be other persons or agencies who take positive action and see that the required health care is provided.

There are no clear criteria for determining just what level of services is due people as a matter of positive right. Despite this difficulty, several considerations seem relevant and useful. First, the things to which people have a positive right are relative to the degree of affluence of a society: the more prosperous the society, the greater the extent of positive rights. In an advanced western society with annual food surpluses, it is reasonable to conclude that everyone has a right to a nutritionally adequate and balanced diet; but in a society with chronic food shortages, food rights might be appropriately limited to the level necessary for survival. Second, those things to which people have a right should fall into the category of *needs,* rather than merely benefits, wants, or demands. What one needs can be thought of as something the denial of which would result in not mere dissatisfaction or inconvenience, but definite harm. For instance, in American society (though perhaps not in certain other societies) it would be definitely harmful to a person to deny him the facilities required for him to obtain a high school education; but to fail to provide the facilities to make postgraduate training in a given field available to anyone who wishes it would be merely failing to provide certain benefits. Failure to provide for needs is tantamount to denying people the opportunity to utilize their abilities to achieve for themselves a decent level of existence.

Obviously, some health services are due people by positive right. Equally obviously, there are limits to the right to health care, both because our society is not capable of providing all of the available kinds of health care to all people and because not all of the available medical services fit into the category of needs. Most of the current debate about health care can be seen as focusing on these two limitations. How much of our society's resources—money, manpower, and educational facilities—should we devote to the provision of health services? Is the absence of particular services such as dental care, psychological counseling, elective surgery, or tranquilizers so damaging that they should be made available to everyone as a matter of basic rights? Regardless of where the limits are set concerning the extent of the right to health care, there will be conflicts among the group-level guidelines of maximization of benefits and respect for rights. For instance, some biomedical research that might bring considerable benefits to patients in general may be restricted if patients' rights to informed consent in experimental procedures are duly respected. In some cases, full information about the experimental procedure may make it more difficult to find patients who will consent to be subjects; in other cases, fully informed consent may influence the participants' behavior and thus render study results invalid. Such circumstances involve a conflict between maximizing benefits and respecting positive rights.

Conflict may also exist between the positive rights of different groups. For example, victims of catastrophic illnesses often *need* very expensive treatment that is not widely available. Yet the expenditure of resources necessary to make such treatment available in all cases would unquestionably hinder the provision of other kinds of care to other people whose claims, in terms of positive rights, are no less substantial. Here there is a conflict between the positive rights of different groups. Additional conflicts may arise in respect to negative rights when families have a negative right to decide for themselves the number of children they will have, and consequently, in the light of the painful facts of the population explosion, this right must be denied or restricted in order to maximize benefits (or minimize harm) for society in general (Leach, 1972). If seriously ill or injured patients have a positive right to blood transfusions, then under conditions of scarcity there may be a conflict with the negative rights of others to refuse to contribute their blood.

Distributive justice

Given the complex conflicts that inevitably arise when policies of action are viewed from the moral perspective, what kinds of guidelines for resolving the conflicts are reasonable or even possible? Since benefits cannot be maximized for everyone, and since all of the rights (both positive and negative) of all the people concerned—rights that we may agree to in the abstract—cannot be granted or respected, what principles are there that will ensure that the fairest or most just distribution of goods and services will be achieved? The search for such principles or guidelines has traditionally fallen under the rubric of *distributive justice,* a subject that has no equivalent among individual-level principles, because it is specifically concerned with the ethical problems that arise in relation to groups of people.

It is commonplace to note that justice requires that equals should be treated equally, and unequals unequally. But since no persons are either equal or unequal (similar or dissimilar) in every respect, this might be better stated: Justice requires that those who are equal in relevant respects should be treated equally and that those who are unequal in relevant respects should be treated unequally. To emphasize the negative: "Injustice is done when individuals who are alike in every relevant respect (not in absolutely every respect) are treated differently, or when individuals who are different in some relevant respect are treated alike" (Feinberg, 1973, p. 100). To illustrate, it is unjust to give voting rights to one group and to deny them to another, when the members of both groups are equal with respect to citizenship (regardless of how they may differ in other ways); those who are equally citizens should be treated equally insofar as voting rights are concerned. In employment situations it is unjust to give equal levels of responsibility and pay to those who are unequal in training and competence; those who are unequal in employable skills and training should be treated unequally insofar as compensation and responsibility are concerned.

In order for considerations relating to justice to be serviceable as guidelines for actual decision making, there must be some specification of the similarities and differences among people that are relevant to the decision-making context. The usual approach is to try to find some characteristic(s) that can fill the place of X in the following schema: The more of X that a person has, the greater is his fair share of the thing being distributed. Proposals about what X should be tend to fall into one of four categories: need, achievement (in a given field of endeavor), contribution to society, or effort. Different choices for X will often lead to rather different conclusions about what social arrangements are compatible with the demands of justice. However, when the "goods and services" under consideration involve health care, the choice of X is at least somewhat less problematic. Feinberg, after noting that characteristics such as race, sex, I.Q., or hereditary caste are inappropriate as bases for discrimination among individuals in the distribution of social benefits because they are differences over which the people involved have no control, says:

> Differences in a given respect are *relevant* for the aims of distributive justice, then, only if they are differences for which their possessors can be held responsible; properties can be the grounds of just discrimination between persons only if those persons had a *fair opportunity* to acquire or avoid them (Feinberg, 1973, p. 108).

To the extent that one's state of health is a result of genetic factors, fixed environmental factors, lack of access to information, or lack of suitable health care facilities, it can be viewed as something for which one cannot be held responsible. Thus, it would seem that, for most health care resources, the relevant characteristic for deciding on distribution is *need;* it would be unjust to make significantly different levels of health care available to persons whose health needs are the same, or to make the same level of health care available to persons who are not equally needy. Recall, however, that needs are to be distinguished from mere dissatisfactions and inconveniences, and also from wants and demands. A need is something the denial of which would be positively harmful to a person; it is something without which he would not have the opportunity to enjoy a minimally decent level of existence. In practice, it is extremely difficult to specify where needs end and wants begin or to divide lesser from greater needs. These difficulties, however, do not render the principle of distributive justice useless in the context of health care decisions at the group level, for at least two reasons. First, approximate justice is preferable to none at all; and second, it is sometimes quite possible to recognize and attempt to correct clear cases of unjust distributions of resources even though one may be unable to say exactly what sort of distribution would be in accordance with "perfect justice." The meaning of the principle of distributive justice in the health care context is simply the maxim that preference should be given to those groups who are more needy. Indicators of greater need would include higher prevalence of or greater risk for contracting a given health problem. For instance, an intervention program for the control of hypertension would be, by this principle, more appropriately aimed at predominantly black than predominantly white populations, since blacks are at significantly higher risk for hypertension.

An excellent example of the application of the principle of distributive justice to the problem of national health insurance has been provided by Jonsen and Butler (1975). Their analysis suggests that a plan involving deductibles and co-insurance, combined with free care for the poverty-stricken, would meet the requirements of justice better than certain alternative approaches because it would concentrate medical assistance on two groups whose health care needs are unusually great: the very sick and the very poor. Taking a similar approach, Davis (1975) shows by a very careful analysis of the distribution of services under the present Medicare system that elderly persons with the poorest health receive the least assistance and that differences in the levels of care provided are correlated with irrelevant factors such as income, race, and geography. She then makes specific recommendations for changes in Medicare policies that would tend to rectify the inequities by achieving higher correlations between services and needs.

CONCLUSIONS

In summary, three ethical guidelines have been discussed that apply to group-level decisions. Two of them—maximization of benefits and respect for rights (both positive and negative)—are extensions of ethical principles that are familiar at the individual level of decision making. The third, distributive justice, is unique to group-level decisions, since it is applicable precisely when the decisions to be made essentially involve consideration of the interests and rights of members of groups. No attempt has been made to rank the principles in any order of priority; there is no formula that will assign the proper weight to be given to each in case they do not all point toward the same choice. Nonetheless, responsible decision making at the group level should involve awareness of and attention to all three. This can be facilitated by rephrasing the principles into questions that can be explicitly considered prior to decisions:

1. Maximization of benefits: Will the envisioned course of action result in as many benefits (or as little harm) to as many people as alternative possibilities would?
2. Respect for rights: To what extent will the envisioned course of action either respect or infringe upon people's rights (both positive and negative)?
3. Distributive justice: Will the envisioned course of action give preference to those whose health needs are greater?

It should be emphasized that these questions cannot be adequately answered simply by taking a few minutes to reflect on them. They require careful consideration of the details of both the envisioned course of action and of possible alternative courses of action, and this in turn typically involves the organized collection and analysis of data. In order to predict who will be benefited or harmed, target populations must be selected, demographic and epidemiological data collected, and probable outcomes (both beneficial and detrimental) estimated; these items must then be compared with similar items for alternative courses of action. "Alternative courses of action" include not only maintaining the status quo but also significant ways of modifying the program or policy under consideration, as well as entirely different uses to which the available resources could be put.

To determine the effect of a program on people's rights, attention must be focused on considerations such as data collection procedures, the uses that will be made of the data, and the persons who will have access to the data. If such matters are considered, program procedures can be evaluated in terms of the rights of privacy, informed consent, confidentiality, and freedom of information. Finally, assessing health needs obviously requires attention to data at the group level (for example, prevalence and incidence data), as well as estimates of the relative seriousness of the health problems under considerations.

Clearly, the ethical aspects of group-level decisions cannot be intelligently considered in a vacuum any more than the financial, legal, administrative, or purely medical aspects can be. It is common for the nonethical (not unethical!) aspects of group-level decisions to be given careful, explicit, and detailed attention. It is no less appropriate for the ethical aspects to be given similar attention and to carry at least equal weight in decision making. In the area of health care almost any decision that will affect groups of people has implications in terms of benefits, rights, and just distributions, and is thus an appropriate subject for ethical reflection prior to action.

REFERENCES

Borhani, N. O., Labarthe, D., Remington, R., and Tyroler, H. A.: The control of elevated blood pressure in the community; an epidemiological perspective, Heart & Lung **3:**477, 1974.

Browne, H. E., and Isaacs, G.: The frontier nursing service; the primary care nurse in the community hospital, Am. J. Obstet. Gynecol. **124:**14, 1976.

Campbell, A. V.: Moral dilemmas in medicine, New York, 1971, Longman, Inc.

Davis, K.: Equal treatment and unequal benefits; the Medicare program, health and society, Milbank Mem. Fund Q. **53:**449, 1975.

Feinberg, J.: Social philosophy, Englewood Cliffs, N.J., 1973, Prentice-Hall, Inc.

Frankena, W. K.: Ethics, ed. 2, Englewood Cliffs, N.J., 1975, Prentice-Hall, Inc.

Fuchs, V.: Who shall live? Health, economics and social change, New York, 1974, Basic Books, Inc., Publishers.

Hiatt, H. H.: Protecting the medical commons; who is responsible? N. Engl. J. Med. **293:**235, 1975.

Jonsen, A. R., and Butler, L. H.: Public ethics and policy making, Hastings Cent. Rep. **5:** 19, Aug. 1975.

Leach, G.: The biocrats. Middlesex, England, 1972, Penguin Books, Ltd.

2 Protection of human research subjects

DORIS BLOCH
THOMAS P. PHILLIPS
SUSAN R. GORTNER

> It would be easier in nursing, or in journalism, or in life
> not to struggle with ethical issues. But the search for moral values is part
> of what makes one human. Respecting the rights of others in their
> search also makes one humane.
>
> *Thelma M. Schorr, R.N.*

RESEARCH—HOPE AND HAZARD

Of all living things, man is the most rational in his approach to reality. Although his degree of success in understanding and dealing with his surroundings has varied from era to era, he has progressed from being defenseless and helpless in coping with the elements to the almost incredible status of traveler in outer space. He has managed to ferret out the secrets of life about him and has moved to structure his surroundings according to his own needs and ambitions. Having successfully provided for the basic needs of shelter and food, he has shifted his emphasis to improving the quality of his life and the stability of his health.

Man's particular gift of rationality allows him to approach health concerns and questions in more than a passive way. He need not merely watch helplessly as disease and disability take their toll. He has learned that he is able to provoke physiological and psychological responses in other human beings and that he can actually witness anatomical and physiological phenomena through surgical procedures. Such capability, while exciting and essential for health protection and investigation, poses certain mental and physical threats to the people who are the research subjects.

In their pursuit of science, it is possible that researchers may overlook the rights of human subjects, or worse yet, may knowingly ignore them. Moreover, scientists may sincerely differ in their conceptions and interpretations of such rights.

Over the years there has always been an element of concern about the protection of human subjects; but perhaps only since the second World War has the public at large been aware of the danger that respect for human beings may be subordinated to the goals of science.

The Nuremberg trials of military war criminals in the mid-1940's focused international attention on such disregard. Testimony and documents relative to the case of the United States vs. Karl Brandt, confirm, for example, that: (1) Poisoned food was administered to some prisoners at the Buchenwald concentration camp, and others were shot with poisoned bullets. Those subjects who did not die as an immediate consequence of this kind of treatment were killed to allow study at autopsy. (2) At Dachau, prisoners were locked in low-pressure chambers to determine the effects of flying at high altitude. Detailed records were kept of the behavior and reactions of dying subjects. (3) At Ravensbrueck, humans were infected with streptococci, gas gangrene, and *Clostridium tetani* in studies testing the therapeutic effectiveness of sulfanilamide (Katz, 1972, pp. 292-306).

The Nuremberg examples epitomize the misuse of human subjects to whom no benefit was intended and who were compelled to serve as living pieces of laboratory equipment; we shall have more to say about this part of human history and its subsequent influence on our code of morality for human research.

A number of studies carried out in this country in recent years have sparked discussion within the scientific community, the public, and the Congress about the rights of research subjects.

Early in 1967, for example, considerable publicity was accorded a study at the Willowbrook State School, an institution for retarded children on Staten Island, where hepatitis had been endemic. It became known that over an 11-year period Willowbrook residents had been injected with live hepatitis virus. As hepatitis proceeded to reach epidemic proportions in the school, newly admitted children were almost certain to become infected. Consequently, the physicians responsible for the study removed certain newly admitted children to a special unit, injected them with the hepatitis virus, and continued in their observations of the disease. At one point, the only available beds for newly admitted residents were on the research unit, and thus, admission implied in a sense coercion as a research subject (Studies with children, 1967, p. 1).

Certain scientists and members of an incensed public charged that there was no possible justification for giving "a disease to a child in order to study the disease" (Studies with Children, 1967, p. 1). The question at issue was whether experimentation on an individual, not for his own benefit, but for that of patients in general, could be justified. Concerned people also questioned whether a parent had the right to consign a child for a medical experiment. The proponents of the Willowbrook study countered that it was to the child's advantage to be injected and treated in a controlled situation; that if the child contracted the disease naturally, the condition might remain undetected and untreated. The researchers also felt that the experimentally induced cases of hepatitis were generally less severe than the natural cases.

Earlier in the 1960s, an experiment at the Jewish Chronic Disease Hospital in Brooklyn had resulted in a series of court cases. Scientists at that institution had injected live cancer cells into patients who were terminally ill with diseases other than cancer, in an effort to determine whether these cells would be rejected as had been the case in previous work involving patients terminally ill with cancer. These patients were not told the nature of the substance they were receiving. Most of the patients did reject these cells; however, some died of their terminal illnesses before it was certain that rejection had actually occured (Cancer Studies, 1964, p. 551).

The research itself was not at issue, for there was little question as to the intrinsic value of the study; at issue, however, was the evident disregard of the patient's rights, the denial of information essential to aware and intelligent participation as a research subject.

The Board of Regents of the University of the State of New York took the view that the two physicians primarily responsible for the study should suffer suspension of license to practice medicine. The suspension was nullified, however, by a subsequent decision to place these physicians on probation (Katz, 1972, p. 62). It is also interesting to note that, although these physicians were adjudged "guilty of fraud or deceit in the practice of medicine and of unprofessional conduct in the practice of medicine," one of them was named president of the American Association for Cancer Research within 3 years (Katz, 1972, p. 65).

Just how much of our current research continues to place the rights of human subjects in jeopardy is difficult to determine. Even thoughtful and responsible persons seem to take differing views. Dr. Donald Chalkley, who heads the Office for Protection from Research Risks within the National Institutes of Health, has expressed the view that there is little unethical human research now in progress in this country (Human Experimentation, 1973, p. 45). On the other hand, a panel appointed by the Department of Health, Education, and Welfare to investigate the Tuskegee Syphilis Study reported that federal officials "are probably the last persons to hear of any infractions once they have occurred, and then only when, as in the Tuskegee Study, they are of major proportions" (Tuskegee Syphilis Study Ad Hoc Advisory Panel, 1973, p. 36).

Barber and his associates reported on a major national survey of institutions involved in biomedical research. As part of the project, a small sample of these institutions was studied intensively. Following these inquiries, which included interviews with scientific personnel, the investigators reported that:

1. Eight percent of their respondents had *volunteered* the information that one or more of their investigations using human subjects had *not come* before the peer review committee, which in each institution should customarily review all proposals for research on humans.
2. A small but significant proportion of respondents *would approve* hypothetical studies entailing unethical use of human subjects.
3. Those biomedical researchers who suffered failure within the social structure of scientific competition—but who were still striving to achieve success in that competition—were the most likely to be permissive with regard to the unethical use of human subjects.
4. The great majority of studies entailing relatively high risks in proportion to their therapeutic benefits used ward and/or clinic patients—not private patients—as subjects (Barber and others, 1973).

Barber and his associates were also quick to see the implications of Merton's work on competition among scientists for priority in scientific discovery and to note its certain impact on present biomedical research (Merton, 1957).

A study undertaken by Gray in a major medical center addressed the question of how and why people became research subjects. Gray concluded that, although the human subjects review committee constituted a very active, conscientious, and effective system within research institutions, it nevertheless could not guarantee that human subjects were completely and correctly informed about their research participation. He identified a host of factors that might motivate an individual to participate in a research project even without full information about its nature and attendant personal risk (Gray, 1975).

SOCIAL AND MORAL CONCERNS

Given the serious human concerns that surround the conduct of research, it is worthwhile to consider why the use of human subjects in research has become standard practice. As far back in time as we are able to probe, certain individuals have been given a mandate by their fellows to attend to that portion of societal work which relates to matters of health. In their attempts to thwart sickness, they have invoked the power of magic; they have been governed by the precepts of trial and error; subsequently—by crude experimentation—they found ways to deal more effectively with sickness, and moreover, built a body of knowledge that others regard with considerable awe. That society values the contribution of science is clearly reflected in the rewards that accrue to its practitioners. This is particularly true of the biomedical scientist, who is part of that "professional complex" which enjoys the highest kinds of monetary and status rewards.

Parsons has described this complex that exists in biomedical science and notes that its members perform in three interacting roles of researcher, practitioner, and educator within the health care arena (Parsons, 1969, p. 326). The intermeshing of three differing roles or functions within a single scientist requires him to recognize that certain activities appropriate to one of these roles may not be appropriate to the others. For example, a physician may have the obligation to prescribe medication for alleviating a patient's disability; he does not, however, have an obligation to prescribe an untried drug to further a research purpose.

Although the professional complex must accept and respect certain restraints, it nevertheless has enviable capability for advancing and accelerating health progress. Society requires and depends on its research contributions. Congress has not only provided that research shall be carried out in certain problem areas but also annually appropriates large sums for research support.

While society and Congress may mandate scientific investigation, the scientists themselves must uncover new knowledge or reaffirm old concepts through the research process. From this responsibility there follow two essential if not problematical premises: (1) that effective, conclusive biomedical research requires the use of human subjects; and (2) that only the professional complex itself—for the reason that it alone is sufficiently knowledgeable—may pass judgment on the proper use of human subjects.

The first of these two premises, although fraught with dilemma and reluctance, may be dismissed as an issue for further discussion because it essentially falls into an area of "no choice." Pellegrino has dealt with this issue:

> Every new treatment or operation ultimately must be tried for the first time in humans; every advance in knowledge of prevention and understanding of disease depends ultimately upon observation in man. Insulin, liver extract, penicillin, smallpox, and polio immunizations—all had to be evaluated in human beings, even after extensive animal trials. Society will not willingly give up these benefits, and so it permits medical research in humans (Pellegrino, 1974, p. 313).

If, then, we are convinced that biomedical research requires the use of human subjects, it becomes increasingly important to observe how the professional complex structures such research. Society does provide a basis for such structuring; it is a basis that has its roots in the value system of society itself. The value system of our particular society arises from a concern with moral issues, which in turn are tied to religious concepts. Although religious denominations and sects tend to abound, and although they differ from each other in some ways, as an entirety they represent the Judeo-Christian tradition, and it is this tradition that governs our society-wide value system.

Beecher (1970) has done a thorough job of coming to grips with value concepts; thus it will be helpful to refer to his work in this area (pp. 185-212). Beecher asserts that those moral values which relate to biomedical research have had best expression in the Roman Catholic Church. He notes that Jewish writings in this sphere are in essential agreement with the Roman Catholic Church, except that organ or tissue transplants from a living donor are never permitted by the Jewish faith, because such donation necessitates personal mutilation. Protestant ethicists, Beecher found, have been less occupied with the issue of human research subjects.

Beecher identified three concepts, which he saw as recurring consistently in the literature: (1) the Judeo-Christian view that man has been created in the image of God, that both the mind and the body were created in this image, and that both are good; (2) the concept that man is not controlled by the whims of fate, but has a free will to act and is, therefore, responsible for his actions; and (3) that it is the duty of each person to approach all others with compassion.

Basic tenets are, of course, relatively easy to set down and quote. It is considerably more difficult to make actual decisions in the realm of research morality. The solution of many research problems and their attendant ethical issues requires the concerted collaborative thinking of the very best minds. The more complex problems may never be resolved to the satisfaction of all members of society, because problems occur for which no precedent is known and also because different value systems exist side by side in our society.

Consider, for a moment, a moral question that may arise in the study of an "intrinsically evil entity." Examples of such a group might include the Mafia or, perhaps, certain medical charlatans. Should the researcher be required to seek the permission of such subjects before studying their activities? Would knowledge gained through deceiving them be of sufficient social value to justify disregard of their right to consent? How should researchers respond to the view that "the failure . . . to uncover corrupt, illegitimate, covert practices . . . because of the supposed prohibition of professional ethics [is] tantamount to supporting such practices?" (Galliher, 1973, p. 96).

Although an answer completely satisfactory to all will continue to elude us now and in the future, society must persist in its pursuit of satisfactory criteria on which to make ethical decisions.

GUIDELINES AND REGULATIONS

Although codes for ethical professional behavior, such as the Hippocratic Oath, have existed for centuries (Beecher, 1970, p. 217), reexamination of such codes was inspired by the publicity attendant upon the Nuremberg trials. These trials, which occasioned world-wide moral shock, also led to the formulation of ten principles applicable to research on human subjects. The document enunciating these principles—although not problem free—has become the basis for a number of later codes, guidelines, and regulations. These principles relative to experimentation on human subjects stipulate that:

1. It is essential to have the voluntary consent of the human subject.
2. The experiment should be such as to yield results which are valuable to society and which are not attainable by other methods.
3. The experiment should be based on the results of animal experimentation and on sufficiently broad knowledge of the disease or problem under study so that the anticipated results justify the use of human subjects.
4. The experiment should be so conducted as to avoid all unnecessary physical and mental suffering and injury.
5. No experiment should be conducted when there is an *a priori* reason to believe that death or disabling injury will result.
6. The degree of risk to the patient-subject should never be so great that it is disproportionate to the humanitarian importance of the problem to be solved by the experiment.
7. Proper preparations should be made and adequate facilities provided to protect the experimental subject against even remote possibilities of injury, disability, or death.
8. The experiment should be conducted only by scientifically qualified persons.
9. During the course of the experiment the human subject should be at liberty to terminate his participation if he feels he has reached the limits of his physical or mental endurance.
10. The scientist in charge must be prepared to terminate the experiment at any point he has probable cause to believe that its continuation is likely to result in injury, disability, or death to the experimental subject (Trials, 1949, pp. 181-182).

The Declaration of Helsinki (1966) developed by the World Medical Association in 1964 has also had a major impact on research ethics. It received the endorsement of major medical associations. Marston has called it "the nearest thing to a universal ethical code" (1972, p. 16). Like the Nuremberg code, it deals with medical research; and like the Nuremberg code, its broad principles have general applicability to nonmedical research. Two types of research are addressed: therapeutic clinical research (that is, research that is justified by its anticipated therapeutic value to the patient-subject himself) and nontherapeutic clinical research (research conducted mainly to advance knowledge rather than to benefit the immediate patient-subject).

The Declaration of Helsinki, like the Nuremberg code, addresses the principle of voluntary informed consent on the part of the research subject. It emphasizes the need to weigh risks and benefits, draw on prior animal experimentation, protect the life and health of the subject, ensure qualified direction of the research project, and allow the research subjects freedom to terminate their participation. In a number of ways, however, this declaration differs from the Nuremberg code. It puts emphasis on preceding a research project with careful assessment of its risks and benefits, taking special precautions to ensure that the experimental subjects do not suffer personality changes, allowing for consent from a legally appointed guardian in the case of a subject's physical incapacity or legal incompetence, and obtaining informed consent in writing.

Many other professional groups have also developed statements of ethical principles for research on human subjects. The American Anthropological Association (1973), for example, stressed the responsibility of the research anthropologist to (1) the people under study, (2) the public, (3) the discipline of anthropology, (4) students of this discipline, (5) the research sponsor, and (6) the researcher's own and/or host government. It calls for protecting the physical, social, and psychological welfare, and the dignity and privacy of the study subjects. It further notes the importance of establishing trust between investigator and subject, of communicating the aims of the study to its subjects, and of deliberating on and openly discussing the research in terms of any possible "repercussions" and "consequences." Clearly, anthropologists regard the hazards of their research from a different standpoint than biomedical scientists: they use the terms "repercussions" and "consequences" in lieu of "risk" and "injury."

The statement of the American Psychological Association on "Ethical Principles in the Conduct of Research with Human Participants" (1973) draws on many examples from actual studies and demonstrates particular concern for the issue of deceit and concealment. It calls for (1) the weighing of scientific and humane values; (2) ethical practice on the part of the investigator and his collaborators, who must accept "parallel responsibility"; (3) informed consent; (4) honesty between researcher and subjects; (5) respect for the subjects' freedom to decline participation; (6) clear agreement between investigator and subject; (7) protection of study subjects from physical and mental discomfort, harm, and danger; (8) full clarification of the study should misconceptions arise; (9) detection and correction of undesirable research consequences; and (10) confidentiality of the research data.

The American Nurses' Association has had an ethical statement concerned with nurses involved in research and with human subjects in research at least since 1968 (American Nurses' Association, 1968, 1975). These guidelines differ from those of other groups largely in that they include discussion of issues relative to the nurse working as a practitioner or as a data collector in clinical settings where others carry out research. The 1975 guidelines address certain rights of research subjects, such as the right to self-determination, the right of freedom from intrinsic risk of injury, and the right to privacy, dignity, confidentiality, and anonymity. Further, the statement calls for the protection of nurses and others employed in research settings and suggests that they be protected by a written statement, at the time of employment, which spells out their potential involvement in research activities—a form of informed consent for the practitioner. The guidelines further state that nurses who care for research patients should be fully informed of the risks to research subjects and of ways to recognize and counteract harmful effects. It is urged that mechanisms be established whereby nurses and others employed in research settings can report violations of patients' rights, so that action can be taken to countermand such violations.

History and the study by Barber and others (1973) have demonstrated that the ethical judgment of scientists may be of uncertain reliability and have pointed out the need for outside checks on research activity. Probably the most potent influence for the protection of human subjects in biomedical and behavioral research has been exerted by federal regulation. In contrast to codes and guidelines of professional groups, such regulations have the effect of law. Margaret Mead (1969) has addressed the issue of necessity for stringent rules for federally supported research. She pointed out that the investment of public funds for an undertaking implies public support as well as public sanction and that society must take collective responsibility for that which it supports (p. 372).

To what extent the federal government should intrude upon the research endeavors of institutions and their investigators has been a matter of considerable discussion. Confrey (1968) pointed out that those who advocate a minimal level of federal responsibility assume the professional integrity of scientists; in contrast, the proponents of maximal federal control see scientists as too preoccupied with the process of discovery to adequately protect their research subjects.

Inasmuch as the Department of Health, Education, and Welfare (D.H.E.W.) is the major funding source for biomedical and behavioral research in the United States, its guidelines for the protection of human research subjects (U.S. Department of Health, Education, and Welfare, 1971, 1975) have had firm impact on institutions under whose aegis research is carried out. First issued in 1966, the guidelines spell out procedures for studies supported by the Department. Many of these institutions, however, apply these regulations to all their projects of biomedical and behavioral research in which human subjects are involved.

The regulations of the Department allow for a system of decentralized control by the recipient institutions. Under this system, each institution is required to provide peer review by an institutional human rights committee. The committee reviews all applications, which are to be submitted for D.H.E.W. support. Each recipient institution is required to provide D.H.E.W. with an "assurance," that is, a document describing its procedures for peer review, as well as with a "certification" for each application, indicating that the study's human subjects will be adequately protected.

The major mechanism presently employed to safeguard human subjects is such a multidisciplinary institutional review committee. Such committees have a great deal of authority in the approval—from a human rights standpoint—of research proposals. The funding agency, however, retains its responsibility. D.H.E.W. staff and its advisory committees may choose to disagree with the institutional committee's approval of a project and may disapprove research proposals if, in their opinion, the research subjects are not adequately protected.

National concern for the protection of human subjects in research resulted in the establishment of an eleven-member National Commission for the Protection of Human Subjects of Biomedical and Behavioral Research. Under Title II of the National Research Act of 1974 (Public Law 93-348), the Commission is instructed to carry out a comprehensive investigation and study to identify the basic ethical principles that should underlie the use of human subjects in biomedical and behavioral research, to develop guidelines to be followed in research involving humans in order to ensure that ethical principles are observed, and to make recommendations for administrative action for the protection of human subjects in federally supported biomedical and behavioral studies.

In carrying out the above broad charge, the Commission was asked to consider (1) the boundaries between research and the practice of medicine; (2) the use and assessment of risk-benefit criteria in research involving humans; (3) guidelines for the selection of humans for participation as research subjects; (4) the nature and definition of informed consent, including requirements for assuring informed consent among children, prisoners, and the institutionalized mentally infirm; and (5) mechanisms for evaluating and monitoring the performance of institutional review boards. The Commission has undertaken special study of the nature and extent of fetal research, of research on children, prisoners, and the mentally infirm, and of the use of psychosurgery. Following its recommendations and final report to the President, the Congress, and the Secretary of D.H.E.W., the Commission will disband; a National Advisory Council for the Protection of Human Subjects in Biomedical and Behavioral Research will then be established to provide advice and to make recommendations on all matters involving the protection of human subjects.

BENEFIT AND RISK IN HUMAN RESEARCH

Risk and benefit are two concerns so basic to any discussion of research with human subjects that they merit careful consideration. In the absence of risk, there would be no need for concern about the rights of human research subjects; and, clearly, without the hope for some type of benefit, there would be no reason to conduct research.

The nature of "benefit"

There are essentially two types of benefits that may derive from research: benefits to the research subjects themselves (therapeutic research) and potential future benefits to society (nontherapeutic research).

An example of therapeutic research in medicine might be the testing of a new drug that, on the basis of animal experimentation, appears to be more effective for treating leukemia than a drug in current use. Such testing is considered "therapeutic research" because of the expected benefit to the participating patient.

In the field of nursing, an example of therapeutic research might be the work by Johnson and Leventhal (1974). These investigators studied the effect of information given to patients prior to undergoing endoscopic examination. One group of patients was told about the sensations they would experience during the examination; another group was supplied information to maximize personal participation during the procedure; a third group received both types of instructions; and a fourth group of patients, which served as control, received no preexamination information. The responses of the groups were compared in terms of such variables as tranquilizers required by the study subjects, their heart rate, gagging, and time needed to pass the instrument. This study is an example of therapeutic research, because the investigators had reason to believe that specially designed preexamination information would have a beneficial effect on patients.

Moreover, if a new drug or new procedure is found on testing to be superior to an old drug or an old procedure, it is reasonable to expect that it will similarly benefit future patients with like conditions. Therapeutic research, therefore, has the potential of benefiting future patients as well as the immediate research subjects themselves. Nontherapeutic research, on the other hand, is not expected to benefit the research subjects themselves. Rather, it is hoped that it will be of benefit to individuals and/or society at some subsequent time.

To give an example of nontherapeutic research from the field of social psychology, we may refer to Milgram's work on *Obedience to Authority* (1974). A series of studies carried out to determine to what extent people will obey commands that are malevolent in purpose. The obedience research was carried out in a laboratory setting and involved volunteer subjects who were ostensibly to function as "teachers" in a learning task study. The "learner" in this study was, in fact, an experimental accomplice. The "teacher" was placed before a "shock generator" panel consisting of 30 switches, each labeled with a voltage designation ranging from "Slight Shock" to "danger: Severe Shock." The "teacher" was instructed to administer a progressively higher voltage each time the "learner" made an error. Appropriate verbal feedback from the invisible "learner"—who did not receive any shocks, of course—

was built into the study. "To our consternation," Milgram reported, "even the strongest protests from the victim did not prevent many [of the teachers] from administering the harshest punishment ordered by the experimenter" (p. 22).

This study provides an example of nontherapeutic research because it was not expected to benefit the research subjects. Rather, its aim was to learn more about human behavior and in this way be of subsequent benefit to society. It might be noted, in passing, that quite a number of Milgram's subjects felt that they had actually profited from their participation.

A good example of nontherapeutic research in nursing has been provided by Glaser and Strauss (1965), who were interested in the experiences, behaviors, and interactions of dying patients, their families, and hospital personnel. This study entailed intensive observation and interviews in the clinical setting. It was designed, not to benefit the study subjects, but to improve nursing education and practice by increasing the knowledge of the phenomenon of dying and of the behavior of persons who interact with the dying.

The nature of "risk"

The major problem in addressing the matter of risk is that it eludes simple definition. Current D.H.E.W. regulations (U.S. Department of Health, Education, and Welfare, 1975, p. 11854) define a "subject at risk" as "any individual who may be exposed to the possibility of injury, including physical, psychological, or social injury, as a consequence of participation as a subject in any research, development, or related activity which departs from the application of those established and accepted methods necessary to meet his needs, or which increases the ordinary risks of daily life, including the recognized risks inherent in a chosen occupation or field of service."

We will be emphasizing concern for nonphysical risks, because (1) such risks have had only infrequent attention in the biomedical literature; (2) they are much more subtle and difficult to characterize than physical risks; (3) in nursing, the risk to the patient is more generally psychological or social, rather than physical; and (4) there is need for heightened awareness of nonphysical risk or injury. However, physical injury as a consequence of nursing research should not be discounted. The components of nursing include the carrying out of technical procedures, physical assessment, and primary care patient management. It is therefore fair to assume that the testing of such procedures may pose an element of physical risk to the human subject. Consider, for example, a study to test the topical administration of insulin as a treatment for decubitus ulcers. The investigator may truly believe, after reviewing the pertinent literature, that no harm will come to the research subjects. And yet it is conceivable that a patient might be adversely affected if the insulin penetrates his broken skin and becomes absorbed internally (Gerber, 1975).

Risk is, to a greater or lesser degree, inherent in the research process, as all conscientious investigators will recognize. Even so simple a procedure as weighing a baby entails the risk of dropping the infant, as Beecher has pointed out (1970, p. 2). It is the obligation of the investigator that contemplates any study involving human beings to ponder and recognize even the most subtle risks that might eventuate to the research subject. However minimal the perceived risk, it is a risk to note and consider, not to ignore.

Barber and his colleagues (1973, p. 48) have noted that investigators may tend to overestimate benefits and minimize risks. Not infrequently, statements discounting the possibility of risk are encountered in grant applications. A proposal to study the parents of abused children is a case in point. The researchers proposed to conduct intensive interviews with the parents to gain insight into their backgrounds, feelings, and behaviors. It would appear that, at the very least, such a study does impose a risk, namely invasion of privacy, which must be addressed with care in the proposed research procedures.

It is equally important to understand that even research of a nonexperimental nature carries a degree of risk for the study subjects. The notion that research has to be experimental to constitute a hazard to the human research subject is fallacious. Even descriptive studies may carry some threat. Certainly there is threat to personal privacy when a research project entails observation, interviewing, or videotaping of its subjects; the child abuse study referred to above is a typical example.

Invasion of privacy is only one of the nonphysical risks that may be incurred by the human research subject. Others may include betrayal of confidentiality and anonymity, embarrassment, surrender of autonomy, and deception with resulting loss of trust.

Inasmuch as practically all studies have the potential for annulling confidentiality and anonymity, it is good research policy to omit the identification of individuals, groups, or institutions under study. Should it be essential, as in the case of longitudinal studies, to preserve the identity of study subjects for a prolonged period of time, the raw study data must not be allowed to fall into the hands of unauthorized persons. The kinds of safeguards that should be taken to protect the data will depend on their nature.

Manheimer and his associates, for example, took unusual precautions in the conduct of a longitudinal study that delved into the use of drugs by college students (Manheimer and others, 1971). The study data were obtained through interviews with the student-subjects. To protect their anonymity, the investigators sent the completed interviews to Canada. There each received a new identification number from a person who had no other connection with the study. The original identifying numbers were retained by the investigators so that they might arrange for future contacts with their subjects.

Particularly in behavioral studies, invasion of privacy is an issue of major concern. In Beecher's words: "As a basic principle, intrusion into a human body or mind under any circumstances is no more permissible than casual search and seizure in a home" (1970, p. 94). Abdellah (1967) addresses the issue of privacy in an equally compelling vein: "The nature of privacy has two conflicting main facets: (1) the right to be let alone or to withhold information and (2) the right to share and to communicate" (p. 317).

It would appear that invasion of privacy differs quite distinctly from other kinds of risks, physical or nonphysical. The very fact of informed consent serves to nullify the invasion and to minimize its hazard. Let us suppose, for example, that an investigator interviews supervisory hospital personnel to obtain information regarding the competencies of staff nurses. If the nurses give permission for the interviews to take place, there is no invasion of privacy. But unless the nurses are properly informed, and their consent is obtained, their privacy is seriously invaded indeed.

Most other types of risks, however, are not annulled by virtue of informed consent. The fact that a patient has consented to a hazardous clinical procedure does not eliminate its hazards, be they side effects from a new drug, death from a heart transplant, or loss of dignity. Informed consent, therefore, cannot usually be equated with diminution of risk, only with the right to freedom of choice and freedom from coercion.

Over the years, certain principles of informed consent have developed. They were derived in part from the Declaration of Helsinki, and these principles are currently embodied in federal regulations that call for:

(1) a fair explanation of the procedures to be followed, and their purposes, including identification of any procedures which are experimental;
(2) a description of any attendant discomforts and risks reasonably to be expected;
(3) a description of any benefits reasonably to be expected;
(4) a disclosure of any appropriate alternative procedures that might be advantageous for the subject;
(5) an offer to answer any inquiries concerning the procedures; and
(6) an instruction that the person is free to withdraw his consent and to discontinue participation in the project or activity at any time without prejudice to the subject (U.S. Department of Health, Education, and Welfare, 1975, pp. 11854-11855).

Although these are sound principles, in practice they may present the researcher with a number of problems. The study subjects may so vary in background and sophistication that it may not be possible to construct a standard explanation. Consent documents, which include a written explanation of the study, should therefore be tailored to fit both the study and the study population. The language should be at a reading level intelligible to the least educated subjects. Unless all subjects are expected to be senior college students or doctoral candidates, sophisticated technical terminology has no place in a consent document. Moreover, a standard medical center consent form, designed for medical research, is likely to be quite inappropriate for most nursing research.

Investigators frequently fail to consider that nurses and/or other professional personnel may in fact be research subjects in addition to patients, and vice versa. For example, the aim of a hypothetical study might be to assess the competence of nurse practitioners, and observation of these nurses as they interact with patients, as well as patient record abstracting, is to be used. In such a case it would be well to obtain consent from *both* patients and nurses because of the risk of invasion of privacy and the matter of confidentiality.

Another issue relates to the use of placebos and control groups. Subjects should be informed that they will be randomly assigned to either an experimental or a control group, and how these differ in terms of treatment. Entry into a controlled study is then contingent upon the subject's willingness to become part of either group. But let us suppose for a moment that too full a disclosure of the research protocol may adversely affect the project. Should that be the case, the investigator must spell out his rationale for less than full disclosure. He must present a special risk/benefit analysis for the scrutiny of his colleagues, the human subject committee of his sponsoring institution, and others in positions of research responsibility, including representatives of the funding agency. Debriefing of subjects after completion of the study should be part of the research plan. For an excellent discussion relative to the problems, issues, and solutions pertaining to the need for "deception" in research, reference is made to guidelines published by the American Psychological Association (1973).

Consent of the subject is one issue. Another is the researcher's use of records obtained for another purpose. Investigators who propose to use such records have been known to assume and declare that they are not using human subjects. Such an assumption is incorrect. In correspondence relative to the legal issues in such a case in the State of Washington, the Assistant Attorney General wrote: "The proposal is inaccurate in its characterization that there are no (human) participants in the experiment. In fact, the 15,000 persons whose records are in the files proposed to be reviewed are 'participants' to the extent that their files are being examined by persons not ordinarily authorized to do so" (Wilson, 1971). The 1971 guidelines of D.H.E.W. further note: "Some studies depend upon stored data or information which was often obtained for quite different purposes. Here, the reviews should also determine whether the use of these materials is within the scope of the original consent, or whether consent can be obtained" (p. 3).

When such materials are used, the crucial question is not simply whether human subjects are involved. They are indeed involved. The crucial question is, rather, *whether such subjects are at risk*. Each use of existing data for new purposes requires individual consideration. No general rule applies, and it may be necessary to obtain legal advice.

Weighing risks and benefits

While there is an element of "moral mathematics" in weighing risks against benefits, no mathematical equation can ever accurately describe the relative risks and benefits in a given piece of research. The risk/benefit ratio results from the application of a conceptual rather than a mathematical scale. Such a conceptual evaluation does not have its source in regulation, although D.H.E.W. policy requires the risks, the benefits, and the risk/benefit ratio to be spelled out in research grant applications. Rather, risk/benefit ratio is the result of a supremely moral process, in which the investigator carefully evaluates the worth of the proposed study against other human considerations. It is a process that must take place in the planning stages of any piece of human research. Ours is a society in which the individual is highly valued. Nevertheless, it is agreed that sometimes, as in the control of communicable diseases, the rights of individuals must be subordinated to the common good.

The weighing of risks to the research subjects here and now against anticipated benefits to unspecified future populations is an ethical necessity, and it is clear that the potential for future benefits must well outweigh any known and unknown risks to research subjects. As expressed by Marston (1972), formerly Director of the National Institutes of Health: "If, in a specific case, I were forced to choose between the individual and the general welfare of society, I would choose to protect the individual. But, in the real world we must have both individual and social welfare" (p. 26).

It should be noted here that the issue of the risk/benefit ratio is closely intertwined with the issue of quality in research design. The question has been raised as to whether the institutional committees that review grant applications from the point of view of human rights should also consider them in terms of scientific merit. In fact, if ethics and science are to prevail, it cannot be otherwise. Ultimately, there can be no benefit from a poorly designed study, because its findings will be invalid. Lack of validity wipes out any possible benefits, leaving only risks in the risk/benefit equation. We are indebted to Rutstein (1969) for the following succinct statement: "A worthless study cannot possibly benefit anyone. . . . Any risk to the patient, however small, cannot be justified. In essence, the scientific valididy of a study on human beings is in itself an ethical principle" (p. 524).

CONCLUSION

There is clearly no simple solution to the numerous issues, some barely touched upon in this chapter, that bear upon the protection of human research subjects. In addition to the general issues discussed, there are special ethical problems posed by certain procedures, such as psychosurgery and genetic manipulation, and by certain classes of individuals, such as children, fetuses, pregnant women, the mentally handicapped, and prisoners. Public forums are being provided for debate of the highly complex bioethical issues relative to use of these procedures and to use of these vulnerable groups as research subjects. Such forums are being provided by the National Academy of Sciences, by other scientific and lay societies, by congressional committees, and by special panels, such as the Commission for the Protection of Human Subjects of Biomedical and Behavioral Research, previously mentioned in connection with ethical guidelines for research.

Central to the issues discussed and currently under debate are two themes: multiple societal values and varying risk/benefit ratios. Societal mores govern the nature and scope of scientific endeavor by imposing sanctions and taboos, sometimes simultaneously, on a given activity. Estimates of risk/benefit ratios can reflect a whole range of judgments from the most individualistic to the most communal. It is when the natural mean of such judgments coincides with the predominant value system that some consensus can be reached on safeguards for the use of humans in research.

Science and ethics find their meeting ground in studies that minimize the risk and maximize the benefit to living individuals or future society. A desirable risk/ benefit ratio can be achieved by maximizing benefit, or minimizing risk, or doing both. Benefit is maximized by constructing the strongest possible research plan. It is maximized by posing research questions of incontrovertible importance to society and by discouraging studies of insignificant societal value.

Risk can usually be minimized with careful planning. The investigator must spell out in advance, and carefully consider, all possible hazards to the subjects. Such ethical conceptualization will sharpen the investigator's awareness of potential problems and serve to fulfill federal requirements as well. A pilot study provides a means of minimizing risk, for it gives the sensitive experimenter, interviewer, or observer early opportunity to note subjects' mistrust or reluctance to cooperate, and to recognize signs of stress and embarrassment. In most cases it should be possible, on the basis of the pilot study, to make appropriate revisions in the research protocol. The introductory explanation might be improved, for example; certain questions directed toward the subjects might be reworded or omitted; and debriefing may be strengthened. Only rarely does a study have to be abandoned because the problem of risk defies solution.

The investigator's contribution to science may well depend on his willingness to devise ways of minimizing risk to the research subject. The ethical investigator is additionally willing to share problems of risk with the research community at large. He does this by publishing reports of his research experience. It has been suggested, in fact, that publications may serve as a policing mechanism. Editors could require research reports to indicate how and to what extent consent of the subjects had been obtained. Journals might refuse to consider manuscripts that have their basis in unethical studies.

We have discussed the ethical responsibilities of the researcher, of the funding body, of institutional review groups, and of federal regulating bodies. Together they are guardians of rights of individuals and of society to informed consent and to maximal benefits with minimal risks from participation in research. The major responsibility and accountability for ethical conduct of research lies with the investigator and his sponsor:

> It is imperative that we be responsive on the one hand to the needs of science for autonomy, for intellectual integrity, and for the detachment from the pressing social, financial, and political concerns that may abort creative efforts, and on the other hand, to the concerns of the public from whom the support for science must inevitably come. It is a delicate balance at best (Gortner, 1973, p. 6).

REFERENCES

Abdellah, F. G.: Approaches to protecting the rights of human subjects, Nurs. Res. **16**:316, Fall, 1967.

American Anthropological Association: Professional ethics; statements and procedures of the American Anthropological Association, Washington, D.C., 1973, The Association.

American Nurses' Association: The nurse in research; ANA guidelines on ethical values, Am. J. Nurs. **68:**1504, July 1968.

American Nurses' Association: Human rights guidelines for nurses in clinical and other research, Kansas City, 1975, The Association.

American Psychological Association: Ethical principles in the conduct of research with human participants, Washington, D.C., 1973, The Association.

Barber, B., Lally, J. J., Makarushka, J. L., and Sullivan, D.: Research on human subjects; problems of social control in medical experimentation, New York, 1973, Russell Sage Foundation.

Beecher, H. K.: Research and the individual; human studies, Boston, 1970, Little, Brown and Co.

Cancer studies, Science **143:**551, Feb. 7, 1964.

Confrey, E. A.: P.H.S. grant–supported research with human subjects, Public Health Rep. **83:**127, Feb. 1968.

Declaration of Helsinki, Recommendations guiding doctors in clinical research, J.A.M.A. **197:**32, 1966.

Galliher, J. F.: The protection of human subjects; a reexamination of the professional code of ethics, Am. Sociol. **8:**93, Aug. 1973.

Gerber, R. M.: Topical application of insulin in decubitus ulcers, Research Grant NU 00501, Division of Nursing, Public Health Service, Department of Health, Education, and Welfare, 1975.

Glaser, B. G., and Strauss, A. L.: Awareness of dying, Chicago, 1965, Aldine Publishing Co.

Gortner, S. R.: The relations of scientists with professional and sponsoring organizations and with society. In Issues in research; social, professional and methodological, selected papers from the American Nurses' Association Council of Nurse Researchers, program meeting, August 22-24, Kansas City, 1973, The Association.

Gray, B. H.: Human subjects in medical experimentation; a sociological study of the conduct and regulation of clinical research, New York, 1975, John Wiley & Sons, Inc.

Human experimentation, Med. World News **14:**37, June 8, 1973.

Johnson, J. E., and Leventhal, H.: Effects of accurate expectations and behavioral instructions on reactions during a noxious medical examination, J. Pers. Soc. Psychol. **29:**710, 1974.

Katz, J.: Experimentation with human beings; the authority of investigators, subjects, professions, and state in the human experimentation process, New York, 1972, Russell Sage Foundation.

Manheimer, D. I., Mellinger, G. D., Somers, R. H., and Kleman, M. T.: Technical and ethical considerations in data collection (paper presented at the first international conference on student drug surveys, New Jersey), Berkeley, Calif., 1971, Institute for Research in Social Behavior.

Marston, R. Q.: Medical science, the clinical trial and society, paper presented at dedication ceremonies for the McLeod Nursing Building and the Jordan Medical Education Building, University of Virginia, Charlottesville, Va., November 10, 1972.

Mead, M.: Research with human beings; a model derived from anthropological field practice, Daedalus **98:**361, Spring, 1969.

Merton, R.: Priorities in scientific discovery, Am. Sociol. Rev. **22:**635, 1957.

Milgram, S.: Obedience to authority; an experimental view, New York, 1974, Harper & Row, Publishers.

Parsons, T.: Research with human subjects and the 'professional complex,' Daedalus **98:**325, Spring 1969.

Pellegrino, E. D.: Humanism in human experimentation; some notes of the investigator's fiduciary role, Tex. Rep. Biol. Med. **32:**311, Spring 1974.

Rutstein, D. D.: The ethical design of human experiments, Daedalus **98:**523, Spring, 1969.

Schorr, T. M.: Editorial, Am. J. Nurs. **72:**61, Jan. 1972.

Studies with children backed on medical, ethical grounds, Med. Tribune **8:**1, Feb. 20, 1967.

Trials of war criminals before the Nurenberg Military Tribunals under Control Council Law No. 10, 1946-1949, Vol. II Nurenberg, Washington, D.C., 1949, U.S. Government Printing Office.

Tuskegee Syphilis Study Ad Hoc Advisory Panel: Final report, U.S. Department of Health, Education, and Welfare, Public Health Service, Washington, D.C., 1973.

U.S. Department of Health, Education, and Welfare: The instructional guide to D. H.E.W. policy on protection of human subjects, Public Health Service, National Institutes of Health, Washington, D.C., Dec. 1, 1971.

U.S. Department of Health, Education, and Welfare: Protection of human subjects, technical amendments, Federal Register **40:** 11854, 1975.

Wilson, J. B.: Unpublished correspondence referring to State ex rel Carroll vs. Junker #79, WN. 2d 12, 482 P 2d 775, 1971.

part II
RESEARCH ISSUES

Interest in research in nursing has reached an all-time high. In academic and nursing service circles, researchers and nonresearchers alike are showing increased interest in documenting both current nursing knowledge and the effects of nursing practice. Besides increased professionalization of nurses and concern for studying the unknown, events internal and external to nursing, such as trends to involve nurses in peer review, the uncertain role of nurses in P.S.R.O. legislation, and national health insurance, have created situations in which nurses are being forced to support their reason for being.

Logically, nursing as a practice profession puts higher research priority on applied (not basic) research. Whereas basic research originates from the desire to know or understand some phenomenon, and its emphasis is on the production of knowledge, applied research is based on the desire to know or understand in order to improve performance. For example, evaluative (or evaluation) research is a type of applied research aimed at providing information for more rational decision making in teaching, training, or some other type of program.

The distinction between inductive and deductive reasoning needs to be made for the profession of nursing to advance. With inductive reasoning, conclusions are drawn from observations or experiences. In deductive reasoning, conclusions are based upon a set of accepted premises or laws. Given the fact that nursing is only beginning to develop a knowledge base, there are few accepted premises or laws by which to explain practice. As a result inductive reasoning must be relied upon for furthering the profession and consequently the development of accepted premises and laws.

Doubtless, nursing has a need for basic research from which to generate a knowledge base for practice. However, it appears premature for the profession to give priority to this direction. Priority should be given instead to applied research using inductive logic that will generate theoretical assumptions and premises for practice. Later, these proposed assumptions and premises can be tested with basic research approaches and deductive logic to develop a substantive knowledge base for the nursing profession. An emphasis on basic research would result in meaningful, long-term benefits for the nursing profession; an emphasis on applied research would result in the profession reaping short-term or immediate benefits. As indicated in the chapters of this section, the greatest research need in nursing is for applied studies. In other words, currently the nursing profession can best be served by research designed to study problems related to nursing practice.

A number of relevant issues and trends for research in nursing are discussed in this section. In summary, these discussions suggest that nursing professionals in service and education must join together in nursing research, and a research model or framework provides an approach for organizing and interrelating variables relevant to nursing practice.

A number of research issues must be addressed for the profession of nursing to advance. The authors who contributed the chapters of this section highlight many of these relevant issues. Dr. Aydelotte's article focuses on clinical nursing research and concept development in nursing. For example, she contends that while nursing practice is lacking in descriptive and explanatory theories, nursing itself is without an accepted "language" that would allow for establishment of meaningful and valid definitions of nursing concepts. She also asserts that research is the responsibility of everyone in nursing, not just the professional elite. The elite should, however, stimulate nursing research, keep it rational, maintain its quality and objectivity, and encourage the use of results in practice.

Dr. Flynn proposes a holistic model for evaluating community health nursing practice. As part of this model, she utilizes the same bidimensional approach of process and outcome suggested by Aydelotte. This model is actually a systems approach evolving from a synthesis of several similar research frameworks. The usefulness of the model is to organize concepts and variables and suggest potential interrelationships among them. To clarify the model, each of the variables proposed in the framework is operationalized. The author also discusses a number of research design issues and suggests solutions to potential problems.

3 Research framework for evaluating community health nursing practice

BEVERLY C. FLYNN

Recent nursing literature includes a number of statements concerning the state of the art in clinical nursing research. Presently it is agreed that nursing practice must be tested and the findings of nursing research applied to the development of nursing knowledge and theory. It also has been suggested that clinical nursing research should generate knowledge that is applicable to nursing practice. A benefit of the validation of nursing practice through nursing research is accountability to the American public for expenditure of public funds on nursing programs.

A nationwide survey was undertaken by Lindeman (1975) to determine priorities for clinical nursing research. Quality nursing care and evaluation of patient outcomes of nursing care were specified in this survey as being among the fifteen most important areas requiring research for the profession. Lindeman's findings concur with the priorities for nursing research indicated by others (Bloch, 1975; Gortner, 1975).

I believe it is imperative that nursing develop conceptual frameworks that are appropriate for the purposes of generating knowledge, utilizing research results in nursing practice, and establishing accountability. A conceptual framework for nursing must be broad yet definitive in order to fulfill these purposes.

My intent is to present one conceptual framework for evaluating the practice of nursing: community health nursing. This framework is a systems approach stemming from four complementary research frameworks found in the health care literature (Bloch, 1975; Donabedian, 1966; Neuhauser and Anderson, 1972; Starfield, 1973).

THE RESEARCH FRAMEWORK

Several issues must be considered before the research framework for community health nursing practice is presented. First of all, community health nurses view their clientele as population groups in the community. Concern is with the entire community, that is, a neighborhood, city, county, or so forth. Population groups served and those not served by community health agencies are considered in the planning and implementation of community health nursing programs. Second, the impact of community health nursing services will need to be examined on the level of families or population groups in addition to the level of individual patients.

Third, community health nurses work in collaboration with interdisciplinary health care providers throughout the community in order to promote the client's optimum level of functioning (Archer, 1975). The interdisciplinary nature of community health nursing may create problems in differentiating the contribution of community health nurses from the work of other health care providers or the overall health care delivery system. The framework proposed for the study of community health nursing practice addresses these issues.

There are four basic dimensions in the conceptual framework for evaluating community health nursing practice: environment, structure, process, and outcome. These four dimensions were proposed by Neuhauser and Anderson (1972) in a research framework for the study of hospitals. Donabedian (1966) first proposed three of these dimensions (structure, process, and outcome) for evaluating the quality of medical care. Starfield (1973) further examines the structure, process, and outcome framework; Bloch (1975) and Gortner (1975) discuss its relevance to the evaluation of nursing care. Because of the compatibility of these frameworks to the study of hospitals, medical care, and nursing care, a combination of these frameworks is viewed as having practical application for research relevant to community health nursing practice.

The conceptual framework that is proposed for community health nursing practice is schematically presented in Fig. 1.

This framework is a systems approach that emphasizes the interdependence of the four major dimensions. The *environment* surrounds structure, process, and outcome. The environment is viewed on several levels of analyses (such as city, county, state, and nation). A wide range of variables are incorporated in the environment: population characteristics, including demography, life-style, and health

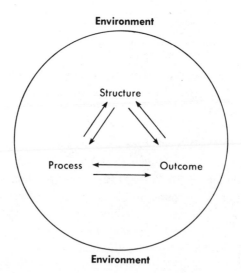

Fig. 1. Conceptual framework for evaluating community health nursing practice.

levels; level of health technology; health legislation; and geographic characteristics, including climate and transportation.

Structure is the particular community health nursing organization under study. It may be a health program, a one-nurse agency, an interdisciplinary community health center, a state health department, or any unit or organization providing community health nursing services. Structure variables include: organization size, policies, finances, staffing patterns, and so forth.

Process incorporates the interface between community health nursing organization or program and the client. Examples of process variables are: nursing-client encounter (for example, home visit, clinic visit, telephone), the client's health problems, the nursing services provided, and the utilization of the services by the client.

Outcome is the result of the community health nursing practice on clients' health knowledge, behaviors, and attitudes. Outcome variables include: morbidity, health knowledge, immunization levels, consumer prices, satisfactions, and so forth.

This framework indicates that structure, process, and outcome interact with the environment of which they are a part. Structure, process, and outcome directly influence each other. Change in any one part of the system creates change in other dimensions of the system.

The four dimensions exist within a time-space framework and as such are influenced by time passing and by the space within which they exist. For example, time and space are influencing the administration of the swine flu immunization program. Legislation was passed and local health departments administer their immunization programs within a specified time in order to prevent this disease in the population. The space of influence has expanded from the city or county surrounding the local health departments to influence from the state and nation that passed this health legislation. In essence, these four dimensions interface in a dynamic acting, reacting, and interacting manner. They are interrelated and interdependent.

THE FRAMEWORK'S EMPIRICAL RELEVANCE TO NURSING PRACTICE

The test of any conceptual framework must be its empirical relevance to nursing practice. Variables that represent a wide range of potentially relevant characteristics of each of the four major dimensions must be identified. Then each of the variables must be operationalized by specifying indicators or information that may be used to measure each variable. The term indicator will be used to depict measurable information of a variable.

Tables 1 through 4 present selected variables and indicators of environment, structure, process, and outcome. It should be emphasized that the variables and their indicators are examples. It is not an exhaustive or all-inclusive listing. For each variable an example indicator is listed. For instance, an indicator of the demography (environment) variable is the age composition of the community; an indicator of the policies and rules (structure) variable is the number of agency job

Table 1. Selected variables and indicators of environment

Variables	Indicators
Demography	Age and sex composition of the community
Life-style	Median income of the community
Attitudes and values	Per capita expenditure on health care in the last year
Economic resources	Methods of financing health care, proportion of private, taxation, contributed monies
Health care facilities	Number of general hospitals, mental health clinics, home care agencies per population
Health levels	Proportion of the population with reportable communicable and chronic diseases
Health technology	Proportion of home and hospital births in the population
Health legislation	Laws that govern professional practice as nurse practice acts, funding for building facilities such as Hill-Burton, funding for services such as Medicare and Medicaid
Geographic characteristics	Average temperature; major transportation utilized

Table 2. Selected variables and indicators of structure

Variables	Indicators
Policies and rules	Number of agency procedural manuals, job descriptions, written reports required per time period; agency purpose, philosophy, goals and objectives
Capital investment	Amount of agency income by grants, fees, insurance, tax support
Facility	Number and type of facility such as neighborhood health center, health department, visiting nurse service; space such as number of personnel per room
Equipment and supplies	Working operation of various equipment used such as automobiles, movie projectors, diagnostic equipment; cost of supplies per personnel
Personnel	Proportion of professional, paraprofessional, and clerical staff positions; educational preparation for these positions
Levels of organizational hierarchy	Number of levels in management hierarchy
Staffing patterns	Administrator/supervisor ratio, supervisor/staff nurse ratio, staff nurse/population ratio
Decision making	Decentralization, that is, the number and content of decisions made at unit level; centralization, that is, the number and content of decisions made at upper management levels
Organizational size	Number of employees and clientele; referrals for community health nursing services

descriptions; an indicator of the clientele problems (process) variable is the extent of difficulty in nursing care needed for home care patients; and an indicator of the longevity-mortality (outcome) variable is the average length of life by sex. Other indicators of each of these variables could have been named. Again they are only examples. It should be noted that the listing of variables is comparable to that

Table 3. Selected variables and indicators of process*

Variables	Indicators
Client's health problems	Range of nursing diagnoses such as anxiety, malnutrition, altered ability of self-care activities (Gebbie, 1974); extent of difficulty in nursing care needed for home care patients
Nurse-client encounter	Number of home visits, clinic visits, office visits, telephone calls
Utilization	Proportion of the population receiving community health nursing services in homes, clinics, and office
Autonomy in service delivery	Number of supervisor/staff nurse conferences per month, number of nurse/physician conferences per week
Length of service delivery	Time spent in the provision of care; number of clientele-provider contacts; length of time before discharge
Communication	Formal communication, that is, number and frequency of meetings, written memos, clientele records kept; informal communication, that is, number of friendships outside of work hours, social gatherings, lunch and coffee breaks among personnel and among clientele
Conflicts/consensus	Intensity of disagreement/agreement between management and staff, staff and clientele

*Services provided are deleted from this table; they are examined in greater detail in Table 5.

Table 4. Selected variables and indicators of outcome

Variables	Indicators
Longevity-mortality	Average length of life by sex; number and cause of deaths in the population
Activity-disability	Extent of activities of daily living and disability of persons 65 years and older
Comfort-discomfort	Extent of physical pain
Satisfaction-dissatisfaction	Number of broken appointments and kept appointments with the community health nurse
Knowledge	Extent of knowledge about medication and diet of population with heart disease
Morbidity	Number of reported measles cases in the population
Human potential	Proportion of infants within normal height and weight ranges
Psychological functioning	Self-concept or ego strength scores
Social functioning	Number of interactions with community groups or number of friendships
Consensus of health care needs	Extent of clientele/community health nurse agreement of health care needs
Compliance	Proportion of families that carry out activities agreed upon in community health nurse/family contract
Prices	Cost of community health nursing services to families

presented by Donabedian (1966), Neuhauser and Anderson (1972), and Starfield (1973). The differences are that several of Neuhauser and Anderson's environment variables have been incorporated under structure. This classification is consistent with that proposed by Donabedian and Starfield.

In the selection of indicators attention must be paid to their appropriateness to the specific community health nursing practice under study. Ideally more than one indicator of a variable should be selected simultaneously and studied. The value of this procedure is discussed in the research design section below.

The health services research literature indicated a number of scales or indexes that may prove useful in measuring outcome variables. These scales will need to be examined for relevancy to the community health nursing practice under study. Modifications of these scales may need to be made. Some examples are: the disability limitation scale developed by the World Health Organization (1970), the comfort-discomfort index utilized by Hulka (1973), the Tennessee Self-Concept Scale (Fitts, 1964), and the I.P.A.T. 16 PF Scale (Cattell, 1970), which measure psychological functioning. For example, the disability limitation scale may be appropriate in developing a family household interview schedule. This interview schedule could then be used to measure the effects of community health nursing on the activities of daily living and disability of persons 65 years and older.

Since the literature indicated that "only an evaluation that encompasses both process and outcome has the potential for great impact on the quality of care" (Bloch, 1975), particular attention was given to process and outcome relative to services provided by the community health nurse. To operationalize the unique services of the community health nurse, an exploration of the basic premises of community health nursing proved useful. A comparison of selected definitions for community health nursing indicated several similarities (Archer, 1975; Division of Community Health Nursing Practice, 1975; Nursing Development Conference Group, 1973; Tinkham, 1972). The focus of the community health nurse's work is the health of the population as a whole. Practice is directed to individuals, families, and groups. Although concern is with the total health-illness continuum, primary focus is on the three levels of prevention: primary prevention, which deals with health promotion and specific protection; secondary prevention, which includes early diagnosis and prompt treatment to limit disabilities; and tertiary prevention, which involves rehabilitation (Leavell, 1965). The scope of practice includes assessment, planning, implementation, and evaluation for the purpose of assisting individuals, families, and population groups toward self-care or helping people to help themselves.

In essence, the three levels of prevention are the basic variables of community health nursing services. Possible indicators of these basic variables are identified and categorized under process and outcomes in Table 5. It is possible to trace the relationship between process and outcomes by reading across this table.

For example, an indicator of the primary prevention (process) variable is assistance in obtaining immunizations and boosters. The outcome indicator of this process variable could be an increased immunization level in the population. An indicator of the secondary prevention (process) variable is referrals to other health team members to meet specialized needs. The outcome indicator of this process variable could be the appropriate utilization of community health resources. A third example relates process and outcomes of community health nursing: An

Table 5. Selected indicators of community health nursing services and outcomes of these services

Process variables and indicators	Outcome indicators
Primary prevention (health promotion and specific protection)	
Assistance in identifying growth and development behavior appropriate for family members	Knowledge of growth and development; expectations of children's behavior appropriate to age and sex
Assistance in social and psychological adjustment to changing life-styles	Social and psychological satisfaction and functioning
Assistance in identifying strengths and weaknesses of communication patterns	Knowledge of family communication patterns
Assistance with planning normal diet within a fixed budget	Adequate family nutrition habits
Assistance in obtaining immunizations and boosters	Increased immunization level in the population and decreased reporting of immunizable disease
Secondary prevention (early diagnosis and prompt treatment)	
Consumer advocate in health planning for health-screening program	Identification of early disease states
Educate to participate in health-screening programs	Increased participation in screening clinics; identification of early disease states
Referrals to other health team members to meet specialized needs	Appropriate utilization of community health resources
Assistance in adjusting treatment regimen to family life-style	Compliance with treatment regimen; reduction of disability limitation
Tertiary prevention (rehabilitation)	
Disease control counseling including medications and special diets	Compliance with medication and special diets; reduction in further complications
Provision of home nursing care to the sick including medication administration, bathing, assistance with exercise	Family maintained as a group without institutionalization of sick member; reduction in discomfort of sick member; maintenance of activities of daily living
Assistance in identifying alternatives in order to cope with illness and management of health care	Family self-help established; appropriate utilization of community health resources

indicator of the tertiary prevention (process) variable is the disease control counseling including medications and special diets. The outcome indicator of this process variable could be the compliance with medications and special diets.

RESEARCH DESIGN LINKING ENVIRONMENT, STRUCTURE, PROCESS, AND OUTCOME

As indicated earlier, environment, structure, process, and outcome are both interrelated and interdependent. In this framework any of the variables of the four dimensions can be the independent or dependent variables. However, each will have to be selected according to the proper conceptualization of the research problem. Structure may be an independent variable whose effect on process and/or outcome is studied, or process may be an independent variable whose effect on outcome or structure is of interest. The environment and structure variables will probably be most frequently studied as independent variables.

Since the empirical relationships among many of these variables have not been tested, research could be designed to answer such questions as: (1) What changes in the services delivered by community health nurses (process) are a result of reduction in capital investment (structure)? (2) Are these changes in capital investment (structure) and services delivered (process) creating significant effects on families' compliance (outcome)? (3) Do the changes in clientele health problems identified by the community health nurse (process) create changes in the nursing staffing patterns (structure)? (4) How does the life-style of the community (environment) influence the immunization level of the population (outcome)? (5) How does the organization size of the community health agency (structure) affect the prices of community health nursing services (outcome)? (6) How does the number of home visits the community health nurse makes (process) influence the disability level of stroke patients recovering at home (outcome)? (7) What health legislation (environment) creates priorities in community health nursing services (process)? (8) Are these priorities in community health nursing services (process) congruent with the community's health levels (environment)? (9) Does an increase in the immunization level of the population (outcome) influence the proportion of agency finances allocated to immunization programs (structure)? (10) Does a decrease in the compliance with treatment regimen for hypertensive patients (outcome) create changes in the health counseling services offered this population group (process)?

Answers to these questions will not only provide information relevant to the nurses in practice (including the nurse administrators) and the community served, but also to the nursing profession as a whole. Moreover, this information may assist community leaders in making rational policy and financial decisions about community health programs. In the analysis of examples such as these, accountability may be established, accountability to the profession of nursing as well as to the public being served.

Each of the indicators noted in Tables 1 through 5 must be measured over time by the implementation of longitudinal, cross-sectional, or comparative studies. For example, in order to make sense out of the life-style variable (environment, Table 1), the indicator, median income of the community, must be set in context. Is the life-style high or low compared with that of other communities of the same size? Has the median income of the population changed significantly in the last 5 years?

How much tax support (structure, Table 2) is allocated to a community health agency? Has this support increased or decreased in the last 5 years? How does this tax support compare with that of other health agencies in the community? Is this tax support higher or lower in other community health nursing agencies across the state or nation?

Has the number of monthly supervisor/staff nurse conferences (process, Table

3) increased or decreased in the last year? How does this number compare with other health professionals? How does this compare with other community health nursing agencies of similar size in the state or nation?

Have the costs of community health nursing services to families (outcome, Table 4) increased or decreased in the last year? How does this cost compare with that of hospitalization? How does this cost compare with that of other community health nursing agencies? Similarly, all the environment, structure, process, and outcome variables selected for a particular research problem must be studied over time in one agency or compared with those of other agencies before any research conclusions can be reached.

Population groups may be compared, such as those receiving and not receiving services of the community health nurse. Research may be designed to measure whether the outcomes of the population served are significantly different from the population not served. This is necessary for answers to such questions as: (1) Does the population 65 years of age and older served by the community health nurse engage in activities of daily living with more or less comfort than the aged population not served? (2) Are referrals made to community agencies by community health nurses as appropriate as referrals made by other health care professionals? (3) Is there greater or lesser family compliance with medications and special diets for families served compared with families not served by the community health nurse? (4) Are the immunization levels in communities without immunization programs higher or lower than in communities with immunization programs? Other intervening variables, such as the introduction of national health insurance, demographic changes in the community population, changes in professional practice acts, and so forth, could be examined to note their impact on variables under study.

Two research designs that permit assessment of independent as well as intervening variables appear to be most applicable (Suchman, 1967). The first is the pretest, posttest, and control group design, which measures the impact of the independent variable (or variables) on the dependent variable (or variables). The second is the Solomon four-group design; it measures both the impact of the independent variables on the dependent variables and the effect of pretesting the population groups under study. The former design has two groups, an experimental and control; the latter design has four groups, consisting of one experimental and three controls.

A cross-sectional study design might be appropriate to measure the impact of selected structure, process, and outcome variables. For example, structure changes may not occur at the same time in every unit of a community health nursing agency. Measurement in a number of different units that have implemented varying changes in staffing patterns may show the effects on services delivered and population outcomes. This research design may be implemented at one point in time and comparisons made across units. Unfortunately, this design does not determine whether the units and population groups were equivalent before the structural changes. In addition, the other intervening variables cannot be clearly documented with this design (Suchman, 1967). These limitations must be seriously considered before selecting this research design.

Difficulties stemming from the developing state of the art for evaluating a practice profession may arise in trying to implement research designs. Researchers and clinical personnel may disagree as to which outcome variables are the result of selected process variables. But instead of creating a barrier to the research, these differences of opinion can be used in establishing the research design. For instance, a number of outcome variables may be simultaneously measured, and any variations therein may be observed. For example, indicators of comfort-discomfort, knowledge, compliance, and ability to cope with adversity could be measured at the same time.

The results of the research can thus be utilized to improve the development of future research. During these early stages of research for a practice profession, no one person or group can specify who is right or wrong; only empirical testing can provide a base of information on which to build knowledge.

Lack of agreement in what, when, and how information should be collected may also arise. A lack of reliable and valid methodologies may prompt consideration of more than one indicator or measure of a variable. A single indicator may provide an insufficient amount of information about a variable; two indicators of the variable, on the other hand, have the potential for not only explaining up to twice as much about the variable but also of determining the reliability or validity of the method of data collection. For example, measurement of the longevity-mortality (outcome) variable could involve both the average length of life by sex and the number and cause of deaths in the clientele population. Correlation of data collected on two or more indicators of a variable may establish the reliability or validity of the indicators selected.

SUMMARY AND CONCLUSIONS

I have presented a conceptual framework for evaluating community health nursing practice. This framework was synthesized from four complementary research frameworks found in the health care literature. The conceptual framework presented here has gone farther than previous frameworks, however, in that it specifically emphasizes the interrelated and interdependent nature of its four dimensions: environment, structure, process, and outcome. These four dimensions interface in a dynamic acting, reacting, and interacting manner.

To suggest the empirical relevance of this framework, selected variables and their indicators (measurable information of the variables) were delineated. Several research design issues were discussed and solutions to potential difficulties were proposed.

This research framework permits, simultaneously, the implementation of innovative evaluative research and the development of a concrete knowledge base for community health nursing practice. Innovative research may take, for example, the form of interdisciplinary research striving to answer complex health care delivery problems that confront community health nursing and other health care professionals. A knowledge base for practice will evolve as the relationships among the variables in the framework are empirically tested and statistically analyzed. It is only through this process that accountability may be established, accountability to the profession of nursing as well as to the American public.

REFERENCES

Archer, S. E., and Fleshman, R.: Community health nursing patterns and practices, North Scituate, Mass., 1975, Duxbury Press.

Bloch, D.: Evaluation of nursing care in terms of process and outcome, Nurs. Res. **24:**256, July-Aug. 1975.

Cattell, R. B., Eber, H. W., and Tatsuska, M. M.: Handbook for the 16 PF, Champaign, Ill., 1970, Institute for Personality and Ability Testing.

Division of Community Health Nursing Practice: Standards of community health nursing practice, Kansas City, Mo., 1975, American Nurses' Association.

Donabedian, A.: Evaluating the quality of medical care, Milbank Mem. Fund. Q. **44:** 166, July (Part 2) 1966.

Fitts, W. H.: Tennessee Self-Concept Scale, Nashville, Tenn., 1964, Counselor Recordings and Tests.

Gebbie, K., and Lavin, M. A.: Classifying nursing diagnoses, Am. J. Nurs. **74:**250, Feb. 1974.

Gortner, S. R.: Research for a practice profession, Nurs. Res. **24:**193, May-June 1975.

Hulka, B., and Cassel, J.: The A.A.F.P.-U.N.C. study of the organization, utilization and assessment of primary care, Am. J. Public Health **63:**494, June 1973.

Leavell, H. R., and Clark, G. R.: Preventive medicine for the doctor in his community; an epidemiologic approach, New York, 1965, McGraw-Hill Book Co.

Lindeman, C. A.: Priorities in clinical nursing research, Nurs. Outlook **23:**693, Nov. 1975.

Neuhauser, D., and Anderson, R.: Structural comparative studies of hospitals, In Georgopolos, B. S., editor: Organizational research on health institutions, Ann Arbor, 1972, University of Michigan Institute for Social Research, pp. 83-114.

Nursing Development Conference Group: Concept formalization in nursing process and product, Boston, 1973, Little, Brown and Co.

Spitzer, W., and others: The Burlington randomized trial of the nurse practitioner, N. Engl. J. Med. **290:**251, Jan. 31, 1974.

Starfield, B.: Health services research; a working model, N. Engl. J. Med. **289:**133, July 19, 1973.

Suchman, E. A.: Evaluative research, New York, 1967, Russell Sage Foundation.

Tinkham, C. W., and Voorhies, E. F.: Community health nursing evolution and process, New York, 1972, Appleton-Century-Crofts.

World Health Organization: International collaborative study of medical care utilization, Baltimore, Md., 1970, World Health Organization.

4 Clinical nursing investigation and the structure of knowledge

MYRTLE K. AYDELOTTE

Although within the last two decades there has been an increase in the number of clinical nursing studies and in the degree of sophistication with which these have been conducted, the need for well-conducted nursing research is vast. Since the current tested knowledge underlying nursing practice is scant and little has cumulated, many areas in nursing practice require study. Lindeman (1975) has identified priorities in nursing research reported by clinicians and investigators and differentiated between those questions of professional significance and others of social significance. She outlines the great need for programs of research of which nursing should take leadership "which could encourage a generation of new knowledge not just for the sake of new knowledge, but because of the potential social benefit associated with that knowledge" (p. 434). Practice problems are immense, real, and urgent.

We should get on with it—the study of nursing practice. We have much in the literature describing theory construction. We have also apologized profusely for the lack of knowledge in nursing and have bemoaned at length our lack of a rich scientific heritage. Now is the time for us to place a high priority on clinical nursing research, to involve many practitioners in that effort, and to fully recognize that the use of scientific inquiry in the study of the discipline of nursing is essential. We cannot achieve our social purpose without knowledge.

The study of any practice discipline requires close interaction between the real world, the practice arena, and theory. In our study attention must be given also to the organization of knowledge as it is built into fields of specialized practice. This organization is necessary to facilitate the communication of knowledge to practitioners and students. But above all, the practical testing of theory (the schema of what is thought to be the pattern and relationships) cannot be overlooked.

THE STATE OF NURSING KNOWLEDGE

The current knowledge base of nursing practice, although becoming more theoretical and less technical in the sense of procedure, is sparse. What knowledge there is has accumulated through a series of unrationalized experiences. Much of it is knowledge common to several of the health professions, derived from the basic physical and social sciences. Although this knowledge has been verified within the domain of those disciplines, a large portion of it has not been studied to learn of its relevance to nursing phenomena.

46

There is a paucity of descriptive and explanatory theories of nursing, although a number of excellent articles on the need for these exist in the literature. Even at the first level of theory development, which is the level of isolating, naming, and classifying activities and objects, little has been accomplished that is rational and validated. This problem of nomenclature and taxonomy confronts us all. Although assumed by many to be positive, the utility of the concepts drawn from other sciences has not been carefully studied to learn if that utility, in fact, even exists.

There is no argument over whether or not nursing is recognized as a discipline. The discipline exists without question within the universities as a field for study. The body of generalizations and principles developed in association with nursing practice is organized in courses and in established curricula. The fact that the knowledge is highly imperfect is known primarily to critics within the nursing community of scholars. Others may have raised the question, but the right of nursing to be within the university disciplines is seldom challenged.

Each discipline has its own social goals, its domain (that is, the phenomena with which it deals), its methods of study, and its structure. In nursing, there continue to be issues about the social goals and the domain. Even among the professional elite in nursing there is no agreement as to its social purpose. There is agreement that nursing has practical consequences and that it has a strong service orientation. Although in Lindeman's study of priorities the question of "What is nursing?" as a research item ranked low, the literature reveals a variety of proposals of social purpose that range from achieving optimal health for all to a less global formulation of purpose. No one has pointed out that social purpose may also change over time as society changes its social mandate, that is, the functions it assigns to professions. Perhaps one reason that nursing research, and consequently nursing knowledge, has been slow to develop is our inability to state in concrete terms that to which we will attend in meeting our social mandate. Gortner (1975) has proposed that "nursing research, in brief, is a systematic inquiry into the problems encountered in nursing practice and into the modalities of patient care, such as support and comfort, prevention of trauma, promotion of recovery, health education, health appraisal, and coordination of care" (p. 193). Is she suggesting that our purpose is to provide strategies that will enable patients and clients through adaptation and learning to care for their own health as they define it? Certainly, her definition of nursing research provides specific direction for the study of nursing practice.

The domain has grown in complexity since the time of Florence Nightingale. The boundaries are vague, confused, and little recognized (Murphy, 1971). Yet if these boundaries continue to be severely blurred, phenomena will be omitted or included without a rational basis for doing so. Do the boundaries include the various structures within which nursing is practiced or not? For example, do they include the variables of cost, such as time and effort? Some discussions of the findings of clinical nursing research would lead one to believe that the world of reality for study is only the nurse-patient interaction. The investigator omits the variables that may limit the use of the findings or fails to propose ways of implementation. There is some evidence that the results of research investigators are not rapidly incorporated into ongoing practice (Ketefian, 1975).

Not only is the question of structure of variables unresolved, but the population of the universe of patients and clients to be studied is ill-defined. First, how are we operationally defining the difference between *patient* and *client?* Is a patient one in an institution who is provided with curative care and a client one in the community who requires primarily health instruction and health appraisal? What is the critical variable or set of variables that differentiates the two? Does nursing serve everybody regardless of their health status? If nursing includes health education and health appraisal for all, how does nursing's study of these differ from that of the health educator and the well-informed citizen? Moreover, how does one answer the question of access to the selected population (for example, the person who believes himself or herself well) when societal endorsement of access to that individual is not present? Is the person included only if the individual seeks access to nursing?

The subject matter of the discipline consists of the concepts and the linkages between the concepts. The structure of the knowledge includes the pattern of the relationships between these concepts, the logic of the relationships, and the methodological approaches used in the study of the discipline, that is, how we look at reality. The "goodness" of the structure is estimated by the degree to which information is simplified for use by members of the profession, by the extent to which new propositions are generated, and by the utility of the concepts and generalizations in practice. If the theory explains and predicts empirical phenomena and thus generates knowledge and guidelines for practitioners, it is useful.

CONCEPT DEVELOPMENT IN NURSING

One of our major tasks, the one that requires clinical nursing investigation, is the establishment of a language in the nursing field that is understood and accepted by practitioners as well as by investigators. Bloch (1974) has aptly described our confusion about the meaning of the terms *nursing approach, nursing intervention, nursing problem, nursing diagnosis,* and others. These terms do not have the same meaning for all of us, because in our usage we have failed to define them. Even the word *patient* conjures up different meanings. Does it mean the same as *client* or not? When we speak of *nurse,* for example, several different meanings again come to mind. In the use of more abstract labels, such as *dependency,* variations in meanings are even greater. The variations are acceptable if, when we read the label, we know how the author intends its use.

The language of nursing includes not only nominal definitions of isolated objects but also operational definitions of concepts. Although the nursing literature contains excellent articles on theory construction emphasizing concept formation, progress has been slow. Since the subject matter of a discipline consists of concepts, in our effort to discover the truth about our world we must first define these concepts so they are reliable, so that there will be agreement about whether or not there is an instance of the concept and if these concepts fit nursing reality. For example, in the nursing literature labels such as stress, adaptation, sensory deprivation, fear, electrolyte imbalance, grieving, compliance, oxygen hunger, and ischemia are used. These are fine words. But have we developed the imagination, precision, and richness in our language to describe them operationally, and do they represent the reality as intended?

Currently, there are efforts to develop a taxonomy of nursing diagnosis that represents theory development at the first level. Bircher (1975), while outlining the dangers and values of a taxonomy system, urges that these diagnoses include critical attributes and responses of the client (or patient) relevant to the nursing situation. My concern centers around the vagueness of definition that may result and the failure to test the operational definition of the concept in clinical nursing situations. The proposal to establish an organized, logical, comprehensive system for classifying nursing diagnoses, health states, and health problems is sound; but to be valuable, the system of concepts must be workable in that it leads to the study of interrelated phenomena. But above all, the proposed nursing diagnoses, health states, and health problems must be validated and tested for utility in the practice arena. They will have to be "cut out, as it were" from the real world (Brodbeck, 1968, p. 3). Since they are concepts formed by abstraction from empirical observations, the antecedent conditions, telling how and in what circumstances the observations are to be made, and from which the existence of an instance of the concept can be inferred, must be precise. These concepts (sets of nursing diagnoses, health states, and health problems) are derived from such observation. If their original derivation was from other bodies of knowledge (for example, *anxiety* from psychology), it is essential that the concept be tested for logical relevance to nursing and be reformulated or modified if necessary to have use in nursing practice.

In the development of concepts we must use our common sense. In nursing, there are many instances of the need to infer underlying states of the patient or constructs. The problem is to employ descriptive terms by which we can describe observations from which that state can be inferred. To do this requires that the individual responsible for the description of the observations have direct acquaintance with the domain and the phenomena. Johnson's (1975) recent publication is an excellent example of the use of theory guiding research design, variables, concept development, and reality testing of operational definitions.

One set of concepts has been given scant attention until recently. The outcomes of effective practice had been greatly ignored until recent legislation required health providers to consider efficacy of various practice strategies. Just as we need to develop a set of concepts describing the properties and attributes of the underlying clinical nursing states of patients, we must give attention to sets of nursing interventions to bring about changes in those states and the outcomes resulting from the interaction between the patient state and the intervention. A schematic model sets forth these ideas (Fig. 2).

In nursing a patient, from observation of the patient and through the use of

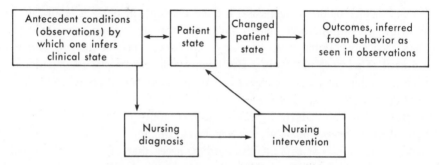

Fig. 2. Patient states and nursing intervention.

operational definitions by which it can be inferred that a state exists (for example, pain), the nurse makes a decision regarding the nursing diagnosis, that is, the need to reduce pain. Using knowledge on which the concept of pain is structured, she selects a nursing intervention that she predicts with a known degree of probability will bring about a change in the state of the patient. Following execution of the intervention, she will infer from the behavior observed in the patient (a changed patient state), such as reporting reduction, sleeping, reading, change in body tension, as she has operationally defined that changed state, whether or not a changed state exists. The scheme involves at least four categories of concepts: undesired patient states, desired patient states, nursing diagnoses, and nursing interventions. Only by the development of operational definitions of concepts within each of these classes can we study the phenomena of the interrelationships of these. If these categories of concepts are built, we move on to the next level of theory construction, the testing of relationships, looking forward to explanation and prediction. Hardy (1974) proposes nine types of relationships that are logical between and among variables.

In our development of nursing interventions (also called nursing approaches and action), I suggest that we develop criteria by which we may evaluate a nursing intervention as well as the effect it produces upon a patient state. For example, we may well look not only at effect, but at its simplicity of execution, the ease with which it can be taught to practitioners, the energy involved on the patient's part, and the technological equipment and the time required. The nursing intervention should be as simple as possible and such that it is feasible in different settings.

OBSTACLES TO CLINICAL NURSING INVESTIGATIONS AND GENERATION OF KNOWLEDGE

In recognizing that clinical nursing investigation is essential to the generation of knowledge and its structure, one is led to ask, "How can study be facilitated? How can obstacles be removed?"

First of all, although we need continued attention given to the nature of theory building, the elite nursing investigators probably should become more concerned that theory be used to guide research and less concerned about whether one or more theories are needed and which theory is preferable. The arguments about types of theories are useful, and discussion and writing about criteria for theory building and evaluation of theory should continue, but we should not become mired in our debates. Several theories may lead to fruitful results. The important matter is that the theories be soundly conceived and that they be used.

Second, in programs of instruction, attention must be given to developing within students a commitment to scientific inquiry. Scientific inquiry must become a part of our daily lives. Unfortunately, to be curious about our world of nursing has been seen as appropriate for only a few well-prepared investigators. Intellectual curiosity must be cultivated, made exciting, and a source of joy. The discovery that the order of phenomena is beautiful should be made possible for all. The student should be so indoctrinated in scientific inquiry that careful, systematic observation of the real world in which he or she practices is a part of daily living and that the ever present opportunity for questioning is taken for granted. In the profession, the use of nursing process has been widely accepted as a practice methodology. Would we be wiser if we used scientific inquiry instead? Scientific study is seen too frequently and by too many as a compartmentalized activity, separate from practice, yet we know that scientific inquiry is an intellectual skill used in all we do.

Third, a closer association between clinicians and investigators must occur. Nursing research must lead to some improvement in practice. The purpose of clinical nursing research is the extension of coherent knowledge that enables the practitioner to practice more effectively. This purpose carries implicitly not only the identification and testing of that knowledge but also the dissemination of it to the practice groups.

Unfortunately, nursing research has been perceived and promulgated by nurses themselves as an undertaking separate and different from practice, administration, or teaching, rather than inherent in these three. Scientific inquiry and practice are not seen as so interrelated that they cannot be separated. They are in essence symbiotic, circular in nature, and of one another. Research has not been a part of all nursing cultures, and there is not a commitment to the generation of new knowledge by all nurses in all settings. In order to conduct clinical investigations in nursing, an amalgamation of competencies is often necessary for the investigator without sound clinical nursing knowledge and knowledge of the health care delivery system. The clinician without research knowledge and skill is also incompetent. We may encounter the fully prepared clinical nursing investigator, but even such an individual needs cooperating individuals of many kinds. Clinical nursing research requires the use of a health care delivery system as its laboratory. Clinical nursing research will be facilitated by the development of teams of researchers and clinicians joining together to study practice. The clinician will serve as the link to the real world of nursing, facilitating the entry of the investigator who brings the theoretical model, the knowledge of methodology, and the orientation and focus to look at the research question. The clinician can also serve as the evaluator of the nursing intervention. Cooperatively, the research will be more easily conducted, and the result should be more useful.

Fourth, at the current state of nursing knowledge, there are very difficult problems of measurement, definitions, selection of level of abstraction to be attained, design, and hypothesis construction. Because of these difficulties, and since in many respects we are beginning from scratch, programs of research built around a set of selected but highly relevant concepts may prove more fruitful than a great diversity of effort. What are some of the different problems of practice? Lindeman (1975) reports high-ranking items of significant social relevance relating to quality of nursing care, reduction of psychological stress, quality of life for the aged in institutions, effective self-care education of patients with chronic diseases, and management of pain. Investigators may wish to follow the model of other successful scholars in selecting a topic in the real world that lends itself to a lifetime of program research. Extensive and thorough acquaintance with an area designated for study is essential to surmounting these problems. The involvement of several individuals working on the same problem from a different perspective who collaborate and communicate with one another may contribute to the resolution of the difficult problems. A few examples of programs of research are now found in the literature. The development of nursing research centers should facilitate the work of groups of nurses dedicated to the same or related research problems.

CONCLUSION

The goal of the research effort is a body of knowledge, tested, validated, and useful in practice. In order to achieve this goal, the full community of professional nursing must become involved, either in the research itself, in the implementation of the findings, or in making its achievement possible. The task cannot be left to the professional elite. The elite has its own role. It is charged with spearheading the movement and exciting others. It is also responsible for maintaining the quality of the research and seeing that objectivity is maintained, that the research is rational, and that it results in generalizing power. All of us must focus upon the utility of knowledge in achievement of nursing's social purpose.

REFERENCES

Bircher, A. U.: On development and classification of nursing diagnoses, Nurs. Forum 14(1):11, 1975.

Bloch, D.: Some crucial terms in nursing; what do they really mean? Nurs. Outlook 22:689, Nov. 1974.

Brodbeck, M., editor: Readings in philosophy of the social sciences, New York, 1968, Macmillan, Inc.

Gortner, S.: Research for a practice profession, Nurs. Res. 24:198, May-June 1975.

Hardy, M. E.: Theories; components, development, evaluation, Nurs. Res. 23:100, March-April 1974.

Johnson, J., and others: Altering children's distress behavior during orthopedic case removal, Nurs. Res. 24:404, Nov.-Dec. 1975.

Ketefian, S.: Application of selected research findings into nursing practice; a pilot study, Nurs. Res. 24:89, March-April 1975.

Lindeman, C. A.: Delphi survey of priorities of clinical nursing, Nurs. Res. 24:434, Nov.-Dec. 1975.

Murphy, J.: Theoretical issues in professional nursing, New York, 1971, Appleton-Century-Crofts.

part *III*
ISSUES IN HEALTH CARE DELIVERY

Trends and issues in American society today have provoked increasing interest in health care delivery. Perhaps one of the greatest controversies concerns the philosophy that health care is a basic right for every citizen. One could debate this issue in light of concerns over the rising costs of health care, maldistribution of health manpower, quality and efficiency of health care, and so forth.

The authors of the chapters in this section emphasize many of these issues and trends in health care delivery, of which nursing is a part. Most of the chapters focus on macrolevel or global issues that confront nursing and health care today. Drs. Henshaw, Gage, and Martinson discuss expanded nursing practice. Dr. Henshaw takes a historical approach to the nurse practitioner movement and focuses on why the concept emerged. The issues of specialization, legal aspects, and quality and efficiency of care are discussed in light of influencing the future of the nurse practitioner movement. Implications for research are drawn from his analysis. Dr. Gage writes on processes common to expanded nursing practice in primary care settings. Three processes highlighted are: role development and reallocation, the legal base for nursing practice, and reimbursement for nursing services. The author suggests that an understanding of these issues is necessary if nurses are to work with physicians and other health care providers to increase accessibility to health and illness care.

Dr. Martinson, in her article on the role of the nurse in home care for the dying child, argues that the care given by health care personnel to the dying patient generally lacks in sensitivity and consideration, in regard not only to the needs of the patient but also to those of his family. As a result, the patient tends to lose his sense of identity, personal dignity, and feeling of worth. Much of this problem is related to the fact that dying patients are treated in hospitals where they are without family support; the family is deprived of interaction with its dying member.

It is pointed out in this article that dying need not be a totally destructive process for the family; to the contrary, if dying is approached by the family with understanding and support as provided by the nurse, the death of a family member may actually act to strengthen the family unit. Dr. Martinson also points out that caring for dying patients (and their families) can be a rewarding experience for the nurse, especially if the nurse actively assists the family with information, support, and help in reorganizing its family relationships.

53

The chapter by Dr. New and associates was originally written for an invitational conference on citizen participation. Although nursing is not addressed specifically in this chapter, the issues raised are most appropriate for the nursing profession. The role of nursing is evolving from one of caring for patients within the hospital to one of responding to community needs. This is especially true for nurses who work in neighborhood health centers and various community action programs that were initiated under the auspices of the Office of Economic Opportunity and continued by community residents and by official and private agencies. These authors take a historical perspective in addressing the new awareness among consumers who feel they should have a voice in health care services. They warn that conflicts may arise if health care providers do not consider consumers in their decision making. An intriguing aspect of this chapter is the presentation of two paradigms that depict how citizens and professionals have different degrees of involvement and different perceptions of optimum involvement in the political and health delivery arenas. The implications of this chapter for nursing are that the nurse may have to become an advocate for the client and be willing to enter into the political world. This is one role nurses have not eagerly pursued. Yet, if the nursing profession is to have any impact on the new consumers, this role (and others too) is one that nurses may have to assume.

Wallston and associates, in a chapter that examines the nurse's role in counseling about sexuality, adopt the patient or microlevel of analysis. The focus of this chapter is nurse-patient communication in an effort to assist nurses to help patients express themselves as sexual beings. The authors emphasize that sexuality can be expressed in a variety of ways. They also differentiate between the nurse's tolerance for the patient's sexual expression and the nurse's attempt to educate the patient about various ways of sexual expression. Events in the health care environment that threaten an individual's sexual expression are examined (such as life events, illness, and treatment). A parallel is drawn between counseling in human sexuality and Dr. Kübler-Ross's work in the area of death and dying.

Although the content areas vary, the authors indicate that the general public is more sophisticated about health care today. The authors focus on innovative roles in nursing within the health care system and, in so doing, may present unpopular conclusions about the future direction of nursing. For example, Dr. Henshaw indicates that the medical practice act is advantageous for nurse practitioners because it exempts the nurse from role constraints. Implied in these chapters is the need for alterations in the education of nurses (such as understanding of patients' sexuality; sensitivity to political aspects of health care; benefits of expanded role in terms of quality of care, productivity, availability, and costs of care; and treatment of the dying patient and his family).

Constraints on the nursing role are also discussed. For example, Dr. Wallston and associates indicate that the nurse cannot proceed too far when there is considerable conservatism regarding overt sexual expression. Drs. Henshaw and Gage contend that nurse practitioners cannot function independently of other health care providers; instead, they must depend directly and indirectly on others.

Several of the authors identify issues of concern to the nursing profession as a whole that provide insights concerning the direction of public policy decisions. For example, Drs. Gage and Henshaw warn that reimbursement for nursing practice continues to be a critical political issue for nursing since this mechanism will control professional autonomy and financial rewards.

In conclusion, a wide range of relevant issues in health care delivery is discussed in this section. These chapters were selected not because they exhaust the issues, but because they are thought-provoking and present unique and insightful implications for the profession of nursing.

5 The nurse's role in counseling patients about sexuality

KENNETH A. WALLSTON
GLORIA CALHOUN
BARRY D. COHEN

Human beings are sexual beings, yet, as recently as 10 years ago, sex and sexuality were taboo topics in most encounters between patients and health practitioners. For a variety of reasons, patients were loath to bring up sexual concerns, and providers were equally reticent to deal with or even discuss sexual matters. Embarrassment and ignorance were prevalent. Lately, however, things have begun to change. Sex has, as it were, come out of the confines of the bedroom. Consumers have become more assertive in demanding that health care providers deal with their totality of needs, and health care providers in turn are recognizing that they must overcome deficits in their own knowledge base and communication skills with regard to sex and sexuality. Lay persons expect the physician and the nurse to be "experts" in the area of sexuality. Yet it has not been uncommon to find health care professionals avoiding this area altogether or bluffing their way through questions because they are reluctant to show their ignorance. In order to keep pace with society's changing norms and expectations, the health care professions are being forced to come to grips with the "sexual revolution."

A fairly recent trend in nursing and other health care professions is toward viewing sexuality in broader terms. Human sexuality is now being recognized as an important component interwoven in the personalities, life-styles, and value systems of all individuals. The sexual dimension of the total person has far-reaching implications for the nurse's approach to total health care. No longer is sexuality defined in strictly genital terms or only as sexual intercourse for the purpose of procreation. The public is being educated through a wide selection of "how to" books and articles in the popular media and is becoming increasingly aware that sexual health is an essential component of an individual's total well-being. Sexuality includes a wide variety of behaviors that range from holding hands, exchanging glances, affectionately hugging and kissing (which may not be overtly sexual) to the more overt expressions of sexuality, such as masturbation, mutual stimulation, and sexual intercourse.

The purpose of this chapter is to define and explore the role that members of the nursing profession can play in helping clients work through a multitude of sexual issues. Nursing has long purported to be concerned with people as total human beings and has adopted a "biopsychosocial" orientation toward delivering total health care. Thus it is our contention that nurses should be in the forefront of any movement concerned with human sexuality and its relation to patients' needs. If we judge by the number of articles that have recently begun to appear in nursing journals, some nurses share our viewpoint and have assumed a degree of leadership in this area. For reasons that will be explored below, however, many nurses have been reluctant to incorporate sexual counseling as part of their role.

A review of the literature (Elder, 1970; Fonseca, 1970; Lief and Payne, 1975; Mims, 1975; Osofsky and Osofsky, 1971; Walker, 1971; Woods, 1975) reveals that education in human sexuality in nursing schools is experiencing a slow beginning, although most schools offer basic content in reproductive biology. Few nursing schools, however, devote sufficent time in their curriculum to sex and sexuality. Education in human sexuality often takes the form of a few hours of lectures to large groups of students with little opportunity for asking questions or small group discussion. Since much of the knowledge and information needed by a nurse who engages in sexual counseling is not provided by the nurse's basic schooling, it is not too surprising that many nurses suffer from a knowledge deficit in this area.

The importance of offering a more broadly based curriculum in human sexuality as an integral part of the nursing school program has only recently been acknowledged by nurse educators across the country. Suggested for inclusion in such a curriculum are the psychological components of sexual development, functioning, and dysfunctioning. If the nurse is to assist the patient with his or her sexual problems, she must acquaint herself with the multicausal psychological elements of sexuality: (1) importance of touch, (2) unconscious factors, (3) sexual anxiety and conflict (including fear about performance or fear of failure), (4) guilt, (5) communication difficulties, and (6) learning theory.

It is not our intent to provide nurses with all the information they would need to counsel clients in regard to sexual matters.* Instead, our purpose is to make the reader aware of the scope of the issues and how they may affect nursing practice in the future.

We begin by briefly providing an overview of the vast array of patients' needs in regard to sexual counseling in order to indicate instances where the nurse could become involved. This is followed by a discussion of the reasons why many nurses may decline active involvement at the present time in counseling patients about sexuality (for example, lack of knowledge and/or communication skills; unfavorable attitudes and/or discrepant values; absence of social support and/or presence of inhibiting pressures or forces from other elements in the system). Finally, we examine some of the issues that nurses need to consider and possibly resolve in order to become involved in counseling patients about sexuality: invasion of privacy, ownership of patients, client-counselor match-ups, and the right not to get involved.

---

*The reader who wishes more in-depth information is referred to the bibliography throughout this chapter.

WHERE THE NURSE CAN BECOME INVOLVED

As the role of the nurse continues to expand in more complex clinical settings with concomitant broad ranges of responsibility, she* will be confronted with a wide range of situations that involve issues of sexuality.

Sexual concerns are very real concerns for a multitude of patients with whom the nurse has contact. In some instances, the sexual concern results where sexuality is the primary problem, as in forms of sexual dysfunction (for example, nonorgasmia, impotence, premature ejaculation, vaginismus). It is obvious that sexuality is a topic for discussion between health professional and patient when the patient presents himself or herself as having a sexual dysfunction. The vast majority of patients, however, are in situations in which sexual concerns are the secondary problem. That is, some aspect of the individual's sexuality becomes involved as a result of medical illness, drug use, or some life event. The nurse may or may not be aware of the potential for sexual concern on the patient's behalf.

Life events

There are certain life events that may prove very threatening to an individual's concept of sexuality. In the health care setting, the very first concern for the individual is the process of becoming a patient and the impact of hospitalization and illness on sexual self-concept and role behavior. The transition from person to patient involves a series of intrusive experiences that have the capability of minimizing sexual dignity as well as human dignity. Some aspects of admissions procedures literally as well as figuratively strip the person of his or her sexual identity. In addition, the physical patient care setting, lack of privacy, and separation from family require changes in the person's sexual behavior patterns. As a result of all these transitions, hospitalized patients may "act out" sexually to test the response of others to their sexuality, to gain control in a situation that makes them feel helpless, or, perhaps, to attract attention. In all cases, though, there exists a need to maintain some sense of self as a sexual being. It is the responsibility of the nurse and the other members of the health care team to promote the sexual integrity of the patient. This can be accomplished by interventions designed to maintain the individual's concept of self as a sexual being and, as much as possible, to promote that individual's "normal" sex role behavior.

Hospitalization is clearly a life event that may be threatening to an individual's sexuality. Pregnancy is another life event obviously involving sexuality. Until recently little was known about women's sexuality during and immediately following pregnancy, let alone the effect of intercourse on the unborn child. In recent years knowledge about the physiological and psychosocial aspects of pregnancy has advanced; thus the nurse can have more of an understanding of sexuality during and

---

*We would prefer to use nonsexist pronouns. However, for the sake of clarity, throughout this chapter nurses will be designated by feminine pronouns, physicians by masculine pronouns, and patients by both feminine and masculine pronouns.

following pregnancy and be able to communicate this information to patients.*

Other life events that entail sexual concern are abortion and trauma resulting from assault such as rape. In both these areas the individual will bring to bear a variety of sexual concerns. Each person will differ greatly on a continuum of biological, social, and psychological concerns and thus cannot be typified. In both instances the sexual concerns of the individual or individuals involved must be dealt with, and it is the nurse's responsibility to at least be aware of these patient needs. The nurse might have difficulty with the patient's sexual behavior, but as health care providers, not theologians, law enforcement officers, or moralists, nurses cannot be committed to total patient care without considering the patient as a sexual being (Zalar, 1975).

Another life event requiring some concern for issues of sexuality is the process of aging. Older people are often asked to conform to a stereotype that society has formed of them. This is most clearly observed in the sexual aspect of life, where a widely perpetuated myth assumes that older individuals just are not interested in, or capable of, sex. One clear example of discrimination in regard to sexuality is the lack of personal privacy many older people have to contend with; homes for senior citizens never have double beds! Information about sexuality and aging has become available,† and nurses need to be informed of new modes of thinking, so that they can educate patients more effectively. Masters and Johnson (1966) found that the process of human sexual response in all phases slows with aging, but at no point does sexual responsiveness stop in either males or females. It may take longer to reach orgasm, the experience itself may be shorter and less intense, and certain physiological changes may occur, but sexual responsiveness definitely continues as the individual ages.

Illness

Some medical conditions more obviously involve sexual concerns than others. Local genital diseases or conditions that may produce pain on intercourse (such as lower back pain, priapism, disease of the penile skin, dyspareunia, vaginal infection, Bartholin cyst infection) may decrease sexual desires and might interfere with sexual functioning. In some cases, alteration of body image, such as results from mastectomy and hysterectomy, will entail sexual concern. In these instances the nurse is usually aware that the patient's sexuality is involved in the illness and should be considered in planning for total patient care.

Medical conditions such as diabetes and heart disease are prevalent in Western society and may have consequences on the individual's sexual functioning as well as on other bodily functions. In these cases, patient sexual concerns may be less obvious to the nurse and therefore require that the health practitioner have some

---

*A good source for information on this topic is Chapter 4 in Woods (1975). See also Solberg and others (1974).

†An excellent discussion of sexuality and the aging process can be found in Scheingold and Wagner (1974), pp. 19-40.

amount of specific knowledge or education, or both. For diabetic men, impotence may be a concern. Some diabetic men may become temporarily impotent when their diabetes is not controlled. However, impotence that occurs in diabetic men who are well controlled is likely to be permanent. Furthermore, as the duration of illness lengthens, so does the chance of becoming impotent. Diabetic women may experience vaginitis or lack of vaginal lubrication, or both, which will contribute to their sexual dysfunction. Disturbances of fertility may also arise in patients with diabetes, and when it does, the concept of self as masculine or feminine may be disturbed. This certainly requires the nurse's attention and most probably will involve careful diagnostic evaluation and therapy. In addition, knowledge of genetic transmission of diabetes also affects the patient's concept of generative sexuality and should be taken into account when counseling patients who have a family history of diabetes.

For the cardiac patient, the road to rehabilitation and recovery involves many fears, doubts, and questions. Resumption of sexual activity often evokes more concern in the cardiac patients than resumption of other physical efforts. Although there is no data to show that heart disease is accelerated by the resumption of sexual activity, a common fear and acceptance of a causal relationship exist.

Delivery of information to cardiac patients seems to decline drastically in regard to sexuality (Cohen and others, 1976). Return to work, diet, and other forms of physical activity are areas that are discussed more thoroughly and in much greater detail. As is the case with many of the conditions already discussed, the nurse or other health care provider's lack of information, combined with feelings of discomfort and insecurity in dealing with issues of sexuality, results in minimal information exchange with patients.

Patients with injured spinal cords form another patient population that requires the nurse's attention to issues of sexual functioning. The level of the spinal cord lesion and the degree of interruption of nerve impulses influence the nature of sexual functioning in the patient with a spinal cord injury. Sexual gratification can be experienced from feelings other than those usually linked to the sex organs during the human sexual response cycle. Therefore, adaptation of previous sexual practices, innovation, and experimentation in sexual activity may be necessitated as a result of spinal cord injury. A wealth of information is currently becoming available concerning the sexual functioning of the patient with a spinal cord injury.*

Treatment

The effects of drugs on human sexual behavior are not readily considered by nurses or other health practitioners involved with patient care. Many drugs tend to have an adverse effect on sexual functioning, and few actually enhance sexual behavior. Drugs that decrease sexual drive and potency often act directly on the

---

*See Rabin (1974) and Chapter 10 in Woods (1975).

mechanisms that control physical performance. Male potency, in particular, seems to be susceptible to the effects of drugs. Ultimately, the effect of any drug on sexual performance is likely to be diminution of interest and capability. The nurse must take this fact into account when involved with patients receiving prolonged drug therapy or in cases of drug abuse. Patients receiving drugs will often voice concerns regarding sexual functioning, and the nurse will be better able to deal with such situations if she is adequately informed about drug effects.*

WHY NURSES MIGHT DECLINE INVOLVEMENT

The health care delivery system is very efficiently geared toward handling specific medical problems. The system, however, fails in most cases to integrate therapy for the "target" disease or disability into the total realm of the patient's social life. Furthermore, disabilities having an impact on the sexual functioning of the individual attract even less attention (Rabin, 1974). In the majority of conditions discussed above, the patient participates in little or no information exchange concerning sexual functioning. Lacking professional advice, patients must make decisions based on their own knowledge or turn to less knowledgeable sources for information. In any case, decisions based on hearsay, fear, and misconception are far from ideal and may even be dangerous. Naturally, the necessity of making uninformed decisions may result in personal frustration, marital tension, and general unhappiness (Griffith, 1973; Tuttle and others, 1964).

Typically, the patient does not initiate discussions with the nurse or with other health professionals. The patient often feels that, "If there's anything I need to know, the doctor or nurse will tell me. I don't need to ask questions." A similar attitude is usually held by the patient's spouse. In fact, the spouse probably feels excluded from any and all participation in planning for his or her spouse's care and recovery (Cohen and others, 1976). In reference to sexuality, spouses may well deny their own sexual needs in order to take "proper care" of their partners. The spouse's emotional stress and anxiety can be alleviated somewhat by increased information and support from the nurse involved with the patient's care.

Role of knowledge, attitudes, and values

In order to have a constructive and beneficial helpee-helper relationships, the nurse or other health professional must be prepared to provide information and answers to many important questions. Many of these questions will involve the patient's sexual functioning. It is hoped that nurses' increasing awareness of these critical issues in total patient care, particularly aspects of the desirability of sexual information exchange, will benefit all those involved.

If the nurse is to help these patients, she must possess a thorough working

---

*Excellent discussions of drug effects on sexual functioning are available in Kaplan (1974), pp. 79-105, and Woods (1975), pp. 175-191.

knowledge of anatomy and physiology of the male and female reproductive systems and the human sexual response cycle. The nurse also needs to expand her knowledge of the interrelatedness of the biological, psychological, sociological, and cultural aspects of human sexuality with corresponding components of growth and development (Woods, 1974). Factual information of this sort is useful in neutralizing the emotional aspect of sexual counseling.

If, for instance, the nurse is aware that vasocongestion and myotonia are two principal physiological components of the sexual response cycle, she can apply this knowledge to counsel a woman who is experiencing menstrual cramps. If the woman can achieve orgasm through masturbation and/or sexual intercourse, she will experience detumescence or loss of vasocongestion, especially in the pelvic area, thus relieving pelvic congestion.

Another piece of information helpful to most women is the explanation and use of the Kegel exercises developed by Dr. Arnold Kegel. Originally he used these exercises to deal with the problem of urinary stress incontinence in his female patients. Quite unexpectedly he discovered that his orgasmic patients developed a greater capacity for experiencing orgasms, and his nonorgasmic patients began experiencing orgasms. For women who desire to become more responsive to genital stimulation, the training of the pubococcygeal muscles is one of the most effective individual techniques in producing the desired therapeutic results.*

It is important for the nurse to be aware of the major role played by anxiety and fear in sexual dysfunction. Fear makes people overly conscious of their actions and reactions, and the more self-conscious people are about their sexual functioning, the less likely they will perform as expected (Masters and Johnson, 1970). A wide variety of techniques and procedures designed to counter anxiety are being used by learning-oriented therapists with good results (Annon, 1974). Behavioral therapy provides a flexible and comprehensive approach that can be adapted to many settings, including hospitals and clinics. One major advantage lies in the brevity of behavioral methods; frequently, only a few therapy sessions are necessary to produce the desired change. Moreover, behavioral therapy can be adapted for use by all levels of health care practitioners; thus it permits a range of treatment choices geared to the level of competence of each practitioner.†

It is our opinion that human sexuality programs in schools of nursing should not attempt to prepare a skilled sex therapist, but should place emphasis on providing: (1) a practitioner who has developed a sensitivity in perceiving potential areas of sexual dysfunction as a result of illness; (2) an educator who can share pertinent information with patients, their families, and other members of the com-

---

*More information concerning these exercises can be found in Kaplan's (1974) book. For further readings on the physiological components of the male and female response cycles, see Masters and Johnson (1966) and Woods (1975), pp. 3-25.
†Further information on behavioral principles and their application to sexual dysfunctions can be found in Annon (1974), Hartman and Fithean (1972), and Kaplan (1974).

munity; and (3) a clinician who has developed communication skills, especially in an active listening role.

Knowledge of human sexuality is important but not sufficient. The clinician's attitudes and values play a major role in whether and how sexual information is communicated to patients. It is essential that a nurse be aware of and comfortable with her own attitudes and values before she can effectively be nonjudgmental in dealing with her patients' sexuality (Zalar, 1975). If a nurse feels that certain forms of sexual expression are "bad," "wrong," "immoral," or "improper," she will have difficulty in hiding these attitudes or values from her patients. On the other hand, if a nurse is confident about her own sexual identity, has developed an awareness of her attitudes and values, and can accept other life-styles and sexual behaviors, she can be an important resource person to her patients, colleagues, and the total community.

Lief and Payne (1975) compared a number of nursing students with practicing registered nurses; they used the Sex Knowledge and Attitude Test (S.K.A.T.) and found that the nursing students were more knowledgeable and more liberal on all four attitude scales of this test. The four attitudinal scales measured: (1) attitudes toward premarital and extramarital heterosexual encounters; (2) acceptance or rejection of commonly held sexual misconceptions, taboos, and fallacies; (3) views on social, medical, and legal aspects of abortion; and (4) views on acceptability or unacceptability of masturbation. This study also concluded that both nursing students and practicing registered nurses were significantly less knowledgeable and more conservative than the women medical students and graduate students with whom they were compared.

Luber (in Lief and Payne, 1975) concludes from data gathered using her Professional-Sexual Role Inventory (P.S.R.I.) that: "It would appear that students who had a more favorable attitude toward masturbation were more comfortable with other aspects of sexuality." Luber further suggests that nurses be screened if they are to work in clinical situations in which knowledge of human sexuality is important (such as family planning clinics) and that selection be based on the nurses' ability to be comfortable and knowledgeable in this area.

Many nurses presently hide behind the safe sexual identity of the "mother surrogate role" as a defense mechanism, denying that they may find a patient's sexuality stimulating. There is nothing wrong with a nurse giving herself permission to accept and enjoy her pleasurable feelings toward a patient, as long as it does not interfere with her ability to make sound nursing judgments. The nurse who is in touch with her attitudes toward sexuality can appropriately control her behavior; this results in a pleasurable situation for both herself and the patient (Zalar, 1975).

It has been our experience that the value of human sexuality as an integral part of total health care is frequently talked about, yet the overt behavior of most health professionals appears contradictory. Too frequently, nurses allow themselves to be dissuaded from exploring the emotionally charged area of their own and their patients' sexuality by peer pressure or submission to authority. The insinuations about the nurse who does sexual counseling, with the implication that perhaps she is "loose," "immoral," or "easy," may be a very real threat to her. If the nurse chooses to become involved in taking sexual histories, counseling, or education, she runs the risk of being labeled the "sex nurse" and can become alienated from the rest of the staff.

Thus there are many reasons why a nurse may be reluctant to get involved in this area. However, if a nurse chooses to play an active role in counseling patients about sexuality and is aware of her knowledge deficits and/or unsure of her attitudes or values, there is much she can do to remedy the situation. For example, she can familiarize herself with textbooks, journals, and current materials that deal with sexual functioning and behavioral patterns. Lectures, courses, films, and workshops will also help the nurse acquire information and communication skills. The use of sexually explicit films, such as those shown during Sexual Attitude Reassessment Workshops (Chilgren and Briggs, 1973), may be helpful in desensitizing the nurse to a broad range of sexual expressions and behaviors. The nurse may view the content of these films as both controversial and debatable, but, hopefully, exposure to these films accompanied by the opportunity to discuss and share her reactions and feelings will result in an increase in the nurse's understanding and acceptance of divergent sexual values and practices.

The nurse may also feel uncomfortable with the sexual language of her patients. A method described by Annon (1974) suggests that the nurse make a comprehensive list of every sexual word or phrase that she knows. After the list is complete and the words defined in a clear manner, the nurse should privately practice saying each word and phrase over and over again. This process should continue until she can say and hear these words without feeling any emotional response.

ISSUES NEEDING TO BE RESOLVED

In the preceding section of this chapter, we discussed the reasons why nurses might not be actively counseling patients about sexuality and concluded with some suggestions for the nurse who would like to broaden the scope of her interaction with patients. Not all nurses, however, will choose or be able to incorporate sexual counseling as part of their role. No nurse should be forced to deal with this area if she does not desire to do so (Zalar, 1975) or if it makes her uncomfortable. But this does not absolve the nurse from the responsibility of seeing that the patient's need for sexual counseling is met; at the very least, the nurse should refer her patients to another health care provider who has the knowledge, ability, and self-assurance to do the job properly.

Ownership of patients

The question, "Who 'owns' the patient?" points to one of the potential conflict areas facing nurses who become involved in counseling patients about sexuality. Can the area of sexual health belong to both the nurse and physician? In most nurse practice settings it is still prevalent for physicians to adhere to the belief that patients "belong" to them (that is, the physicians) and that they are in charge of and responsible for all aspects of patient care (Thompson and others, 1975). Given this belief, the nurse's role is primarily one of carrying out the physician's orders, which may or may not designate what the nurse is free to discuss with patients. Whether implicit or explicit, the nurse may get the message that certain topics, such as sexuality, are either taboo or belong strictly in the realm of the physician-patient relationship. It is, for example, considered part of the physician's role to inform a patient of a diagnosis of cancer once such a diagnosis has been confirmed. Nurses are often placed in the position of having to interact with a cancer patient who has not yet been informed of the diagnosis by his or her physician. Thus the nurse is bound to a conspiracy of silence until the physician decides to tell the patient of the diagnosis.

A situation of this nature imposes a strain on the nurse-patient relationship that is often resolved only by the nurse avoiding the patient at a time when she is most needed. Because the nurse subscribes to the concept that it is the physician's prerogative to inform the patient of his or her diagnosis, the best she can do under such circumstances is encourage the physician to disclose the information to the patient as soon as possible. Many nurses have difficulty in this role.

The issue of whether or not it is part of the nurse's role to initiate discussions or respond to statements concerning sexuality and sexual behavior with patients is less clear-cut than in the above example concerning the patient's diagnosis. Only in rare instances will a physician explicitly forbid nurses to talk with "his" patients about sexual concerns. Nurses do, however, receive many subtle cues as to what is and is not expected of them. How many times have nurses been chastised by physicians for saying something to patients that the physicians wished had not been said or felt should only have been said by themselves? Some physicians believe that certain information in itself would be harmful to patients. Others feel patients would only accept certain information if presented by a physician. It is difficult, however, to find any hard evidence that supports these beliefs; instead, one suspects they are based on the physician's need to retain power and control over what happens to "his" patients. Doubtless, not all physician power dynamics are motivated by physicians' need to increase the sense of their own importance; genuine concern about their patients and the threat of malpractice suits may be very valid reasons for practicing "safe" medicine.

In order to minimize conflict over the "ownership" issue, the nurse must somehow work with physicians to determine how active a role she is to play in counseling patients about sexuality. This would entail a recognition by all parties involved that a potential conflict exists. The nurse should discuss with the physician, openly and frankly, how she is to behave if the patient brings up sexual concerns or if she makes a nursing assessment that the patient needs to be counseled in this area. Should she first consult with a physician, or can she proceed on her own? Nurses do, after all, spend considerably more time with patients than do physicians. Thus, they are in an excellent position to share, at least, the role of sexual counselor with physicians. It is not inconceivable that once physicians are convinced that nurses have the necessary information and skills, they will delegate to them most of the responsibility for dealing with patients' sexual concerns. Mutual respect between physicians and nurses will be the inevitable result of cooperative teamwork.

Matching counselors to patients

Another issue concerning counseling patients about sexuality is whether the demographic match-up between counselor and client has any impact upon the social psychological nature of the relationship. Is it better for men to counsel men and women to counsel women? Is it preferable for the counselor to be at least as old as the person he or she counsels? Would the embarrassment attendant upon a discussion of sexual issues be diminished if an attempt were made to match clients and counselors according to age and sex, and perhaps even cultural and/or socioeconomic factors? Little, if any, attention has been given to these questions in the literature, although Cohen and others (1976) did discover that most of the patients they interview would prefer to discuss sexual matters with a health professional (generally a physician) of the same sex and the same age (middle-aged or older).

Most nurses are women, and the majority are younger than the typical adult patient with whom they interact. It seems reasonable that a 45-year-old married man would have less difficulty discussing his sex life with a middle-aged physician who is a man than with a 22-year-old, attractive, single staff nurse who is a woman, although for many men it might still be difficult to talk about sex with another man. However, the importance of these factors has never been determined. An increasing number of women are voicing complaints that they do not feel comfortable interacting with their gynecologists, who, as a group, are predominantly men. There is a movement toward educating women in our society about the functioning of their bodies in order for them to have more control in this area and to enable them to assert their rights for adequate health care (Boston Women's Health Book Collective, 1973). This is one area where nursing should be taking the lead.

In many situations it is impractical to consider matching providers to consumers; the client is fortunate if anyone is willing or able to discuss his or her sexual concerns. We mention the problem to draw it to the reader's attention—not to suggest that there is any practical solution. Much can be accomplished by health professionals who are sensitive to the differences between themselves and their clients and who take whatever steps are possible to ensure that such differences do not create difficulties in their relationship with their clients.

Invasion of privacy

What about the patient who is not ready or chooses not to discuss matters of a sexual nature with nurses or other health professionals? The patient's right to privacy is a crucial issue for health care consumers and providers. Nurses are expressing concern that questioning the patient about his or her private sexual experiences may indeed be considered prying. People have a right to information; do they also have a right not to be exposed to information? A respect for a person's privacy entails making certain that the person is not coerced into revealing personal information that he or she would prefer not to disclose. Does a concern for privacy, however, extend to protecting people from hearing something that they do not want to hear?

Patients are typically quite unassertive in standing up for their rights; rarely would a person come out and say, "I do not wish to discuss this topic with you!" Instead, the nurse is forced to depend on more subtle cues in assessing how far to pursue sexual concerns with a particular patient. The nurse's perception may or may not be accurate. In most cases the proper way to proceed is to check things out with the client: "I sense you are feeling uneasy when we discuss matters of sexuality. Would you prefer we drop the matter for the time being?" This assures the client that the nurse is aware of his or her feelings. It also allows the client the freedom to make a decision about the nature of the continuing interaction. Nurses will be surprised to discover that, in most instances, such an intervention leads to a deeper exploration of the client's problem. But some patients will decline the invitation to be exposed to sexual information. Just as nurses have the preogative not to become sexual counselors, patients have the right not to be involved as counselees.

Conclusions

There are few valid reasons why, within limits, patients in hospitals cannot be permitted freedom to express themselves as sexual beings. Obviously, one of the limits must be the protection of the rights of other persons, including the nursing staff, who might be the unwilling targets of sexual acting out or who might be embarrassed by having to witness sexual behavior. Many patients in hospitals are just too sick to even care about having their sexual needs met. On the other hand, many hospitalized patients resent the fact they are forced to adopt all the trappings of the "sick role."

It is important to remember that sexuality can be expressed in a multitude of ways other than actual sexual intercourse. For some people it can be the opportunity to participate in decision making relevant to their care; for others, it can be a chance to be productive by helping other people who are in need; for still others, it can be expressed by touching or being touched. Despite papal pronouncements, masturbation is a perfectly appropriate form of sexual stimulation, acceptable to many people; all it requires is privacy. The important thing to recognize is that sexual behavior is normal and, in most cases, healthy. If a nurse is truly concerned with helping patients lead as normal a life as possible, she must be prepared to accept the fact that some patients will meet their sexual needs in whatever way is comfortable for them.

There is a difference between nurses actively promoting a patient's sexuality and giving "permission" for the occurrence of sexual expression. The former involves nurses helping patients either to find the means of expressing themselves or to change patients' beliefs and value systems so that patients increase their desires to so express themselves; the latter involves accepting patients' desires and/or behavior without inducing shame or guilt. Since the trend in nursing has been toward a greater awareness of the importance of human sexuality in the lives of patients, it is probable that nurses will become more tolerant of patients' expressions of sexuality; in other words, if and when it occurs, nurses will be better prepared to deal with it.

Zalar (1975) cautions nurses about the "frying pan effect" when setting up or becoming involved in human sexuality programs. She states that some individuals may become so zealous and enthusiastic about developing human sexuality programs that the result is "clobbering everyone over the head with it" (p. 43). She recommends starting out small and informing people of the program's intentions in order to obtain their support. This involves being sensitive not only to patients' needs but also to the attitudes and values of the community, opinion leaders, administrators, and colleagues. It should also be noted that programs in human sexuality, at least initially, might be more readily accepted in some parts of the country (such as the East and West coasts) than in others (for instance, the Deep South or the Bible Belt).

Before Elizabeth Kübler-Ross's (1969) pioneer work in the area of death and dying, few nurses felt comfortable in responding to patients' inquiries about dying, much less initiating discussions with them about their experience. Just as the trend in the area of death and dying has been toward the preparation of nurses to deal with this previously avoided topic, so it will be in the analogous area of sexuality. Today it is an accepted part of the nurse's role to initiate counseling with the dying patient; tomorrow it will be acceptable for the nurse to initiate discussions about sexuality. It is ironic, in fact, to realize that the trend toward greater openness in communicating with patients about dying predated that toward dealing openly with sexuality. The question that used to be a joke, "Is there sex after death?" turns out to be a prophecy when applied to trends in communication between health providers and consumers.

REFERENCES

Annon, J. S.: The behavioral treatment of sexual problems, Honolulu, Hawaii, 1974, Kapiolani Health Services.

Boston Women's Health Book Collective: Our bodies, ourselves, New York, 1973, Simon & Schuster, Inc.

Chilgren, R. A., and Briggs, M. M.: On being explicit; sex education for professionals, SIECUS Rep. 1:1, 1973.

Cohen, B. D., Wallston, B. S., and Wallston, K. A.: Sexual counseling and cardiac rehabilitation, Arch. Phys. Med. Rehabil. 57:473, 1976.

Elder, M. S.: The unmet challenge; nurse counseling on sexuality, Nurs. Outlook 18:38, 1970.

Fonseca, J. D.: Sexuality; a quality of being human, Nurs. Outlook 18:25, 1970.

Griffith, G. C.: Sexuality and the cardiac patient, Heart & Lung 2:70, 1973.

Hartman, W. E., and Fithean, M.: The treatment of the sexual dysfunctions, Long Beach, Calif., 1972, Center for Marital and Sexual Studies.

Hellerstein, H. K., and Friedman, E. H.: Sexual activity and the post-coronary patient, Cardiac Rehabil. 3:43, 1972.

Kaplan, H. S.: The new sex therapy, New York, 1974, Brunner/Mazel, Inc.

Kübler-Ross, E.: On death and dying, New York, 1969, Macmillan, Inc.

Lief, H., and Payne, T.: Sexuality; knowledge & attitudes, Am. J. Nurs. **75:**2026, 1975.

Masters, W., and Johnson, V.: Human sexual response, Boston, 1966, Little, Brown & Co.

Masters, W., and Johnson, V.: Human sexual inadequacy, 1970, Boston, Little, Brown and Co.

Mims, F.: Sexual health education and counseling. In Mims, F., editor: The nursing clinics of North America, Philadelphia, 1975, W. B. Saunders Co.

Osofsky, H., and Osofsky, J. D.: Let's be sensible about sex education, Am. J. Nurs. **71:** 532, 1971.

Rabin, B. J.: The sensuous wheeler, Santa Ana, Calif., 1974, JOYCE Publications.

Scheingold, L. D., and Wagner, N.: Sound sex and the aging heart, New York, 1974, Human Sciences Press.

Solberg, D. A., Butler, J., and Wagner, N. N.: Sexual behavior in pregnancy, N. Engl. J. Med. **288:**1098, 1974.

Thompson, L. F., Miller, M. H., and Bigler, H. F.: Sociology; nurses and their patients in a modern society, St. Louis, 1975, The C. V. Mosby Co.

Tuttle, W. B., Cook, W. L., and Fitch, E.: Sexual behavior in post–myocardial infarction patients, Am. J. Cardiol. **13:**140, 1964.

Walker, E. C.: Study of sexuality in nursing curriculum, Nurs. Forum **10:**18, 1971.

Woods, N. F.: Human sexuality in health and illness, St. Louis, 1975, The C. V. Mosby Co.

Zalar, M.: Human sexuality; a component of total patient care, Nurs. Digest **3:**40, 1975.

6 "New consumers" meet the establishment

exploration of issues in health care delivery

PETER KONG-MING NEW
WILFRED E. HOLTON
JUDE THOMAS MAY
RICHARD M. HESSLER

There is a new awareness among consumers of services that they should have something to say about the types of services rendered, the satisfaction or dissatisfaction they feel about these services, and decisions made regarding these services. The awareness itself is hardly new. Citizens in different eras have all had to learn how to make their plaints felt. Just as the citizens in the eighteenth century had to learn that they did not need to stop short of the railroad platforms that were only accessible to first-class train passengers during a Vienna uprising, the citizens of the twentieth century had to learn that they do not need to confine their unrest to certain areas. The way that consumers go about making their awareness felt in the 1970s is certainly very different from the hunger marches of the 1930s or the mass protests of suffragettes of the previous era. The demands for and the responses to changes have taken many turns through the years. These have been documented elsewhere (Greenstone and Peterson, 1973), and in this chapter we hardly need to elaborate on any of these. We focus on one group of consumers—those who serve on citizen boards or councils of neighborhood health centers or community mental health centers—and discuss some of the problems they face as they voice their concerns, raise issues of dissatisfaction, and demand power to make decisions over the types of services to be rendered by these health centers.

Much of our current concern about consumers who want participation in health affairs goes back to 1969 when we received a 2-year contract from the National Center for Health Services, H.S.M.H.A., to study the process of citizen participation in 12 neighborhood health centers throughout the United States. During the study we interviewed approximately 150 staff and citizens in these centers to ascertain

Revision of a paper prepared for the Sub-committee on Consumer Participation in Health Care, Association of Teachers of Preventive Medicine, John E. Fogarty Center in the Health Sciences, Public Health Service, Washington, D.C., April, 1974. Many of the ideas for the paper were generated from results of two contracts, HSM-110-69-255 and HSM-42-70-99, Health Services and Mental Health Administration. The studies cited were undertaken in the Department of Community Health and Social Medicine, School of Medicine, Tufts University, 1969-1971.

the problems they encountered in attempting to institute citizen paricipation in these centers (Bellin and New, 1972; May, 1973; New and Hessler, 1972; New, and others, 1973). In 1970, we received a 1-year contract from the National Institute of Mental Health to study the same process in six community mental health centers serving geographic areas covered by six of the neighborhood health centers being studied (Holton and others, 1971, 1973). We are still in the process of analyzing much of the data collected during that time, and two of us are engaged in collecting additional data (May and New, 1974, 1975).

When we were engaged in these studies, neighborhood health centers were at the peak of their operation, with over 70 centers throughout the U.S. (Hollister and others, 1974). These centers were receiving enormous amounts of money from both the Office of Economic Opportunity and the Public Health Service, and they were rendering very necessary services to hundreds of thousands of residents. Some of the centers, sponsored initially by various medical schools or hospitals, were already shifting away from their parent bodies to become independent centers, with funds coming directly to neighborhood corporations. Thus, on the surface, most of the centers seemed healthy, and titles such as "mature centers" were being bestowed on some. Some of the many community mental health centers being funded by the N.I.M.H. were in poverty areas. The community mental health centers were designed to deliver comprehensive services, including some in-patient beds in the centers or in affiliated agencies. Because the N.I.M.H. legislation did not define citizen participation narrowly, the centers' boards varied from elite groups (similar to hospital boards described below) to those pressing for a degree of control.

As researchers, we were not as sanguine about the health or maturation of the centers, especially when it came to consumer participation. We began to see cracks in the veneer that have been documented elsewhere (Kisch, 1972; Davis, 1971). The faults cannot be summarized in a sentence or two, because the weaknesses of citizen participation in neighborhood health centers reflect, in part, weaknesses in the provision of health care in the wider system. In this chapter, we examine some of these problems.

We begin by examining an ideal model of traditional health care, as represented by a hospital and its board, made up mainly of persons respected in their communities. The goals of the hospitals pretty much parallel the goals of the board members, most of whom come from middle-class backgrounds and are chosen precisely because they share the values of the hospital staff.* The hospital looks to these members for assistance and guidance in various endeavors. At the same time, the "lay" (nonphysician) members respect the staff in their areas of technical competence and, in most instances, do not dispute the medical decisions made by physicians, nurses, and other health workers in the hospital.

---

*Although hospital boards are now quite stable, when they were first formed, members of the board were also faced with many problems such as their relationships to each other as well as to other health institutions. Many of these problems centered on the differential goals of the hospitals and their members. For an elaboration of some of these differences, see Davis and Dolbeare (1968), pp. 224-240.

The hospital itself relates to other institutions and agencies in the community, attracted to some and repelled by others, depending on the exchange of services that may arise on a day-to-day basis or on a special basis. Since members of the board are themselves members of boards of other agencies, the relationships thus created are of a fairly stable nature. These hospitals, health agencies, or other institutions throughout the community are aligned in various hierarchical or horizontal patterns, each knowing its place. (Here, we are portraying a decidedly ideal type model, since we recognize many exceptions to the rule.)

One could almost portray this set of relationships in physical terms, using the analogy of positive or negative forces that align themselves around a magnet. In this analogy, the institutions are represented by metal balls with magnetic charges of their own that attract them to or repel them from the hospital. When the neighborhood health center is introduced as an innovation in health care, the previously aligned forces are disturbed. The types of medical and nonmedical activities that are carried out in these centers certainly do not conform to traditions. However, in the system that we envisage, given time, even the traditional health care system could cope with it. The neighborhood health center itself would begin to marshall supporters and identify detractors of its way of delivering health care services. The positive and negative forces would probably soon realign themselves to accommodate this novel institution.

When citizen participation is introduced, with a totally different concept from traditional hospital boards, it becomes much more difficult for the traditional health system to adjust to it. By nature of its character, we would portray citizen participation as a wooden ball (with no magnetic attraction of its own) that darts through the magnetic field, upsetting all previous alignments. Further, this ball does not come to rest (we realize we are going against Newton's principles) and creates a great deal of havoc by colliding with other institutions. As we examine the disruptions created by the introduction of citizen participation, we note several factors that render the analogy of the perpetually moving wooden ball as ideal.

First, the consumers on the citizen health boards in the neighborhood health centers do not necessarily subscribe to the goals of the center. In many instances, they have personal reasons for serving on these boards.

Second, these consumers are not as homogeneous as the middle-class board members, since they come from different social backgrounds with different experiences. Some operate on more concrete levels, while others can relate to more abstract issues.*

---

*Heterogeneity of consumers may have other consequences as well:
  Where the heterogeneity of the consumers is most significantly expressed in class or ethnic divisions, a systematic pressure towards differentiation within the occupation exists. One of the consequences of such divisions may be to produce within the field of health separate and even competing organisations of health provision—a public hospital for the less well off and a private system for the rich. These organisations compete for resources, and practitioners develop divergent interests in the struggle for resources (Johnson, 1972, p. 60).

Third, many of these consumers are trying to build up constituencies of their own, whereas hospital board members have worked out their constituencies previously. The neighborhood health center provides a convenient vehicle for consumers to make themselves more visible while they attempt to work out some method of procedure.

Fourth, because neighborhood health centers are sufficiently unstable, consumers on the boards have ready access to any number of issues that are potentially explosive. Some of these issues can become focal points for specific or general grievances directed to the neighborhood health center or other community agencies.

These four points, seen in the context of citizen participation, create conditions whereby consumers of the neighborhood health center boards look for allies to their causes. Thus, as the wooden ball moves within the constellation of agencies, it will create disturbances among the previously aligned forces. First, some of the institutions that have never been attracted to each other may join forces for mutual protection against citizen participation. Second, some individuals within previously dormant agencies may become so attracted to the notion of citizen participation that they create ripples of their own, or these members may join forces with the neighborhood health center board members. An infinite number of combinations may be created by the ever-moving ball, citizen participation.

We recognize the danger of carrying this analogy too far: We would end up being too ethereal. Nevertheless, we deliberately pose the issue of consumer participation in this fashion to show that consumers who participate change through time, but the system in which citizen participation is evolving is also attempting to adapt to this concept. Now, we shall be more concrete in discussing who this "new consumer" is, what he is trying to accomplish, and how he goes about accomplishing his goals. In turn, we shall also pay some attention to the milieu in which the consumer resides and what forces within this milieu or the neighborhood health center help or hinder the consumer in obtaining what he wants.

The early version of this "new consumer" was a hesitant, bewildered, respectful individual. Traditionally, charity medicine had taught him to mind his own business, even with the knowledge that all was not well with his health care. He had been treated in a cavalier fashion by those who provided his health care. In 1965, with the advent of O.E.O. neighborhood health centers, he was forced onto center stage, because maximum feasible participation pretty much "dictated" that he become a consumer who would actively participate in his own welfare. The health center boards that were established never made clear how much power this "new consumer" had to decide on policies relating to the center. At most of the early meetings of these boards, the "new consumer" was puzzled by the parliamentary procedures that had to be followed, the agendas that were discussed, and the decisions that had to be made. The health providers who came from middle-class backgrounds (and many from academic settings) assumed that everyone thought and acted on issues the way they did: They dispassionately discussed various issues before any decisions were made. They assumed that everyone would trust each other and be open in considering alternate solutions.

For both the consumers and health providers, the first meetings were frustrating (Davis and Tranquada, 1969). Many issues had to be settled while few guidelines existed. The ultimate authority often did not rest with anyone in the health centers; yet the granting agencies had high expectations of these health centers to "deliver" within a very short time. The consumers found that early expectations for decision making on policies that govern the operation of the health centers were not realized, and providers often were equally disenchanted to find that a larger portion of their time was spent on nonmedical problems for which they were not trained. As time went on, consumers began to identify structural weaknesses in the neighborhood health centers: rapid turnover of staff, fiscal instability and crisis, dominant philosophy of funding agencies (expressed through project assistants who came from Washington) or benign neglect, lack of clear direction, and a host of major or minor problems. Some of the consumers and staff found that they could manipulate the center personnel for their own purposes. During different stages of the health center development some consumers on the board adopted various disruptive tactics because they felt the establishment was not responding to their needs (New and Hessler, 1972; New and others, 1973; Zurcher, 1969). In extreme situations, the neighborhood health center became the focal point of community conflicts because there were no other similar agencies as visible.

These events occurred at the time when the consumer movement had extended to community control of law enforcement and educational institutions. In other words, the "new consumer" in the health area found kindred souls who also wanted control over their destinies. Within the health field, consumers from the neighborhood health centers began to organize. A conference was held in San Francisco in 1970, which a few of us attended only after much negotiation with various organizers who did not really encourage outsiders to look in. About that same time, the Medical Committee on Human Rights also held a conference in New Orleans, with the focus on neighborhood health centers. The directors of these health centers organized, with Clifton Cole of the Watts Health Foundation assuming a position of leadership. All these efforts signaled the emergence of the "new consumer" into the more "middle-class" mold of health care delivery.

The noble visions of the Kennedy-Johnson era gave way to the more limited scope of the Nixon administration. Many of the "new consumers" who were actively engaged in the neighborhood health center movement began to slip away to other activities. Because of their visibility, some of the "new consumers" took on other careers. The character of the neighborhood health center also began to shift from one of innovation to one that was more traditionally oriented. Part of this, of course, was caused by the push by the government to have these centers adopt the Health Maintenance Organization stance, the prepayment plans that were successfully carried out by organizations such as Kaiser, Group Health of Seattle, H.I.P. in New York, Harvard Plan, and others. Although we have not kept in close touch with the various neighborhood health centers and mental health centers since our study ended in 1971, we know that a few of these have closed their doors while most of the remaining centers are now quietly performing their work. At the same time, the consumers of the health center boards are behaving in somewhat the same manner as hospital board members.

In community mental health centers, the "new consumers" were a minority. "Elitist" boards predominated, but there was a divided trend or strain toward the opposite pole of consumer control. The pressure for this change came from two sources: general community interest in affecting the policies of local agencies; and dissatisfaction with services, elite boards, or professionals in the centers. We have discussed this previously at length and proposed a "transitional model" for moving toward consumer control in community mental health centers (Holton and others, 1973). Here we will briefly discuss the emergence of the "new consumer" in relation to mental health in some poverty areas.

Professional orientations in mental health tend to favor the medical and middle-class models of services and the monopolization of control of professional and administrative issues. At a recent meeting where citizen participation was discussed, a psychologist stated, "You are asking us to perform psychopathic behavior in giving up some of our power." We feel, in contrast, that the real issue is fear of unknown territory. In our experience elements of consumer control and new-careers involvement are often very acceptable to professionals after the initial fear and uncertainty have passed.

Community residents have been somewhat less concerned about community mental health centers than about neighborhood health centers and other local services. This relative lack of interest suggests that, especially in poverty areas, mental health does not have high priority. The consequences are twofold: Centers' services are often not well known or adequately utilized, and community residents do not strongly demand a voice in decision making. There is, however, a perceptible change in poverty areas.

"New consumers" can arise in community mental health as a result of specific dissatisfactions, when local issues become sharply defined and controversial. In one city, an old nursing home was purchased by the City Health Department for use as a community mental health center; a number of residents saw this as "second-class treatment" and picketed to demand a voice in decision making. This group became an "activist advisory" board for the center. In a second center new-career employees and other community residents became very concerned with what they believed to be irresponsible behavior by the director; they called open meetings that led to a special advisory committee that challenged the total power of the director and the elitist governing board. In these and other centers where "new consumers" emerged, a facilitating role was played by N.I.M.H. site-visit teams that stressed the desirability of participation by catchment area residents. Underlying this trend has been a growing desire to affect the policies of service agencies in poverty areas.

All this may not be bad. The ever-moving wooden ball may be slowing down to rest at some point of equilibrium. The negative and positive elements that scrambled for allies may have now coalesced and found ways of adapting to citizen participation. Within a few short years, the neighborhood health centers have become part of our "establishment" and deliver health care to a large segment of our population. Some of the "new consumers" have also been absorbed into the system and have themselves become managers of these centers.

CITIZEN INVOLVEMENT IN HEALTH CARE*

The issues we have raised regarding the "new consumers" concern their involvement in health care. In turn, we may raise a series of related questions, more directly posed with regard to the neighborhood health centers and all that they stand for: Are these centers community-run? Do these centers service a wide spectrum of community residents and their health problems? Do they deal with outpatient or inpatient services? Do they perform outreach services? Do they provide health care for the populations that lack this, such as rural populations or the population of the central city? Are these health centers purely for health care delivery, or are they established for political reasons as well?

Community health centers, of course, can contain elements of all that we have mentioned above. In recent years, many neighborhood health centers were created as a response to political unease, citizen demands for health care, medical and other health-professional student unrest, general disenchantment with the medical establishment, and a desire for local control. The growth of the health centers is partly due to the general decentralization process of health services and partly to health problems encountered by specific population groups, such as drug use among youths or the poverty cycle among the poor.

Thus, a neighborhood health center is not just another health care delivery service that consists of clinical and organizational components, but a political organization as well. It is a place where both concerned citizens and health professionals would like to exert some control over the management and operation of the services. Up to now, most health service organizations have been controlled by the professional staff. To be sure, hospitals and social agencies dealing with health have "lay" boards that deal mainly with financial planning and possibly interagency problems. Seldom do they deal with internal operations of the health institution. Now, an increasing number of citizens want control over the day-to-day operations of health institutions, especially those with "community" attached to their names. However, citizens and professionals have different degrees of involvement and different perceptions of "ideal" amounts of involvement in the political and health delivery aspects.

For the types of involvement by the "new consumer" that we have described, we propose the following paradigm as a way to view these centers:

*Part of this section is adapted from New (1974).

TYPES OF ACTIVITIES

| | Political | Health delivery | |
		Clinical	Organizational
Persons involved Citizens	Participation	Noninvolvement	Minimal participation
Persons involved Professionals	Noninvolvement	Control	Participation

Paradigm I: Perception of professionals on control of activities in neighborhood health centers

TYPES OF ACTIVITIES

| | Political | Health delivery | |
		Clinical	Organizational
Persons involved Citizens	Control	Participation	Control
Persons involved Professionals	Involvement	Advocate	Minimal control

Paradigm II: Perceptions of citizens on control of activities in neighborhood health centers.

While we recognize the dangers involved in the use of paradigms to explain events, they may help us to understand the concerns of the "new consumers" as against the health professionals. The paradigms best represent what takes place in centers that (1) have evolved out of community demands or (2) have been established by forces outside of the community and, at a later date, have been subjected to community demand for control.

Citizens and professionals perceive problems of control differently. The professionals are most concerned with control over clinical aspects of health delivery. They are well trained in this area and justifiably feel it is their domain. The closer the practice of physicians working in neighborhood health centers approximates solo medical practice, the happier they are. When it comes to the matter of controls, physicians act as a close corporate group over clinic operations. The preferred mode of operation is indeed that citizens keep "hands off."

At the opposite extreme, most health professionals, especially physicians, prefer noninvolvement in the political sphere. Because they have little emotional investment in the political arena, they may feel comfortable when citizens become more involved in this area. As far as management of health delivery is concerned, professionals want some participation, but not necessarily over all spheres of organizational management. They would probably tolerate minimal participation from citizens, such as in the choice of paraprofessionals or the allocation of space in the waiting room.

The perception of interested citizens is quite different. The ones most involved want total control over the political and the management spheres. In the clinical area, they would like to have some participation but recognize that many strictly medical routines are beyond their capabilities; however, a new movement is now under way among citizens who feel that everyone should know something about his own body. Citizens do not view health services narrowly as only involving a select group of health professionals. They feel that appropriate functions could be carried out by others as well, such as neighborhood aides or other new-career persons.

Citizens also feel that health professionals should be involved in the political area because they can use their prestige to obtain funds or to influence legislators or can hold press conferences to tell the world how good or bad current medical services are. Citizens would like health professionals to be their advocates in the clinical area and to have some participation in the management of the health center.

These paradigms may help to explain some of the issues that "new consumers" are concerned with. The goal of delivery of health care to all may be shared by citizens and health professionals, but they differ in their methods of achieving this goal. Neighborhood health centers and citizen participation grew out of a fairly tense political situation in the mid-1960s, and it is well for us to keep that in mind as we move into a more "quiet" period in the mid-1970s. Through attempts at new legislation, Congress is trying to win over the "new consumers" by providing more funds for various human resources services. Some of the issues that we have raised, implicitly or explicitly, will not evaporate quickly. The "new consumers" have become more sophisticated in regard to problems of control and accountability. For instance, they have learned something of the possibilities of pooling financial resources and energy to deal with external forces that have not been identified clearly before. At any moment, political alliances can be mobilized to create yet another disturbance among these aligned forces.

REFERENCES

Bellin, S. S., and New, P. K.: Neighborhood health centers. In Haring, J. E., editor: Urban and regional economics, Boston, 1972, Houghton Mifflin Co.

Davis, J. W., Jr.: Decentralization, citizen participation, and ghetto health care, Am. Behav. Scientist **15:**94, 1971.

Davis, J. W., Jr., and Dolbeare, K. M.: Little groups of neighbors; the selective service system, Chicago, 1968, Markham Publishing Co.

Davis, M. S., and Tranquada, R. E.: A sociological evaluation of the Watts Neighborhood Health Center, Med. Care **7:**105, 1969.

Greenstone, J. D., and Peterson, P. E.: Race and authority in urban politics; community participation and the War on Poverty, New York, 1973, Russell Sage Foundation.

Hollister, R. M., Kramer, B. M., and Bellin, S.S., editors: Neighborhood health centers, Lexington, Mass., 1974, Lexington Books, Inc.

Holton, W. E., New, P. K., and Hessler, R. M.: Citizenship participation and interagency relations; issues and program implications for community mental health centers, National Technical Information Service, Report PB 210-093, Washington, D.C., 1971, Department of Commerce.

Holton, W. E., New, P. K., and Hessler, R. M.: Citizen participation and conflict, Admin. Ment. Health **1:**96, 1973.

Johnson, T. J.: Professions and power, Toronto, 1972, The Macmillan Co. of Canada Ltd.

Kisch, A. I.: The U.C.S.D. (University of California, San Diego), O.E.O. Comprehensive Health Program story (unpublished paper), School of Public Health, University of California at Los Angeles, 1972.

May, J. T.: Public funds and the fate of voluntarism; some notes on a neighborhood health facility, Hum. Organization **32:**248, 1973.

May, J. T., and New, P. K.: Shifting patterns of authority and control in the neighborhood health centers (unpublished paper presented to the American Anthropological Association, Mexico City, November 20, 1974).

May, J. T., and New, P. K.: Shifting patterns of authority and control in neighborhood health centers (unpublished paper presented to the Society for the Study of Social Problems, San Francisco, Calif., August 24, 1975.)

New, P. K.: Community health centres; five danger signals, Community Health Centre Project, Monograph No. 5, Ottawa, 1974, Canadian Public Health Association.

New, P. K., and Hessler, R. M.: Neighborhood health centers; traditional medical care at an outpost? Inquiry **9:**45, 1972.

New, P. K., Hessler, R. M., and Cater, P. B.: Consumer control and public accountability, Anthropol. Q. **46:**196, 1973.

New, P. K., and New, M. L.: Health care in the People's Republic of China; the barefoot doctor, Inquiry **12**(Suppl.):103, 1975a.

New, P. K., and New, M. L.: The links between health and political structure in New China, Hum. Organization **34:**237, 1975b.

New, P. K., and New, M. L.: The barefoot doctors in China; healers for all seasons. In Landy, D., editor: Culture, health and disease; a reader in medical anthropology, New York, 1976, Macmillan, Inc.

Zurcher, L. A., Jr.: Stages of development in poverty program neighborhood action committees, J. Appl. Behav. Sci. **5:**223, 1969.

7 The nurse practitioner movement

STANLEY K. HENSHAW

A dramatic recent development in health care delivery has been the movement to transfer some primary ambulatory care responsibilities from physicians to mid-level health workers, specifically nurse practitioners and physician's assistants. Mid-level health workers have the potential to alter radically the delivery of ambulatory care, and nurse practitioners have already had an impact on the nursing profession and nursing education. This chapter gives a brief overview of the nurse practitioner movement and discusses three issues that will vitally affect its future.

There is no universally accepted definition of the term *nurse practitioner,* and some nurses use it in its literal sense to apply to any nurse providing direct patient services. Increasingly, however, the term is being used to refer to the expanded nursing role; for the purposes of this discussion it will be defined as an ambulatory care nurse with "advanced skills in the assessment of the physical and psycho-social health-illness status of individuals, families, or groups in a variety of settings through health and development history taking and physical examination."* In addition, nurse practitioners are usually trained to do the following with more or less assistance from physicians and protocols: evaluate the assessment data to make treatment decisions; order and interpret laboratory tests; and manage the care of selected patients, which includes prescribing and providing care, making judgments about the use of accepted pharmaceutical agents, and assuming responsibility for patient education and counseling. This definition includes some nurses with other titles such as "clinician" and "specialist."

The transfer of responsibilities from physicians to nurse practitioners may be viewed as a continuation of a long-term process that extends from the time when nurses were not entrusted with reading the clinical thermometer. However, the nurse practitioner role represents a quantum jump in this process, seen most dramatically in nurses' use of physical examination techniques and management of drug therapies. The significance of these changes is enhanced by the fact that they obliterate some of the traditional distinctions between nursing and medicine and leave no simple way to reestablish the professional boundaries.

The first nurse practitioner programs were in pediatrics, and pediatric nurse

The research reported in this chapter was supported by Grant No. HS01366 from the National Center for Health Services Research of the U.S. Department of Health, Education, and Welfare.
*From the definition adopted by the Congress for Nursing Practice of the American Nurses' Association in May, 1974.

practitioners are now the most numerous and well-accepted type of nurse practitioner. An American Nurses' Association study identified 2,300 pediatric nurse practitioners and associates as of May 1974, and this undoubtedly understates the true number (American Nurses' Association, 1975). Pediatrics has been particularly receptive to the nurse practitioner concept because of the large proportion of physician time spent on routine well-baby examination, treatment of minor illness, and counseling. The success of the pediatric nurse practitioner programs led to experimentation with adult and family nurse practitioners. This movement received an added impetus when MEDEX and other physician's assistant programs were started, accompanied by much publicity and support from organized medicine (Sadler and others, 1972). By 1975 the combined number of adult, family, and maternity nurse practitioners approximately equaled the number of pediatric nurse practitioners (Sultz, 1975) and was of the same order of magnitude as the number of physician's assistants. Nurse practitioners are now being trained at a greater rate than are physician's assistants.

There is wide variation in the extensiveness of training of nurse practitioners. The most common type of program provides 3 to 6 months of intensive didactic and clinical training to registered nurses with varied backgrounds, followed by a preceptorship period of supervised practice. Some nurse practitioners have been trained individually by physicians or in in-service programs. At the other end of the spectrum, an increasing proportion are being trained in master's degree programs.

The special skills of nurse practitioners lend themselves to a variety of roles and functions in different health care settings. Theoretically, the family nurse practitioner provides primary care to a caseload of selected families with a collaborating physician or team available for consultation and backup. The nurse is the person of first contact for the individuals in her caseload, and she handles many minor acute and stabilized chronic illnesses with little physician assistance. She performs complete screening examinations as well as the traditional nursing functions of prevention, patient education, and counseling. The patient care activities of the collaborating physician are concentrated on more serious and complex medical problems.

The benefits expected from the nurse practitioner role are somewhat different for the various participants in the health care system. The rationale used most frequently in public and official statements has emphasized the shortage and maldistribution of physicians. Midlevel health workers are seen as a way of increasing the availability of primary health care at a moderate cost and within a reasonable length of time. For example, the following statement appears in the report of the Secretary's (H.E.W.) Committee to Study Extended Roles for Nurses (1971):

> There is a growing recognition of the importance of physician-nurse collaboration in extending health care services to meet increasing demand . . . . A basic problem is that many nurses are not practicing at their highest potential nor receiving training and experience that would enable them to extend the scope of their practice and thereby extend the availability of health services (p. 4).

Some groups give greater emphasis to nurse practitioners' potential for improving the quality of health care, and others are most concerned with reducing the cost of care.

In fact, nurse practitioners may have a number of different effects, depending on how they are trained and used: (1) Quality of care may improve because physicians are freed to spend more time on complex cases; psychosocial care, education, and counseling, which the nurse can provide more effectively when she is also the primary care provider, may improve; continuity and coordination of care, especially in clinics with a high turnover of parttime physicians may be improved; the quality of traditional nursing services such as patient evaluations in a visiting nurse home visit may improve. In addition, an increase in the availability of services also affects quality by making it possible for more attention to be given to secondary problems and follow-up and by facilitating early access to care: (2) The availability of care can be increased by permitting physicians to increase their patient loads, establishing nurse clinics in areas without physicians, and reducing waiting times for patients. (3) The cost of certain health services can be reduced by substituting nursing manpower for more expensive physician time. The financial saving may go to the patient in the form of lower fees, to the nurse's employer, to the nurse practitioner herself, to a third-party payer, or a combination of these. This potential benefit is given particular emphasis by government agencies responsible for underwriting health care and by certain employers. (4) Satisfaction of the participants in the health care system may be increased. These participants include patients, the nurses who enjoy increased responsibility and rewards, and physicians, who may be relieved of unwanted tasks and have increased time for more rewarding activities.

The actual impact of nurse practitioners and physician's assistants has been the subject of research, but as yet there are no conclusive answers, due in part to the uncertainty of generalizing from the particular cases that have been studied. A number of studies have found the technical quality of medical care provided by nurse practitioners to be "adequate" or comparable to physician care (for example, Duncan and others, 1971; Sackett and others, 1974; Schlesinger and others, 1973), but only one controlled study has shown a significant improvement in quality of care resulting from the use of nurse practitioners (Lewis and others, 1969). Most research has not attempted to measure the aspects of care in which nurse practitioners might be superior to physicians.

A number of conditions have contributed to the growth of the nurse practitioner movement (Bullough, 1975a). From a sociological perspective, it is not surprising that an important segment of the nursing profession would support a move to incorporate medical functions into nursing, inasmuch as these functions confer prestige and material rewards. The incorporation of these functions conforms to an important value held by nursing in that it may result in more and/or better care for patients. In contrast, the willingness of physicians to relinquish their exclusive right to these functions seems rather surprising and is the result of a special circumstance, the excessive demand for primary medical care in relation to the number of physicians providing such care. This demand for care has provided physicians with such economic security that they do not generally perceive midlevel health workers as a competitive economic threat. In fact, some physicians expect a beneficial effect, that of a reduction in public dissatisfaction with the medical care system. In addition, some physicians have realized an economic advantage from the employment of nurse practitioners. Should the demand-supply situation improve even modestly, which is easily conceivable, it could have an economic effect on physicians, who would then move to protect their interests. Midlevel health workers and foreign medical graduates would be the most likely targets. The power of organized medicine has decreased somewhat in relation to nursing but is still adequate to retard further expansion of the nursing role or force retrenchment in some states and localities.

Physicians have made an important contribution to the nurse practitioner movement. Early experiments were initiated by two physicians, Henry Silver in Colorado and Charles Lewis in Kansas, in cooperation with nurses. The American Academy of Pediatrics furnished leadership in the development of pediatric nurse practitioners (Bullough, 1975a). In addition to the need to improve patient care, an important motivation for physicians has been the desire to be relieved of certain tasks that they find relatively unrewarding professionally. Among these are the examination of asymptomatic patients, routine patient care in general medical clinics where the physician's time is volunteered, and work in diagnostic and distribution clinics.

Presently, the nurse practitioner concept is firmly established within organized nursing and is gaining increased acceptance by health care providers. The number of nurse practitioners is increasing rapidly, due in large part to the financial support of the Department of Health, Education, and Welfare. The following sections discuss some issues whose resolution will shape the future of the movement.

DEGREE OF SPECIALIZATION

Discussions of the nurse practitioner concept have given little explicit consideration to the question of specialization in the training and roles of nurse practitioners. Three degrees of specialization can be distinguished:

1. Least specialized is the family nurse practitioner, who has primary care responsibility for patients of all ages and the full range of health care functions, including chronic disease care, treatment of minor acute problems, health maintenance, and prevention.
2. Intermediate in specialization are pediatric and geriatric nurse practitioners, whose patients are limited in age range, and nurse practitioners with a limited range of functions, such as health maintenance of chronic disease patients only and staffing a walk-in clinic.
3. Some nurse practitioners work in still more specialized areas, such as family planning, diabetes, or surgery, or have a single function, such as

performing screening and preemployment examinations. Nurses may work in two or more of these specialty roles or combine a specialty with a more general nurse practitioner role.

A specialized role in this sense does not imply a lower level of responsibility or competence to exercise independent judgment and, therefore, is not analogous to the Type B physician's assistant described in a report of the National Academy of Sciences (1970). The training required is not always less than that for a generalist, because a greater depth of knowledge may be needed in the area of specialty.

The rationale for the most general role, family nurse practitioner, is twofold. First, nurse practitioners are needed to work in general practices and nurse clinics in remote areas where the physician shortage is most severe. Second, even where patient care is concentrated so that specialization is possible, family-centered care may be preferable to the fragmented care provided by specialized nurses and physicians. In addition, general training gives a nurse more flexibility in the types of positions she can fill. However, there is a tendency for nurse practitioners with general training to gravitate toward more specialized roles. A survey of the graduates of six family nurse practitioner programs (Henshaw, 1976) found that over half are limited in the age range of their patients, in most cases seeing only adults. About half are also somewhat specialized in their functions. Thus it is evident that pressures for specialization are affecting nurse practitioners. These results suggest that nurse practitioner training could be profitably oriented toward particular settings and roles rather than based on a practice model that is rarely realized. Specialization could in some cases reduce training costs and the time needed by trainees to reach a satisfactory level of proficiency. An additional consideration is that generalized training creates expectations on the part of the nurses that may not be realized in specialized roles, resulting in dissatisfaction and job turnover.

The fact that physicians with specialty training seem to be more receptive to midlevel health workers than do general practitioners also bears on the question of specialized roles for nurse practitioners. A survey of physicians in Wisconsin found that more surgeons and internists than general practitioners saw a need for physician's assistants (Coye and Hansen, 1969). In the Cornell survey (Henshaw, 1976), physicians with medical school affiliations were more favorable to their nurse practitioners than were other physicians. One explanation is that midlevel health workers can relieve specialists of unwanted peripheral duties; however, their skills overlap a large segment of the skills of general practitioners. Record and Greenlick (1975) in reporting the experience of a Kaiser-Permanente health plan concluded that a threat to the status of physicians exists where midlevel health workers are capable of performing functions regarded by physicians as central to their role, even where no direct economic threat exists. The example given was that of obstetricians who would not permit nurse midwives to perform normal deliveries. In addition, general practitioners may be more sensitive than specialists to the possibility of economic competition from midlevel health workers.

In conclusion, although there are many situations in which family nurse practitioners are needed, most nurse practitioners are assuming more specialized roles. Evidence indicates that the effectiveness of specialized nurse practitioners is equal, if not superior, to that of family nurse practitioners. The nurse practitioner movement, including the training programs, would benefit from greater awareness of the advantages of specialization.

LEGAL ASPECTS OF THE NURSE PRACTITIONER ROLE

Many nurse practitioners have found that legal restrictions on the practice of nursing have prevented them from assuming some of the responsibilities for which they were trained. Efforts to conform to nurse and medical practice acts, as these are interpreted by nurse practitioners and their employers, sometimes result in truncated roles and inefficiencies. For example, many nurse practitioners cannot prescribe or renew medications in the absence of a physician. In a nurse satellite clinic, this means that some patients must make unnecessary return visits to obtain a prescription. Another example is the practice in many settings of having a physician sign the chart of each patient before the patient leaves the clinic. Nurses and patients may spend a significant amount of time waiting for a physician to be available to review the chart.

Interpretations of statutes limiting the practice of nursing are highly variable and uncertain, particularly in the states without explicit provision for nurse practitioners, and there are few court decisions to provide guidance. Many nurse practitioners and physicians participate in activities potentially subject to legal challenge, either in the belief that they are in fact legal or with a conscious willingness to take a limited risk. For example, some nurse practitioners use presigned prescription blanks provided by their collaborating physicians, and a few have found pharmacies that will honor their signatures. Many diagnose and treat illnesses in a manner that could be construed as the practice of medicine. It should be emphasized that it is impossible to know in advance whether a particular act can legally be performed by a nurse; what is legal is what a court would decide, and this is largely unpredictable except in extreme cases.

Experience to date suggests that under present conditions the risk of suit for malpractice or prosecution for illegal practice of medicine is extremely low. It is well known that for years nursing practice exceeded the bounds of outdated statutes without repercussion. There have been very few malpractice suits or other legal actions against nurse practitioners. It is reported that, in 1971, graduates of the Duke University physician's assistant program had experienced no legal problems even though they were practicing in ten states that had no authorizing legislation (Barkin, 1974). The absence of legal problems can be best understood by looking at the groups who might challenge nurse practitioners. Physicians and institutions benefit from the right to delegate responsibilities to nurses, and they are not likely to challenge this right unless nurse practitioners begin to pose an economic threat or to practice independently. Consumer acceptance of midlevel health workers has been good, and consumers are not likely to file complaints as long as they have the option of being seen by a physician. Malpractice suits involving nurse practitioners will occasionally occur, but possibly at a lower rate than for physicians because nurses usually take time to show more personal interest in patients.

In spite of the favorable legal experience of nurse practitioners, they would benefit from legislative change that would clearly establish their authority to diagnose and treat medical conditions within their capability. In recent years most states have liberalized their nurse practice acts to some degree, and additional changes are occurring rapidly (Bullough, 1975b; Kelly, 1974; Sadler, 1974). However, most of the new statutes have not lifted restrictions on nursing to the extent that all nurse practitioners are unambiguously authorized to utilize their full capabilities. State legislatures are influenced primarily by organized nursing and organized medicine, and the latter at best has preferred to move cautiously in surrendering the physician monopoly on medical care. Physicians are especially anxious to retain ultimate control over medical functions either as individuals or in the state boards of medicine.

From the point of view of nurse practitioners, ideal legislation would authorize them to exercise their skills with a minimum of bureaucratic red tape and physician control. A proposal in New York State that came close to this ideal would have allowed nurses to perform all functions for which they had gained competency in certified educational programs. The only bureaucratic control would have been in the certification of the educational programs; this would probably not have been a major obstacle, although it could have created complications for nurses trained out of state. The proposal proved to be unacceptable to physicians because of the degree of independent authority granted to nurses and is being modified accordingly.

An approach adopted by a number of states is to expand the definition of nursing practice and eliminate specific prohibitions on the practice of medicine. These statutes tend to be unclear in defining the functions nurses may and may not perform. For example, the widely copied New York act defines professional nursing to include "diagnosing and treating human responses to actual or potential health problems." While this would not seem to authorize the diagnosis or treatment of disease, its vagueness and the use of the phrase "diagnosing and treating" provide the basis of a legal defense of expanding nursing roles.

By 1974, 13 states had established regulatory mechanisms for authorizing and overseeing expanded nursing roles (Bullough, 1975b). In these states the boards of nursing alone or jointly with the boards of medicine may promulgate rules and regulations authorizing nurses to perform certain acts otherwise restricted to physicians. This approach has the advantage of being legally unambiguous, provided that the regulations are clear, but it has major disadvantages in some states. First, the regulations may involve a considerable amount of delay and red tape in establishing the qualifications of the individual nurse, the appropriateness of the practice setting, the type of physician supervision required, and the particular acts authorized (Roemer, 1975). The boards may require the filing of protocols covering all situations in which the nurse is authorized to act; such protocols, besides being difficult to create, can never cover all the situations the nurse will encounter, particularly with elderly patients with chronic diseases. Second, in all but 1 (Oregon) of these 13 states, the board of medicine must agree to the rules promulgated or must recognize the functions authorized as properly belonging to nursing. Thus, organized medicine retains effective veto power over the transfer of functions. Furthermore, the boards of medicine are often dominated by older general practitioners, the group within the medical community most likely to feel threatened by nurses providing primary care. The legislation does not assure that the regulations will not be impossibly restrictive; for example, in California the regulations written to implement the physician's assistant law rendered the concept practically inoperable (Sadler, 1974). The existence of such regulations can prohibit acts that would otherwise have been defensible under the more flexible wording of the nurse and medical practice acts.

A different approach adopted in some states is to allow nurses to assume an expanded role under delegatory authority granted to physicians. In Connecticut, for example, the medical practice act exempts from legal responsibility "any person rendering service as a physician's trained assistant, a registered nurse, or a licensed practical nurse if such service is rendered under the supervision, control and responsibility of a licensed physician." This approach has a number of advantages: No bureaucratic red tape is involved; it clearly conveys the necessary legal authority; it is more flexible and less potentially restrictive than a regulatory approach; and it is likely to be acceptable to physicians and institutions in that it increases their organizational flexibility. It has the disadvantage of not specifying the standard of care required of physicians in determining the adequacy of the nurse's training or the quality of her performance.

Nurses have not been generally receptive to the concept of delegated authority because of resistance to control of their practice by physicians. They argue that the expanded nursing role is nursing, not medicine, and as such should be supervised by nurses rather than physicians. After a long-term struggle to establish nursing as an independent profession, it seems to nurses to be a move backward to accept physician supervision of part of their activity; this problem has caused some nurses to oppose the incorporation of medical functions into nursing. Many nurses do not like to see their role divided into two segments, a medical component supervised by physicians and a nursing component supervised by nurses.

In practical, as opposed to symbolic, terms, it does not appear that expanded role authority based on delegation would be detrimental to most nurse practitioners, except for the few who might wish to establish independent practices. Effective patient care presupposes a nurse-physician relationship based on trust and mutual respect. A physician cannot work effectively with a nurse practitioner who cannot, in his perception, perform competently, nor should a nurse collaborate with a physician whose competence she does not trust. The relationship and its basis of mutual respect are not likely to be affected by legislation. As for supervision, many nurse practitioners prefer to be supervised in the clinical area by physicians. However, the regulatory approach holds little superiority in this regard since physician supervision is usually required, and the degree of supervision specified may be greater than that practiced by many physicians operating under general delegatory authority.

Even in the absence of special legislation, the nurse practitioner role can eventually establish a legal basis under the principle of "custom and usage." As the role becomes widespread and generally accepted as good medical practice, it will become less vulnerable to legal challenge. This being the case, existing legislation may be preferable to legislation that recognizes nurse practitioners but provides for close, restrictive regulation.

The reaction of the medical profession is a critical factor in determining the extent to which nurses will move into primary care roles. At the individual level, nurses can seek out physicians and health care organizations favorable to the expanded role even if these are in the minority. On the level of the state legislature, the problem is somewhat more difficult, but here organized nursing has increasing political influence and may be able to mobilize support of institutions, consumers, and third-party payers, provided that the value of the expanded role has been demonstrated to these groups. The most unfavorable arena for confrontation with medicine is in the boards of medicine and the medical societies. The growth of the nurse practitioner movement will be most vulnerable to physician opposition if power over its future is vested in these groups.

The second legal problem affecting nurse practitioners is the fact that their services are not usually reimbursable under Medicare, Medicaid, and private insurance plans. To get around these restrictions, many employers require that a physician see every patient, however briefly. Some believe it is sufficient for a physician to sign each chart and the necessary forms. Most do not believe they can bill third-party payers for services provided in nurse clinics without a physician present, which inhibits one of the most valuable uses of nurse practitioners.

Legislative remedies for the third-party payment problem raise some difficult questions. Should all nurse services be reimbursable, or only physician-substitution services? The high cost of reimbursing all nurse services poses a severe obstacle to this approach, but otherwise there must be a procedure to determine which services are of the physician-substitution type. This may involve physician delegation, nurse practitioner certification, and other regulatory mechanisms.

QUALITY VERSUS EFFICIENCY

Most of the possible advantages of nurse practitioners can be seen as either improvements in the quality of care or increases in the efficiency with which care is delivered. Quality improvements include better patient education, more continuity of care, more thorough patient assessments, and so forth. Increased practice efficiency can be manifested by a higher patient load, improved accessibility of care, better use of physician time, and economic benefits. To a large extent these two types of benefits are mutually exclusive—the more emphasis is placed on improving the quality of care, the fewer efficiency-related benefits are likely to be realized.

Some observers have suggested that an exception to the conflict between quality and efficiency will occur in the case of patients with chronic diseases, for whom better nursing care could reduce episodes of illness and hospitalization and thereby reduce the overall cost of care. On the other hand, it could be argued that improved care would result in the detection and treatment of more medical conditions and, consequently, in more hospitalization. Research has not been conclusive on this subject but has not generally found reduced hospitalization (Gordon, 1974; Spector and others, 1975) or improved patient functioning (Sackett and others, 1974). One widely quoted study reported reduced hospitalization (Lewis and Resnik, 1967), but the differences were not subjected to a test for statistical significance and may have been random error. The authors did not report hospitalization data for a replication of the study (Lewis and others, 1969). If further research demonstrates that under certain conditions primary care by nurse practitioners results in reduced hospitalization, this will constitute an important exception to the following observations.

The nurse practitioner movement is confronted with conflicting expectations with respect to quality and efficiency. Quality of care tends to be emphasized by educators in nurse practitioner training programs and others in the nursing establishment. They stress the importance of combining nursing and medical care and feel that nurse practitioners should maintain their identity as nurses rather than function as physician's assistants. Nurse practitioners do not like to feel that their purpose is to save physicians' time, though this is an important prerequisite for efficiency-related benefits. There is also a desire to avoid falling into the pattern of some physicians who provide fast technical care at the expense of psychosocial care. The emphasis of quality over efficiency also has the advantage of being less economically threatening to physicians.

On the other hand, the publicly stated rationale for nurse practitioners as described earlier is based on the shortage and maldistribution of physicians, which implies that the physician-substitution aspect of the role is most important. Individuals and organizations that bear the cost of health care as well as many potential employers of nurse practitioners are most concerned with the efficiency-related benefits of the role. Medicaid and Medicare coverage for nurse practitioner services will depend to a large extent on the outcome of studies of the effect of such coverage on the overall cost of care. Thus, the use of nurse practitioners will depend in large part on their measured cost-efficiency, while the nursing community transmits to nurse practitioners a value system that emphasizes quality of care.

A number of studies have attempted to assess the productivity and economic impact of nurse practitioners. The results for pediatric nurse practitioners in private medical practices suggest that their productivity can usually justify their salary and expenses (Charney and Kitzman, 1971; Kahn and Wirth, 1975; Merenstein and others, 1974; Yankauer and others, 1972a). The largest of these studies (Yankauer and others, 1972a) found that 27 pediatric nurse practitioners working in private practices handled an average of 65 patient encounters a week without physician assistance. These services were valued at $2,500 more than the salaries and expenses of the pediatric nurse practitioners, but only about half the practices actually increased their patient loads (Yankauer and others, 1972b). Most of these and other nurse practitioner studies were conducted within the first year after training, before most nurse practitioners probably reach peak proficiency, and thus tend to underestimate their productivity.

Studies of family nurse practitioners have produced somewhat different results. Office nurses given additional training have been found to increase practice efficiency (Lees, 1973; Spitzer and others, 1974), but the increase was smaller than that found in the previously cited studies of pediatric nurse practitioners. Two studies of nurse practitioners caring for patients with chronic diseases in hospital clinics found that the total cost of clinic care was higher than that provided by physicians, in part because the nurses ordered approximately twice as many patient revisits (Lewis and Resnik, 1967; Spector and others, 1975). Another study employing random assignment of patients reported increased patient contacts for the nurse but did not give cost data (Gordon, 1974).

These research findings suggest that productivity and efficiency may emerge as a problem for nurse practitioners, particularly family nurse practitioners. High productivity for family nurse practitioners may be difficult to achieve because of the wide range of medical problems encountered and knowledge needed. The pediatric nurse practitioner role may be more conducive to high productivity because a large proportion of pediatric patients are asymptomatic or have minor acute illnesses that are relatively simple to treat. A more narrowly defined role with adult patients might be desirable from this point of view; for example, the Kaiser-Permanente health plans in Oakland and Sacramento have found that nurses are effective and efficient in performing screening physical examination (Henriques and others, 1974; Taller and Feldman, 1974).

Data from Henshaw's (1976) study of family nurse practitioners show that they tend to work in settings that place little emphasis on productivity. Few of the graduates studied work in private fee-for-service practices, and many of the graduates work in hospital clinics where neither physicians nor administrators know the cost per visit in the nurse's subunit, and no cost-benefit studies of nurse practitioners have been performed. Further evidence of the low value placed on economic considerations is the fact that most of the respondents in the questionnaire survey were unable or unwilling to give an opinion regarding the financial impact of their nurse practitioners. Studies of productivity in such settings are likely to produce results that are unfavorable to nurses and do not reflect their potential contribution. A remedy is for nurse practitioner programs to attempt to place their trainees in more efficiently run medical settings.

In conclusion, support for the nurse practitioner movement is likely to be strongly influenced by its perceived effect on health care costs. This is an area that is given little emphasis by the nurses involved in the movement but is a major concern at all levels of government due to the rapid rise in public expenditures for health care. The few studies reporting nurse practitioner productivity may have underestimated the nurses' contributions; nevertheless, decisions will be influenced by the data available, however inadequate. Most of the reports show nurse practitioners increasing the productivity of physicians by 50% or less. At this rate, nurse practitioners can be economical if their remuneration is less than half that of physicians, depending on their overhead costs and assuming that they do not order more services for their patients than do physicians. The salary demands of nurse practitioners are likely to increase as more of them obtain master's degrees as a result of the trend toward the merging of nurse practitioner training into academic programs. In some areas nurses may find themselves competing for institutional positions with young physicians who are disinclined to enter private practice. If the momentum of the nurse practitioner movement is to be maintained, it may be necessary for more attention to be given to productivity and financial impact.

CONCLUSIONS

The number of nurse practitioners is increasing rapidly, due in large part to federal support for training programs, and their acceptance is good despite legal restrictions and resistance of some physicians. At this point the only real dangers to the continued growth of the movement appear to be economic problems with the role, including restrictions on third-party payment, and physician opposition resulting from the threat to the income and prestige of general practitioners. The legal system poses a major obstacle only insofar as it is influenced by physicians opposed to expanding the role of nurses in primary care.

The nurse practitioner movement would benefit from more adequate research in the areas of productivity and quality of care. The few studies reporting data on productivity suffer from the following shortcomings: (1) Measurements were made within 1, or at most 2, years of training, although there is evidence that proficiency continues to increase beyond that point; (2) productivity is affected by such factors as the demand for services and the practice setting's emphasis on efficiency, which makes it difficult to distinguish the effects of the nurse's capacity from extraneous influences; and (3) the traditional nursing services provided by nurse practitioners are frequently overlooked. The premature evaluation of nurse practitioners is a result of the fact that most research is tied to new training programs, which makes it necessary for data collection to begin soon after training is completed.

The quality of nurse practitioner care has been demonstrated to be adequate in laboratory-like situations, but further studies are needed to determine the effects of experience and role routinization. Perhaps even more important from nursing's point of view, more effort should be devoted to the measurement of aspects of quality of care in which nurses may make a special contribution rather than simply substitute for physicians; prevention, psychosocial care, and health maintenance of patients with chronic diseases, which entails the possibility of reduced hospitalization. If nurses can significantly improve care in these respects, it is further justification of the nurse practitioner role even at increased cost; if not, nurse practitioners should emphasize the physician-substitution aspects of their role.

REFERENCES

American Nurses' Association: Pediatric nurse practitioners; their practice today, Kansas City, Mo., 1975, The Association.

Barkin, R. M.: Directions for statutory change; the physician extender, Am. J. Public Health **64:**1132, 1974.

Bullough, B.: The third phase in nursing licensure; the current nurse practice acts. In Bullough, B., editor: The law and the expanding nursing role, New York, 1975a, Appleton-Century-Crofts.

Bullough, B.: Factors contributing to role expansion for registered nurses. In Bullough, B., editor: The law and the expanding nursing role, New York, 1975b, Appleton-Century-Crofts.

Charney, E., and Kitzman, H.: The child health nurse (pediatric nurse practitioner) in private practice, N. Engl. J. Med. **285:**1353, 1971.

Coye, R. D., and Hansen, M. F.: The doctor's assistant; a survey of physicians' expectations, J.A.M.A. **209:**529, 1969.

Duncan, B., Smith, A. N., and Silver, H. K.: Comparison of physical assessment of children by pediatric nurse practitioners and pediatricians, Am. J. Public Health **61:**1170, 1971.

Gordon, D. W.: Health maintenance service; ambulatory patient care in the general medical clinic, Med. Care **12:**648, 1974.

Henshaw, S. K.: Survey of clinical supervisors of graduates of six PRIMEX family nurse practitioner programs (unpublished report), Cornell University–New York Hospital School of Nursing, New York, 1976.

Henriques, C. C., Virgadamo, V. G., and Kahane, M. D.: Performance of adult health appraisal examinations utilizing nurse practitioner–physician teams and paramedical personnel, Am. J. Public Health **64:** 47, 1974.

Kahn, L., and Wirth, P.: The modification of pediatrician activity following the addition of the pediatric nurse practitioner to the ambulatory care setting; a time-and-motion study, Pediatrics **55:**700, 1975.

Kelly, L. Y.: Nursing practice acts, Am. J. Nurs. **7:**1310, 1974.

Lees, R. E. M.: Physician time-saving by employment of expanded-role nurses in family practice, Can. Med. Assoc. J. **108:**871, 1973.

Lewis, C. E., and Resnik, B. A.: Nurse clinics and progressive ambulatory patient care, N. Engl. J. Med. **277:**1236, 1967.

Lewis, C. E., and others: Activities, events and outcomes in ambulatory patient care, N. Engl. J. Med. **280:**645, 1969.

Merenstein, J. H., and others: The use of nurse practitioners in a general practice, Med. Care **12:**445, 1974.

National Academy of Sciences: New members of the physician's health team; physician's assistants, Washington, D.C., 1970, The Academy.

Record, J. C., and Greenlick, M. R.: New health professionals and the physician role; an hypothesis from Kaiser experience, Public Health Rep. **90:**241, 1975.

Roemer, R.: Nursing functions and the law; some perspectives from Australia and Canada. In Bullough, B., editor: The law and the expanding nursing role, New York, 1975, Appleton-Century-Crofts.

Sackett, D. L., and others: The Burlington randomized trial of the nurse practitioner; health outcomes of patients, Ann. Intern. Med. **80:**137, 1974.

Sadler, A. M., Sadler, B. L., and Bliss, A. A.: The physician's assistant; today and tomorrow. New Haven, 1972, Yale University School of Medicine.

Sadler, B.: Recent legal developments relative to physician's assistants and nurse practitioners, P.A. Journal **4:**35, 1974.

Scheffler, R. M., and Stinson, O. D.: Characteristics of physician's assistants; a focus on specialty, Med. Care **12:**1019, 1974.

Schlesinger, E. R., and others: A controlled test of the use of registered nurses for prenatal care, Health Serv. Rep. **88:**400, 1973.

The Secretary's Committee to Study Extended Roles for Nurses: Extending the scope of nursing practice, Washington, D.C., 1971, Department of Health, Education, and Welfare.

Spector, R., and others: Medical care by nurses in an internal medicine clinic, J.A.M.A. **232:**1234, 1975.

Spitzer, W. O., and others: The Burlington randomized trial of the nurse practitioner, N. Engl. J. Med. **290:**251, 1974.

Sultz, H. A.: Role preparation and expectations of nurses in extended roles (paper presented at Nurse Practitioner Research Conference II, Hartford, Conn., April 30–May 2, 1975).

Taller, S. L., and Feldman, R.: The training and utilization of nurse practitioners in adult health appraisal, Med. Care **12:**40, 1974.

Yankauer, A., and others: The costs of training and the income generation potential of P.N.P.'s, Pediatrics **49:**878, 1972a.

Yankauer, A., and others: The outcomes and service impact of a P.N.P. training program; nurse practitioner training outcomes, Am. J. Public Health **62:**347, 1972b.

8 Partners in primary care

LOIS W. GAGE

Over the past few years, the need for change in the health care system has mounted. The federal government has supported the need for primary health care, complementary to secondary and tertiary care, in order to increase accessibility and availability for continuous coordinated care. Legislation to increase the "substantive and technological knowledge and skill of nurses in primary care" has passed (*Federal Register,* 1976). Nurses, along with physicians and other health care providers, can and must augment preventive, restorative, and health maintenance services currently denied large segments of the population. The utilization of nurses, particularly in primary care settings such as outpatient clinics, health maintenance organizations, and public health and community health settings, is the subject of discussion. Specifically, this chapter deals with nursing processes common in all sites, such as role development and reallocation, ensuring a legal base for nursing practice, and reimbursement for services, rather than the effect of organizations on practice.

ROLE DEVELOPMENT AND REALLOCATION

As nursing education, technological advances, and population needs have changed, new nursing tasks and roles have evolved. For example, nurses in expanded roles provide direct patient care to both patients and families. They make independent decisions regarding their patients' nursing care needs and participate with a variety of other health care providers in making decisions about their patients' medical, social, nutritional, and other requirements. Moreover, they work in an increasingly large number of health care settings (for example, primary, acute, and chronic). Finally, these nurses are involved in the planning of health care programs (Wise, 1974).

The road to role development and reallocation is complicated. Basic changes in nursing identity are required. First, there are multiple roles to be assumed that are ambiguous to the practitioner as well as to those with whom she interacts. Second, the knowledge and skills to be acquired are largely medical, and hence, an identity crisis is precipitated. Third, the lack of dissemination of levels of expected training outcomes provides little role support from colleagues. Fourth, the dispersion of nurses in expanded practice is such that many are isolated by location or scheduling patterns, or both. Last, the lack of nursing leadership in policy making complicates nursing administrative support, essential to the clarification of role expectations and the obtaining of nursing rewards.

It may be important to emphasize that the phases in role development are

94

interrelated, not discrete. Conceptualized from learning theory, role development follows a pattern beginning with awareness of need, tryout, adoption, and integration.

During the awareness stage, there is an initial enthusiasm quickly followed by generalized feelings of loss of professional identity that trigger fear and anxiety. Questions proliferate. Who am I? How can I learn all the skills I need to make accurate judgments? What is happening to my nursing knowledge and skills; they are gone. How could I possibly miss so much, not ask more questions—simply not hear? Frequently expressed, these questions reflect fear of failure and diffuse anxiety. It is not surprising that much of the learner's mental and emotional energy is directed toward physical skill acquisition (VandenBroek and others, 1975).

Some educators, such as Lynaugh and Bates (1975) and Chapoorian (1976), state that learning expanded nursing practice is optimized when the physician-nurse faculty team plan, implement, and evaluate the entire educational experience collaboratively. By so doing, the nurse and physician can demonstrate nursing-medical practice as well as role development and reciprocity, both in the classroom and in the community/outpatient clinical laboratories. The nurse can learn medical diagnostic skills and extend her knowledge of management of conditions from the physician; she can pattern her interventions and learn to collaborate with the physician preceptor in a manner useful for later team practice. The preceptor team should select the patients according to the student's need to acquire a broad range of diagnostic and treatment skills. The patients should be representative of the entire ambulatory population; therefore, faculty should avoid focusing only on patients who have particular categorical complaints or those who have multiple and complex problems. In the first instance, nurses will acquire specialized rather than primary care skills, and in the latter, they may become overwhelmed or discouraged.

As a nurse learner begins to practice new tasks, she is gradually able to try out expanded skills with increased freedom, to test her abilities, and to participate collaboratively with physician and nurse mentors. As she gains increased self-confidence, she learns to answer challenging medical questions more easily and to exchange data and plan treatments more openly.

Once nurses become more accountable, responsible, and autonomous, other changes occur in nurse-physician dyadic relationships. Stereotyped responses surface, power struggles open to scrutiny, and anxiety increases. The doctor-nurse game is in full play, but now it is open rather than covert. Hopefully, the contest is held in a climate that allows for openness, genuineness, behavioral tryout, and acceptance, so that the partnerships can build on mutuality and trust rather than competition and suspicion. As the physician benefits from the nurse's knowledge of the patient's life space, the nurse gains from the physician's diagnostic and treatment skills. Thus, the third phase of learning, integration, can unfold.

Newly acquired knowledge and skills become part of individuals in such a way that their functions begin to overlap comfortably, and they can rely on each other for backup as needed for patient welfare. They may ask for assistance from other health and social workers and integrate their functions and knowledge in the patient/family total plan for care. Physicians provide medical diagnostic and prescriptive functions directly or in consultation with nurses. Nurses take histories, assess health and illness states, manage conditions by using established guidelines, and usually assume the major responsibility for the coordination of care within the health plan, for individuals and families. Both physicians and nurses provide continuity of care.

In an academic interdisciplinary primary care program with which I am familiar, the exchange of information is threefold. First, each master's-prepared nurse practices primary care with a physician partner. They consult each other about patient diagnostic and treatment problems as well as share knowledge and skills relative to counseling and educational interventions. Second, nurses and physicians develop, evaluate, and reformulate organizational policies to meet changing program needs. Third, nurses and physicians participate equally in formal peer review in weekly clinicians' meetings where practice problems such as hypertension, sexual dysfunction, and urinary tract infections are reviewed. While medical and counseling treatments of common primary care problems vary to some extent, their joint effort contributes not only to the development of standing orders agreeable to both physicians and nurses, but also to documentation of the relationship between care processes and outcomes, such as Williams (1975) advocates. In this case, the participating nurses were both experienced and had master's degrees, the setting was academic, and the health maintenance and counseling needs of the population served were generally greater than the medical needs. To what extent the educational preparation of nurses, the organizational structure, and the population needs influenced each other is not known. Such studies are critically needed if we are to improve educational and service programs to help meet future population health care needs.

LEGAL BASE FOR NURSING PRACTICE

A key element in any health organization is the guarantee of a legal base for practice. During the past decade or so, there has been much controversy among both nurses and physicians about the ability of nurses to make autonomous decisions, particularly when they concern medical practice. This subject has been covered by Bullough (1975). Briefly, the problem is twofold. Many physicians have been socialized to expect assistant rather than independent nursing functions, and many nurses have such a low opinion of themselves that they avoid the responsibility of autonomous decision making. For years public health and hospital nurses have collected relevant data, necessary for diagnosing and treating emergencies, but unfortunately many nurses have not and still do not take credit for their practice. Their recordings, reflecting well-learned instructions, are filled with statements such as *seems appropriate,* which are neither scientific nor professionally accountable. The physician-nurse games described by Bates (1975) continue to be played from fear of legal consequence or deference to continued traditional physician power.

Aside from physician and nurse attitudes toward autonomous practice, it is interesting to note how few instances there have been when nurses were indicted for exceeding the scope of practice, unless negligence was cited. What, then, is the real barrier to extending the scope of practice? Bullough (1976) contends that state nursing licensure laws that prohibit diagnosis and treatment are the block. She believes, however, that this problem will be remedied after all states enact amendments to their nurse practice acts to increase nurse diagnostic and treatment functions. (Thirty have done so between 1971 and 1976.) Moreover, some states are including provisions for increased training so that nurse practice can expand legally as competence is assured. No clear discernible pattern among state regulatory approaches is identifiable yet, but the overall pattern is facilitative rather than constrictive.

Nurses are continuing to prove their effectiveness in providing health assessments and treatments for persons who are well or who have minor or uncomplicated acute and chronic conditions. They are also counseling individuals and families for emotional and social problems as well as teaching them how to prevent illness and sequelae from chronic or acute conditions. In so doing, they have, according to Cohen and others (1974), (1) performed as well as the physician with whom they are compared, (2) increased physician productivity, (3) been profitable to employers, and (4) been accepted as practitioners by consumers.

Nurses are increasing the health manpower pool necessary to distribute health care services, including preventive and health maintenance, more equitably. In rural areas, for example, some nurses have negotiated with local physicians for medical backup and sought the sanction of the local medical society to develop primary care centers to provide health assessment, preventive, and restorative services. In many instances, the medical societies have given their approval; but occasionally, the request is denied because the society questions the adequacy of the medical support even though the county may not have basic health services, such as obstetrical care, within a radius of 100 miles. Such maldistribution of health manpower is serious, and it behooves community and professional leaders to work effectively with medical boards to develop the needed health care services that can utilize the unique capabilities of both professions.

Another example of improved access to care through a nurse-staffed health evaluation service is described by Garfield and others (1976) at Kaiser-Permanente Health Maintenance Organization in California. Nurses, with minimum involvement of the physician, separate and analyze multiphasic screening data and divide consumers into three groups: (1) the well and worried well, (2) the asymptomatic sick, and (3) the sick. The majority (72.3%) are well, worried well, and asymptomatic sick and, according to Garfield and others (1976) are "most appropriately handled by entry through the health-evaluation service." This conclusion is exciting and provocative, for it documents the need for the utilization of primary care nurses in prepaid systems. The cost saving could be measured in thousands of dollars, and concomitantly, physicians would be freed to care for the more seriously ill and provide medical support when needed.

While all the legal issues are far from solved, it is reasonable to expect a ripple effect to occur. As nurses continue to expand their knowledge and skill, their nursing practice will continue to grow, thus increasing the manpower pool for providing health care to the population.

Meanwhile, federal and professional support from the Department of Health, Education, and Welfare, the American Nurses' Association, and the National Joint Practice Commission, in the form of descriptive and advisory statements, helps. In 1971, H.E.W.'s Ad Hoc Committee on Health Professions issued a report that included current practices and functions for which nurses were being prepared in acute, long-term, and primary care.

Two years later, the American Nurses' Association (1973) published *Standards of Nursing Practice,* which provided a "basic and general model for nursing practice . . . by which quality of general nursing practice may be measured." Specific standards have also been established by the divisions on practice of the American Nurses' Association.

In 1974, the National Joint Practice Commission (established 1972) issued a statement on medical and nurse practice acts in an effort to improve health care established by action of the American Medical Association and the American Nurses' Association. Their principal recommendations were that (1) the best practice acts of medicine and nursing permitting flexibility be maintained and (2) those practice acts that by definition constrain role flexibility, even though they are "within the limits of legality," be reconstituted in order to provide for practice flexibility. Resolution of issues of role realignment and readjustments might then be initiated by state joint practice committees or other joint bodies of medicine and nursing (Report of the National Joint Practice Commission, 1974).

To date, progress toward mutual understanding between medical and nursing organizations has been sporadic. On the positive side, a major collaborative effort between the American Nurses' Association Division on Maternal-Child Health Nursing Practice and the Nurses' Association of the American College of Obstetricians and Gynecologists resulted in joint certification in maternal, gynecological, and neonatal nursing. Paradoxically, the American Academy of Pediatrics reaffirmed the traditional view regarding nurse practitioners when it stated its "support of the role of the pediatric nurse associate, *functioning under the direction and supervision of the pediatrician,* as one of several models of delivery of primary health care to children" (italics in original, American Academy of Pediatrics, 1976). Clearly, continued efforts for joint professional understandings are needed to support the ability of nurses to make autonomous decisions within their learned competence.

REIMBURSEMENT

Payment for health care service is an important issue requiring immediate assessment since it puts financial reward primarily in the hands of the medical profession and, importantly, fosters coercive power rather than collaborative partnerships between physicians and nurses. It is paradoxical that the federal government has increased its support for preparation of registered nurses to provide primary care, and yet, physician sanction for payment continues to be necessary for reimbursement even for services that, by training, nurses are competent to deliver.

One facet of this problem stems from the plethora of training programs in expanded nursing practice whose objectives frequently do not reflect the extent— depth and breadth—of expected competency. Second, it is not entirely clear what the criteria for reimbursement should be. Third, support for expanded nursing practice comes from the attempt to make health care services more equitable.

The issues surrounding reimbursement are, according to Cohen and others (1974), whether reimbursement for nurse practice should be aimed at redistributing health care personnel to underserviced areas; whether reimbursement should be a function of education and training or of the tasks performed, regardless of educational preparation; and whether reimbursement should be equal to physician fees or only at a percentage of physician fees. In other words, should the amount of payment for service be based on site of practice, profit sharing, education, or kind of task? These questions have not yet been answered, but the American Nurses' Association is conducting a study to examine the issues in order to develop a policy position. Meanwhile, staff and members of the American Nurses' Association and the National League for Nurses continue their dialogue with legislators regarding this critical problem.

In primary care, there are differences in reimbursement policies between prepaid and fee-for-service settings. In the former, nursing salaries are generally covered as organizational expenses and, thus, are not dependent directly on generated income. To what extent financial incentives include nursing as well as medicine is not known, but such a notion is interesting in view of studies that suggest that expanded nursing practice is of the same quality as that of physicians (Schiff and others, 1969).

Where the payment mechanism is fee-for-service, there are differences among third-party payers. Government reimbursement for nursing services through Medicare and Medicaid, for example, differs among institutional settings. Payment to certified community nursing agencies is set relative to the current rather than projected costs of general and line items. Such a fiscal procedure has inherent difficulties, especially in periods of high inflation, because a lag between operating costs and revenue occurs. Present regulations prevent reimbursement for services traditionally ascribed to physicians when performed by a nurse independently. Hence, payment for health care is predominantly dictated by insurance and government regulations.

Third-party payments, both goverment and private, also depend on physician verification for the need for service as well as submission of a plan for care. Payment may be either for direct bedside care, for teaching a household member to administer medication, or for providing nursing assistance to the patient. In these events, reimbursement for nursing practice is dependent on medical or illness care rather than on preventive and rehabilitative services. Payment generally is denied for counseling and teaching, frequently cited as the major purview of nursing. Such exclusions interfere with educational efforts deemed necessary both for management of conditions and efficient utilization of services that, in turn, affect morbidity statistics and health care costs. Is it any wonder that compliance with medical regimens continues to be an unresolved issue and that overused and crowded emergency rooms plague health care providers, hospital administrators, and consumers?

A part of the reimbursement problem is fee setting, a varying procedure. Although there is evidence that in some office practices a fee differential occurs between nurse and physician services (Charney and Kitzman, 1971) in order to pass on the savings that accrue from the increased income from nurse practice, this is the exception. Most studies indicate that the fee remains the same regardless of professional provider (Cohen and others, 1974). This practice stems from the belief in one quality of care that can be rendered either by nurses with medical backup or by physicians. In other words, the fee reflects the service provided rather than the provider.

Currently, the fact that reimbursement issues are complicated and serious cannot be denied. The problems are interrelated and include the discrepancy between expected training outcomes and rewards for practice and differences in physician and nurse, entrepreneurial and organizational, employer and employee role expectations. It is mandatory that an understanding both of the nature of these problems and of their relationships be developed so that true partnerships between physicians and nurses in primary care may grow out of rational thinking rather than competitive striving or capitulation.

SUMMARY

Briefly, this chapter has described the nature of role development and reallocation necessary so that nurses might contribute with physicians and other health care providers to increasing accessibility of health care for populations in health and illness. Expanded nursing practice creates stress for both nurses and physicians, particularly in areas where their professional roles overlap and thus causes a spiral effect of evolving role changes of self and others. Nursing practice is legitimated through nurse practice acts that are also undergoing considerable change. Reimbursement for nursing practice continues to be a critical issue because this mechanism holds much of the power over professional autonomy and equitable rewards.

REFERENCES

Ad Hoc Committee on Health Professions: Expanding the scope of nursing practice (a report to the Secretary of Health, Education, and Welfare, September 8), Washington, D.C., 1971, U.S. Government Printing Office.

American Academy of Pediatrics: Academy policy in relation to the pediatric nurse practitioner, Pediatrics **57:**467, April 1976.

American Nurses' Association: Standards of nursing practice, Kansas City, 1973, The Association.

Bates, B.: Physician and nurse practitioner; conflict and reward, Ann. Intern. Med. **82:** 702, May 1975.

Bullough, B.: The law and the expanding nursing role, New York, 1975, Appleton-Century-Crofts.

Bullough, B.: The law and the expanding nursing role, Am. J. Public Health **66**:249, March 1976.

Chapoorian, T.: Personal communication, 1976.

Charney, E., and Kitzman, H.: The child-health nurse (pediatric nurse practitioner) in private practice; a controlled trial, N. Engl. J. Med. **285**:1353, Dec. 9, 1971.

Cohen, E., and others: An evaluation of policy related research on new and expanded roles of health workers, New Haven, Conn., 1974, Yale University School of Medicine.

Federal Register, Nurse practitioner training, II, January 23, Washington, D.C., 1976, U.S. Department of Health, Education, and Welfare.

Garfield, R. S., and others: Evaluation of an ambulatory medical care delivery system, N. Engl. J. Med. **195**:426, Feb. 1976.

Lynaugh, J., and Bates, B.: Clinical practicum in ambulatory care, Nurs. Outlook **23**:444, July 1975.

Schiff, D., and others: The pediatric nurse practitioner in the office of pediatricians in private practice, Pediatrics **44**:62, July 1969.

Report of the National Joint Practice Commission: Statement on medical and nurse practice acts, Washington, D.C., Feb. 1974, U.S. Government Printing Office.

Vandenbroek, D., Shepard, A., and Gage, L.: Primary care nursing in an academic interdisciplinary setting (paper presented at Michigan State Nurses' Association, Lansing, Michigan, 1975).

Williams, C.: Nurse pracitioner research; some neglected issues, Nurs. Outlook **23**:172, March 1975.

Wise, H., and others: Making health teams work, Cambridge, Mass., 1974, Ballinger Publishing Co.

9 The role of the nurse in home care for the dying child

IDA M. MARTINSON

As recently as a generation ago, dying and death were as much a natural part of the total family life cycle as childbirth, illness, and growing old. Most of our parents can recount experiences of a sibling who died from communicable disease. Since each household usually consisted of several generations, the dying process, as well as death itself, took place within the family circle. Thus, the young were able to see the process of dying, death, grief, and bereavement as a natural part of the total life experience.

This is generally not true of the present generation. Most of these processes have been isolated from the total family life and the members separated from the dying-death experience. The hospital, with its increasing technical resources, has become the accepted place to send all who are sick and those who are dying. Today, when a health crisis arises, the afflicted member is rushed to the hospital, at times arriving just minutes before dying. But is the hospital with all its highly developed technical equipment and impersonal machines the only place to receive death?

While in the hospital, these patients live their last moments or days in a largely artificial environment. In most hospitals no one under age 14 is allowed to enter, thus excluding the younger family members from visiting. The request for quiet results in hushed voices. The atmosphere is regulated and controlled. Even machines seem to encroach on the patient's personal worth. Some time ago when my uncle had his second heart attack, I was allowed to visit him for 5 minutes every 2 hours. But I found my eyes drawn toward the machines and my attention turning to the wavelength shown on the EKG receiver. Only with conscious deliberation was I able to concentrate not on the machines but on the patient, my uncle.

Thus, the environment provided by the hospital deprives dying and death of any semblance of a normal experience and often makes it a dehumanizing process. We may find ourselves routinely not accepting that death is a natural part of life by treating it as some form of failure. Though trained in a health care field that must deal with dying and death, we may come to realize that we have not after all received the education and the experience necessary to best help the dying patient. There is a great need for organized care for the dying patient that will protect his sense of identity, ensure his personal dignity, and give him a feeling of worth.

We may begin with the realization that dying is an inevitable part of life, that helping someone to die is a positive aspect of responsibility in the health care delivery system, and that dying and death may even have a beneficial effect in strength-

102

ening the family unit. Suffering and death are an inescapable part of human existence and demand acceptance as such, both for ourselves and for others. One solution to another's suffering, as Edna Hong (1970) suggests in *Turn Over Any Stone,* is indifference. The alternative is to care and support, but this must be done without self-destructive feelings of guilt and failure. To support a concerned family before the death arrives, to help the family through the actual death event, and to aid in the necessary reorganization of relationships are a legitimate part of our nursing function and can be very rewarding.

There are many settings in which the nurse may help the dying person and his family. Emphasis in this chapter will be on the home setting for the dying child, a setting that needs to be considered as a viable alternative to the hospital during dying and death. In the home setting, however, the nurse may find herself in a role quite new to her in certain aspects. She will probably find a shift both in the type of care that she gives and in the focus of her care.

One attempt to explore the home setting for the dying child in the final phase of illness was the Home Care Project, begun in 1972 at the University of Minnesota School of Nursing. Since that time, eight families have participated in the study. Of the eight children involved, five died at home; the sixth lived only 2 hours in the hospital before death. The other two children were hospitalized and died in that setting.

The average length of a nurse's involvement with each family was 45 days (range of 5 days to 6 months), and the mean total hours of direct professional service through home visits, telephone calls, and clinic visits was 20 hours, ranging from 15 to 40 hours. The number of home visits by the nurse ranged from 3 to 10 per family; these visits were supplemented with an average of 10 telephone calls per family.

This study indicates an acceptance by the parents of home care of the dying child. They report feeling relief in knowing that their child need not be separated from his parents or from a familiar setting at a time when cure is still unknown and a favorable change in the child's condition cannot be expected. Not only may the dying child remain with his family at one of the most crucial periods in life—death—but the parents are provided with an opportunity for emotional and physical involvement with their child during the dying process in a way not possible in the hospital setting.

That this active involvement is an effective help for the parents as well as the child was evidenced through the Home Care Project. In the five families whose children died at home, the parents found little or no use for sleeping pills, tranquilizers, or alcohol before, during, or following the death of their child. These observations are reinforced by statements of the parents themselves. The parents in the first family to become involved wrote the following after their son's death:

> It was a very deep and meaningful experience to our family to have been able to personally take care of and be with him through the end when he needed us the most . . . We had not considered nor did we know it was possible to make it 'all the way'

until Dr. Martinson began her home visits with us . . . seventeen days before [our son] died. Without her aid and reassurance, to both ourselves and [our son], I doubt that we could have suceeded in this venture (Kuhlenkamp and Martinson, 1974).

A nurse, in writing of another family who cared for their dying child at home, wrote:

They seemed to benefit very greatly from having D. with them for those last two weeks because they were able to feel very strongly that they had done everything they possibly could for him, that he was made as comfortable as he could have been in the hospital, that nothing they could do in the hospital was greater than what they were able to do at home and this seemed to alleviate a lot of their frustrations quite considerably (University of Minnesota School of Nursing, 1975).

Similar psychological needs of the adult patient and his family are also met through care at home. In spite of the physical and emotional stresses encountered by one family in caring for their terminally ill husband and son, they felt the experience to be a positive and meaningful one for them all.

They kept thanking us for making death easier, not only for Jerry, but for them as well. It hurt and they would grieve, but they would not suffer from guilt. As Jerry's mother said, "His death was a beautiful experience for all of us" (Kobrzychi, 1975, p. 1313).

The role of the nurse in the home care setting may be quite different from that in the hospital setting. In the latter the nurse finds her care and concern concentrated on the dying patient, for whom she is the principal care giver. Although the family members may aid in the care, it is the nurse who administers the medications, changes the bed linens, provides food and comfort. In short, it is primarily the nurse who gives the necessary psychological and physical care to the child.

Lacking control in the care-giving process, the family members may feel superfluous, except for the moral support they are able to give. They may, in fact, suspect they are "in the way" and a hindrance to the care process. Surrounded by expert care givers, the parents of a dying child may feel they are considered by the professionals to be much less knowledgeable than they actually are. Normal relationships at home based on interdependence have been interrupted, and parents of young patients have to adjust rather suddenly to their loss of control and their right to decision making. Often the parents watch as their child, in recognizing the shift in primary care giver from parent to nurse, adjusts his direction of trust accordingly.

In the home care setting much of this is changed. The general focus becomes more clearly care and comfort rather than cure (recognized as no longer possible) or the prolonging of life, and quality of life becomes the goal. The focus of the nursing role shifts from the patient to the parents, the role itself from primary care giver to supporter. The nurse becomes teacher, advisor, and supporter, and the parents become the primary care givers.

As a teacher the nurse may instruct the parents in the administration of medications, such as injections for pain. That this can be very successful was seen during one clinic visit when the child requested that her mother, rather than the nurse, give her the shot. The nurse may also inform the parents of symptoms in the child's condition and of possible complications, such as hemorrhaging, and suggest how best to prepare for and cope with such a situation. Whether these complications actually occur or not, the parents are able to understand their situation more completely and feel more confident and in better control. The nurse's function as a source of information extends also to advice regarding the type of death the child will probably experience. The nurse is able to alleviate the parents' anxiety by informing them of the probable situation and preparing them for it.

Suggestions for the patient's increased comfort are given. In one case, for example, the child had become edematous and was experiencing difficulty in breathing. The nurse then helped the parents by explaining ways of making her comfortable: By keeping her in a sitting or semisitting position she would be able to breathe more easily because of the lowered diaphragm; positioning her head to keep it from falling one way or the other when she fell asleep in this position would also help. The parents took these suggestions and were able to keep their daughter quite comfortable.

The nurse's role as supporter, though ambiguous, is nevertheless of extreme importance. Much of the support is emotional and psychological. Several parents have mentioned that just to be able to talk with someone who understands their situation, to feel free to ask questions is essential. Another mother mentioned how the nurse had increased their confidence in their care of their child immeasurably. She had explained carefully the care measures to be given and then let the parents do it themselves rather than taking over with her own skill. Any lack in expertise and experience there may have been was made up for by the child's security in his parents' love and presence. This support extended also to decision making. The option was always left open that the child was free to be admitted to the hospital again at any time, and it was made clear that such a decision was to lie with the child and the family. In most cases, both child and parents chose home care through the death.

Sometimes the support given by the nurse was more concrete. When a hospital bed was needed for a child in one instance, the nurse was able to procure it through the American Cancer Society. When another family needed a wheelchair, the nurse was able to obtain one through the same source. Lamb's-wool pads were provided for the child's comfort. At times a family needed or appreciated help in making necessary arrangements at the time of death, such as calling the mortician or aiding with funeral arrangements.

Sometimes further help from other professionals may be needed, such as the clergy, social worker, psychiatrist or psychologist, as well as the physician. In some situations the family may feel free to contact the doctor directly if their relationship is very close. However, this is often not the case, and the parents feel more comfortable requesting the nurse to act as liaison.

Support from the professional nurse is also needed at times in face of the expectations of the society surrounding the family. Often when relatives and friends are still not admitting the possibility of death, by suggesting various folk cures or making statements of hope for reversal, the family needs the support of the nurse in facing and accepting the inevitability of death. When social pressures are for the "proper" care of the dying through hospitalization, the family needs support in its affirmation of the quality of life, made possible for the child at home.

In striving for this quality of life, most families attempt to maintain as much normalcy in their life-styles as possible. In one family the child was carried downstairs to eat each meal with the family in spite of the bruises easily caused by his father's hands while being carried. The same child, not too long before his death, went golfing a few holes with his father, although he upset onlookers who saw him lose his balance and fall. Another child had her school friends into her room for a birthday party. Others had their pets as well. One child accompanied her mother in a wheelchair while shopping; another went on a family camping trip over the Labor Day weekend. Another child died at the kitchen table while watching her mother prepare the evening meal. Through these activities the dying children were able to remain a part of the human community. They and their parents, while recognizing the tragedy, pain, and suffering of life, were also able to affirm its fun and its joys until the end. To do this, given their mental and physical fatigue, they needed support.

A very important aspect in this attempt to maintain as much normalcy as possible is the involvement of the siblings in the life of the child. Not only is it meaningful to the child to have his or her brothers and sisters nearby, but they too have the opportunity of feeling useful and of being an integral part of this very important family event. One nurse records that the older boys and girls in the family were a great support and help to the parents. The family had always been very close. Now during their sister's fatal illness, they were also able to show their love and concern for her by doing whatever they could to help make her comfortable and to keep her as happy as possible during her last days.

One parent reported that the key to the success of the family in caring for its dying child at home was the availability of the nurse both day and night. Several telephone calls were made during the night, though seldom were requests made for a visit by the nurse. Even more significant to the parents was the knowledge that such calls were possible. They found this to be immeasurably reassuring and strengthening. Sometimes the questions regarded rather minor matters according to professional opinion, but for a family without previous experience with home care these problems could become large and, without support, difficult to cope with.

Thus, the role of the home care nurse has changed in the type of care, and the focus of that care has shifted from direct physical care of the child to psychological support of the primary care givers, the parents. However, a clear description of the role of the home care nurse is still not possible. But indications are that it will involve the functions described above and that the need for this nursing role will expand. Nurses who have already experienced this role are strong in affirming the value of home care for the families who choose it. In spite of the grief and tragedy to be borne, there are beautiful moments to be lived, and the nurse and the family may come through the experience stronger people.

REFERENCES

Hong, E.: Turn over any stone, Minneapolis, 1970, Augsburg Publishing House.

Kobrzychi, P.: Dying with dignity at home, Am. J. Nurs. **75:**1312, 1975.

Kuhlenkamp, E., and Martinson, I. M.: Eric, University of Minnesota, Minneapolis (unpublished material), 1974.

University of Minnesota School of Nursing: Home Care Project (unpublished data), 1975.

part IV
ISSUES IN NURSING ORGANIZATION

The future of nursing as a viable profession is dependent on the profession's ability to draw together its rather heterogeneous constituency (for example, diploma, associate degree, and baccalaureate; public health and institution-bound; medical-surgical, obstetric, psychiatric, and so forth; old and young) into a unified voice for nursing. Unlike other health care professions, especially medicine and dentistry, nursing is without a professional organization projecting "a consistent image to the public and . . . offering effective guidance to the thousands of American nurses."* Instead, nursing has a professional organization with a membership level of 20% of all employed registered nurses and an exceedingly large number of special interest groups. The problem, as pointed out in the three chapters of this section, is that the American Nurses' Association lacks wide support among the individual members of the profession.

In Chapter 10 Dr. Miller examines the power struggle in nursing among the various organizations serving nursing needs. Miller shows that present-day factionalism among nursing organizations is not a new development; to the contrary, factionalism characterizes nursing's history as well as the history of most, if not all, professions. Dr. Miller conducted a mail survey of the leadership of nurses special interest groups; he concludes that these groups would not have grown to their present extent (17 organizations with 114,000 members compared with 180,000 for the A.N.A.) if the A.N.A. had not failed to support nurses' varied nursing practice needs. The proliferation of nurse special interest groups is so extensive (and groups continue to be created) that Miller projects that their membership will exceed that of the A.N.A. by 1980. This may not occur if the Federation of Special Interest Groups and the A.N.A. is successful in its efforts to merge the organizations.

Dr. Miller and Dr. Flynn use a cost-benefit analysis in Chapter 11 to assess the basis of the fact that 80% of all employed registered nurses decline membership in the A.N.A. They show, by comparing demographic characteristics of A.N.A. members and nonmembers, that registered nurses who have the most education, positions in teaching, administration, and supervision, and who are 35 years of age or older, single, employed in schools of nursing, in public health, and as school

---

*Lysaught, J. P.: An abstract for action, New York, 1970, McGraw-Hill Book Co., p. 144.

nurses, are overrepresented among the A.N.A.'s membership. This so-called nursing elite belongs to the A.N.A. because, the authors contend, the benefits of membership to them are greater than the costs. Conversely, the majority of nurses do not join the Association because the perceived (and real) costs of membership outweigh the benefits. Miller and Flynn conclude by questioning whether the nursing elite really wants to make membership in the A.N.A. beneficial to nonelite nurses.

In Chaper 12, Miller and Dodson analyze 103 nurse work stoppages occurring during the period from 1960 to 1974 by type of stoppage, reason for the action, location, number of nurses involved, and so forth. The authors discover that only in recent years have nurses identified their work stoppages as strikes, preferring in earlier years to use other terminology. Work stoppages were confined primarily to urban centers and were attributed to wage inequities. The emergence of nurse work stoppages is related to changes in nurses' education, the A.N.A. salary goal of 1966, contagion, and community size.

10 Special interest groups or the A.N.A.

an analysis

MICHAEL H. MILLER

Factionalism characterizes professions in the United States. Bucher and Strauss (1961, p. 325) contend that professions, instead of constituting stable communities, are, in reality, "loose amalgamations of segments, pursuing different objectives in different manners and more or less deliberately held together under a common name at a particular time in history." Divisions within professions may be a function of sex, age, race, ethnicity, religion, technology, specialty, residence, or other differences between the members (Gilb, 1966, p. 159). Specialty or splinter groups* within a profession originate to represent divergent (usually minority) interests and perspectives of members and are likely to challenge "the goals and means of the larger profession in line with their own objectives and technologies" (Epstein, 1970, p. 155). Although it is not common, a specialty group, by attracting a larger membership than the professional association,† may increase in prestige to the point that it comes to represent the objectives of the larger profession.‡ In this case, the specialty group may assume professional association status and become the spokesman for the profession.

As might be expected, professional associations do what they can to restrain or diminish the "formal articulation of specialty interest" by such tactics as merging the various specialty groups in a profession into a single large association, providing the specialty group with divisional affiliations within the association, and/or allowing the groups to have representation in the government of the professional association (Gilb, 1966, pp. 159-160). Like other professional associations, the American Nurses' Association has attempted to diminish the influence and number of specialty groups within the nursing profession. But despite its efforts, specialty groups continue to organize and flourish.

Before 1950, registered nurses in the United States were represented by seven

---

*Specialty groups are frequently referred to as splinter groups by members of the professional association because they break off from the professional association to establish their own organization.

†A professional association ostensibly represents the interests and goals of all members of a profession (that is, professional, economic, political, and social) regardless of individual special interests or needs. Most members of the profession regard the association as the official spokesman for the profession.

‡See Gilb (1966) for a discussion of specialty groups in education and engineering.

occupational associations. The professional association was the American Nurses' Association with more than 170,000 members. The specialty groups were the National League of Nursing Education (N.L.N.E.) with more than 10,000 members, the National Organization for Public Health Nursing (N.O.P.H.N.) with nearly 10,000 members, the American Association of Industrial Nurses (A.A.I.N.) with 2,500 members, the National Association of Colored Graduate Nurses (N.A.C.G.N.) with more than 2,000 members, the Association of Collegiate Schools of Nursing (A.A.C.S.N.) with 43 member schools, and the American Association of Nurse Anesthetists (A.A.N.A.) with about 7,000 members. Beginning in 1950 a series of mergers occurred among five of these seven organizations that resulted in the dissolution of three of them. First, in 1950 the N.A.C.G.N. was absorbed by the A.N.A.; then in 1952 the N.L.N.E., N.O.P.H.N., and A.C.S.N. were reorganized into the National League for Nursing. Although the A.A.I.N was also expected to become a part of the AN.A.–National League for Nursing, it decided against dissolution in favor of retaining its independence and integrity. The A.A.N.A. made no effort toward merging with the other associations (Roberts, 1961).

The N.L.N. was created by the nursing leadership more as a nursing foundation than as a special interest group. Primarily, the decision to create the N.L.N. stemmed from the A.N.A's decision to admit only nurses and its inability, as a politically active organization, to receive tax-deductible gifts. Since the N.L.N. was separate and distinct from the A.N.A., it could receive tax-deductible donations to nursing. In addition, the N.L.N. encouraged nonregistered nurse membership (Roberts, 1961).

Within 3 years of the 1952 mergers, the Association of Operating Room Nurses (A.O.R.N.) and the American College of Nurse Midwives (A.C.N.M.) were founded. The foundings of these special interest groups are significant because they occurred even though the A.N.A. established a special groups section* as part of the A.N.A. reorganization. The special groups section was organized, interestingly, to eliminate the need for separate special interest groups by providing a forum within the A.N.A. for these groups to discuss their problems (Griffin and Griffin, 1973, p. 23). Following the emergence of the A.O.R.N. and the A.C.N.M., there was a 13-year span before any additional special interest groups were organized. Then, beginning in 1968, special interest groups began forming until, by 1975, there were at least 13 additional groups. (See the chronology of nurse associations.)

Based on the research of Gilb (1966) and Epstein (1970), we would predict that the extent to which nurse special interest groups flourish will be a function of the manner in which the American Nurses' Association deals with the issues that result in the founding of specialty groups. In this chapter, the relationship of nurse special interest groups to the A.N.A. is examined in an effort to provide a better understanding of the evolution of the many special interest groups in nursing.

---

*In 1968 the A.N.A. changed the name of this section to the Division of Practice.

CHRONOLOGY OF NURSE ASSOCIATIONS

1893 American Society of Superintendents of Training Schools for Nurses founded (Renamed—National League of Nursing Education in 1912)

1897 Nurses Associated Alumnae of the United States and Canada founded (Renamed—American Nurses' Association, 1911)

1900 American Federation of Nurses organized

1908 National Association of Colored Graduate Nurses organized

1912 A.F.N. (dissolved)—National Organization of Public Health Nursing founded

1931 American Association of Nurse Anesthetists organized

1932 Association of Collegiate Schools of Nursing organized

1942 American Association of Industrial Nurses organized

1950 National Association of Colored Graduate Nurses merged with A.N.A.

1952 National League for Nursing organized
National Organization of Public Health Nursing ⎫ Reorganized into
National League of Nursing Education ⎬ the National League
Association of Collegiate Schools of Nursing ⎭ for Nursing

1954 Association of Operating Room Nurses founded

1955 American College of Nurse Midwives organized

1968 American Association of Nephrology Nurses and Technicians founded
American Association of Neurosurgical Nurses founded
Nurses Association of the American College of Obstetricians and Gynecologists founded

1970 Emergency Department Nurses' Association founded

1972 American Indian Nurses' Association founded
Association for Practitioners of Infectious Control founded
Orthopedic Nurses' Association founded
National Black Nurses' Association founded

1973 Gay Nurses' Alliance founded
Nurses Concerned for Life founded
Federation of Nurse Specialty Groups and the A.N.A. organized

1974 Association of Pediatric Oncology Nurses organized
Association of Rehabilitation Nurses founded

Moreover, an assessment is made of the long-range implications of special interest groups for nursing.

THE SAMPLE

A list of nurse special interest groups was obtained from the 1974 *American Journal of Nursing Directory*. In all, 17 groups or associations were listed.* A questionnaire was mailed to the executive director, president, or secretary of each

---

*Since this time, a number of other nurse special interest groups have been organized.

association as listed in the Directory, requesting their assistance in providing information about their organization. After the initial mailing and four mail follow-ups, all 17 groups had returned usable questionnaires.

The 17 nurse special interest associations that returned questionnaires (see Table 6) had a combined membership in 1975 of more than 113,000. The A.A.C.C.N. had the largest number of members with 25,000, followed by the A.O.R.N with 22,000, the A.A.N.A. with 17,546, the N.A.A.C.O.G. with 11,931, the N.C.L. with 10,000, the E.D.N.A. with 9,984, and the A.A.I.N. with more than 8,000 members. Considerably smaller were the O.N.A. (3,100), the A.A.N.N. (nephrology nurses) (2,200), the A.P.I.C. (1,700), the A.C.N.M. (945), the A.A.N.N. (neurosurgical nurses) (525), the A.R.N. (350), the A.P.O.N. (350), and the A.I.N.A. (185). The G.N.A. was unable and the N.B.N.A. unwilling to provide accurate membership data. Membership figures for the years prior to 1975 show that all associations (except the A.R.N. and the A.P.O.N., which were founded in 1974) experienced a substantial growth in membership. For example, the membership of the N.C.L. increased by 150% between 1974 and 1975 as 6,000 new members joined the association.

Special interest groups are highly attractive to staff nurses. Staff nurses constitute only 35% of the A.N.A. membership (*A.N.A. in Profile,* 1974) compared

Table 6. Membership of nursing special interest groups returning questionnaires (1975)

Special interest groups	Number of members (1975)
American Association of Critical Care Nurses (A.A.C.C.N.)	25,000
Association of Operating Room Nurses (A.O.R.N.)	22,000
American Association of Nurse Anesthetists (A.A.N.A.)	17,546
Nurses' Association of the American College of Obstetricians and Gynecologists (N.A.A.C.O.G.)	11,931
Nurses Concerned for Life (N.C.L.)	10,000
Emergency Department Nurses' Association (E.D.N.A.)	9,984
American Association of Industrial Nurses (A.A.I.N.)	8,000*
Orthopedic Nurses' Association (O.N.A.)	3,100
American Association of Nephrology Nurses (A.A.N.N.)	2,200
Association for Practitioners in Infectious Control (A.P.I.C.)	1,700
American College of Nurse Midwives (A.C.N.M.)	945
American Association of Neurosurgical Nurses (A.A.N.N.)	525
Association of Rehabilitation Nurses (A.R.N.)	350
Association of Pediatric Oncology Nurses (A.P.O.N.)	350
American Indian Nurses' Association (A.I.N.A.)	185
Gay Nurses' Alliance (G.N.A.)[†]	—
National Black Nurses' Association (N.B.N.A.)[†]	—
Total	113,816

*Actually, there are more than 8,000 members in this group. The exact figure was not provided, however.
[†]No membership figures were provided.

with more than 60% of the special interest group membership. Since only 56% of all employed nurses are staff nurses (*The Nation's Nurses,* 1974), it is clear that these groups provide various services and benefits that are highly desired by this type of nurse. Supervisory and administrative nurses comprise 15% of the special interest group membership, followed by instructors with 10%, and consultants and all others with 14%.*

RESULTS

All but one of the special interest groups indicated that they were neither founded with nor had any future interest in assisting their members with their economic pursuits. Twelve of the seventeen said that their principal reason for being was to provide a forum for sharing ideas, experiences, and problems related to their particular nursing specialty or interests. Three of the five exceptions were associations that were founded solely to disseminate information to colleagues. The others were organized to deal with inequities in the health care of Indian and Black people. Eleven of the associations indicated that their organizational goals also included developing educational resources to promote the continuing education of members. Other goals mentioned were updating nursing standards, increasing expertise of members, promoting a nurse specialty, and maintaining the honor and character of the nursing profession. Overall, the goals of the groups have remained stable even in the cases of the A.A.N.A., the A.A.I.N., and the A.O.R.N., founded 44, 35, and 21 years ago, respectively.

For 13 of the specialty associations, initial relationships with the A.N.A. were not advantageous. Six said that they were unable to establish a working relationship with the A.N.A., and seven said they would describe their initial encounter with the Association as poor. Two recently organized groups that had a favorable initial relationship with the A.N.A. pointed out that they requested and received guidance in establishing their specialty organization. Most specialty groups surveyed attempted unsuccessfully to establish ties with the A.N.A. Almost without exception, the groups said that the A.N.A. felt special interest groups should participate within its structure. For instance, the A.A.C.C.N., originally the American Association of Cardiovascular Nurses, sought to become a specialty organization within the A.N.A. The A.N.A. said, however, that it was not prepared structurally for autonomous specialty organizations. Because the A.A.C.C.N.'s planning committee thought that the A.N.A.'s Division of Medical-Surgical Nursing Practice "could not meet the needs of the cardiovascular nurse," an independent special interest group was established.

Fourteen of the 17 associations said that their organization was founded in response to an action or nonaction of the A.N.A. For example, the O.N.A. replied that the A.N.A. did not have organized activities in continuing education for orthopedic nurses; the A.O.R.N., A.A.C.C.N., and A.P.I.C. all stated that because the

---

*These data are based on information supplied by only 10 of the 17 special interest groups. Those not providing these data said the data were unavailable.

A.N.A. did not encourage their affiliation as specialty groups; they were forced to establish independent associations; the N.C.L. pointed out that it was founded because the A.N.A. was unable "to come to grips with the profound ethical dilemmas caused by changing social mores and technology"; and the N.B.N.A. indicated that it was organized because of the "failure of all existing organizations to meet the needs of Black nurses and Black health problems."

The relationships between specialty associations and the A.N.A. appear to be improving. Indeed, only 4 of the 17 associations indicated that their present relationship to the A.N.A. was neither good, warming, or cooperative. Most of the 13 with a "positive" orientation to the A.N.A. indicated that they wanted more contact with the A.N.A. as members of the Federation of Nurse Specialty Groups and the A.N.A. To this end, a number mentioned that they were pursuing issues of mutual interest with the A.N.A. through their membership in the Federation. Included were such collaborative efforts as standards of practice for specialty groups, certification, and quality assurance.

The special interest groups appear evenly divided over their future relationship to the A.N.A. Seven groups stated that it will be either collaborative or cooperative. Five others indicated that they intended to wait and see with regard to establishing a closer affiliation with the A.N.A. The A.P.I.C. and G.N.A. were not hopeful, however, about the possibilities of increased cooperation with the A.N.A. "unless the A.N.A. decides to accept and recognize specialty groups." Three other groups pointed out that while they might work or communicate with the A.N.A. on programs and projects of mutual benefit, they fully intended to retain their independence.

Most special interest group members do not hold joint membership in the A.N.A. Whereas 20% of all employed registered nurses belong to the A.N.A., only 18% of the special interest group members belong.* Apparently, A.N.A. membership penetration among special interest groups is less than among employed nurses in general. Basically, registered nurses do not join both a special interest group and the A.N.A., because most do not have sufficient time for two organizations or cannot afford both membership fees.

DISCUSSION

The findings of the present study show that a rise in nurse special interest group membership accompanied a substantial decrease in the A.N.A.'s membership. Between 1968 and 1975, membership in special interest groups rose from about 20,000 to more than 113,000, an increase of more than 450%. Moreover, in 1968 the ratio of registered nurses in special interest groups to registered nurses in the A.N.A. was 1 to 10; in 1975 the ratio was more than 6 to 10. It is apparent that special interest groups attracted members at a substantially higher rate during this

---

*The percentage of dual (special interest group–A.N.A.) membership is based on data from 8 of the 17 special interest groups. The other groups did not have these data or would not provide them.

period than did the A.N.A., which saw its penetration of employed registered nurses shrink from 31% in 1968 to 20% in 1974. This decline in A.N.A. membership is particularly significant because it followed a 6-year period (1962-1968) of increased membership penetration (*Facts about Nursing,* 1950-1974). Although 18% of the special interest group members hold A.N.A. membership, it is clear that if the total membership of these groups continues to grow, it will exceed the A.N.A.'s total membership by 1980.

According to Strauss (1963), there is a continuum of occupational associations that range from unions at one extreme to professional associations at the other. The difference between the two is mainly that unions are oriented toward assisting members in gaining economic benefits; "pure" professional associations attempt only to disseminate information and upgrade the knowledge of their members. The occupational associations between the extremes overlap in these objectives to the extent that they engage in both goals with emphasis generally on one or the other. The data show quite clearly that the nurse special interest groups, except for the A.P.I.C.* fit Strauss' definition of "pure" professional associations, whereas the A.N.A. fits his conception of a "mixed" occupational association because of its heavy emphasis on economic benefits for nurses.

The A.N.A.'s decision to work for the economic and social welfare of nurses was influenced by a small group of registered nurses, members and nonmembers, who pressured it to repeal its no-strike policy in 1968 and to engage more aggressively in collective bargaining (Miller, 1975; Miller and Dodson, 1975).[†] This change was effected by the A.N.A. in order to retain its vanguard position in nursing. However, the A.N.A. decision illustrates that it could not be all things to all people. To concentrate its efforts on improving the economic welfare of nurses, the A.N.A. had to relinquish some of its important professional functions. This transition occurred at a time when nursing was striving to establish a professional identity and develop a more clinical orientation. Nurse special interest groups evolved to fill the special needs of nurses for professional activities, which were subordinate to the A.N.A.'s decision to provide other services.

The findings of this study suggest that if the A.N.A. had decided not to change its orientation from almost entirely professional to strongly economic, and if it had continued to address and provide for the special interests of registered nurses, special interest groups probably would not have evolved to the extent they did during the late 1960s and early 1970s.

In addition, the data suggest a change beginning in 1974 and 1975 in the A.N.A.'s orientation toward special interest groups. The A.N.A. recognizing the rapid growth of special interest groups, began to exhibit a more affirmative attitude

---

*The A.P.I.C., a multidisciplinary organization with members in infectious diseases, epidemiology, public health, microbiology and so forth, indicated its intention to become a bargaining agent for its members in the future.

†The A.N.A. has engaged in collective bargaining activities since 1946, but not to the extent to which it has participated since the late 1960s.

toward these groups. With the creation of the Federation of Nurse Specialty Groups and the A.N.A., nursing associations appear on the threshold of Gilb's (1966) so-called final stage of professional development. In this stage, the "differentiated and articulated parts of the system are more closely integrated into the whole while retaining their separate identity, with consensus reached through negotiation and bargaining" (p. 158). If the relationship between the A.N.A. and the special interest groups continues to move toward integration and consensus, and the data suggest that it will, nursing again will have a professional organization that represents a majority of all employed nurses.

CONCLUSION

From 1955 to 1968 the A.N.A. was able to contain the propagation of new nurse special interest groups. Then, beginning in 1968 and continuing through 1974, nursing succumbed to the same strong centrifugal forces that gave rise to the formation of independent, special interest associations in nearly every other profession (Gilb, 1966, pp. 162-163). In this second period the competing interests within nursing began to assert themselves and engage in what Gilb (1966, p. 158) calls "formalized combat over principles and power." Thus, after 1968, nurses came to recognize that their special professional interests and needs were not being adequately represented by the A.N.A., and, as a result, they began to establish alternative professional organizations.

The A.N.A. decision to emphasize the economic and general welfare of registered nurses, rather than their special professional interests, appears to have been the major factor in the subsequent emergence of special interest groups in nursing. If the A.N.A. goal in making that decision was to represent a large segment, if not the majority, of employed nurses, it is obvious that the decision was erroneous. Even though the A.N.A. wanted to benefit nursing by pressing for better economic and welfare conditions, the economic status of registered nurses has not improved since 1968 at a greater rate than it did in the few years prior to 1968. In fact, salary increases for registered nurses have actually lagged behind those for teachers and social workers during the period from 1968 to 1974, whereas they were increasing at a greater rate before 1968 (see Chapter 12).

The A.N.A. has initiated many changes in philosophy and operation over the past two decades. According to Alutto (1971, p. 115), each structural alteration has been founded on the desire of the A.N.A. "to design a voluntary organization that is both effective and truly responsive to its members' wishes, *i.e.,* a democratic and voluntary association capable of efficiently achieving the professional goals of all nurses." The decision of the A.N.A. to work with nurse special interest groups suggests that the association does want to represent the major interests of all nurses. It must, however, pursue basic nursing interests "if it is to remain a professional association of nurses and not simply a special interest group" (Alutto, 1971, p. 117).

REFERENCES

Alutto, J. A.: The professional association and collective bargaining; the case of the American nurses. In Arnold, M. F., Blankenship, L. V., and Hess, J. M., editors: Administering health systems; issues and perspectives, Chicago, 1971, Aldine Publishing Co.

American Nurses' Association: Facts about nursing, Kansas City, 1950-1974, The Association.

American Nurses' Association: A.N.A. in profile, Kansas City, 1974, The Association.

American Nurses' Association: The nation's nurses, Kansas City, 1974, The Association.

Bucher, R., and Strauss, A.: Professions in process, Am. J. Sociol. **66:**325, 1961.

Epstein, I.: Specialization, professionalization and social-worker radicalism; a test of the "process" model of the profession, Appl. Soc. Stud. **2:**155, 1970.

Gilb, C. L.: Hidden hierarchies; the professions and government, New York, 1966, Harper & Row, Publishers.

Griffin, G. J., and Griffin, J. K., editors: History and trends of professional nursing, St. Louis, 1973, The C. V. Mosby Co.

Miller, M. H.: Nurses' right to strike, J. Nurse Admin. **5:**35, Feb. 1975.

Roberts, M. M.: American nursing; history and interpretation, New York, 1961, Macmillan, Inc.

Strauss, G.: Professionalism and occupational association, Industrial Relations **2:**7, May 1963.

11 The American Nurses' Association

to join or not to join

MICHAEL H. MILLER
BEVERLY C. FLYNN

The American Nurses' Association is widely considered to be a professional association. It is so defined because as a multipurpose organization it works "for the continuing improvement of professional practice, the economic and general welfare of nurses and the health needs of the American public" (American Nurses' Association and National League for Nursing, 1956). Professional association status also has been ascribed to the A.N.A. because it is the oldest and largest organization representing registered nurses. Moreover, the association is well organized and has an effective political lobby. Be this as it may, there is still some question about the professional association status of the A.N.A. and whether it actually represents "the policies of at least a majority of nurses" (Alutto, 1971, p. 117).

Professional associations perform many diverse but interrelated functions with important consequences for individual members of the association, the profession itself, and society (see Merton, 1958, for a complete description of the various functions of a professional association). But, interestingly, members of a profession who do not belong to the professional association typically receive "unearned increment of social, moral, and economic gain from the work of their professional colleagues in the association" (Merton, 1958, p. 52). Those professionals who remain outside the association are freeloaders, according to Merton, since they receive benefits from the association even though they choose not to hold membership in it. Merton also points out that nonpaying and nonparticipating members do not perceive themselves as freeloaders. They choose not to belong to the organization, because either they are not cognizant of the benefits they receive (or could receive) from the efforts of the association or they do not consider the benefits of membership as outweighing the costs to them of joining.

Over the past three decades, the proportion of registered nurses belonging to the American Nurses' Association has decreased significantly. In 1949, for example, 57% of all employed registered nurses belonged to the A.N.A.; in 1958 membership dropped to 41%; to 31% in 1968; and to 21% in 1972 (*Facts about Nursing,* 1950-1974). Similar but less severe declines in membership have occurred in many other professional associations (Moore, 1970). For instance, membership in the American Dental Association declined from 85% in 1960 to 82% in 1973 (Oshin, 1962; American Dental Association, 1973).

120

In general, membership in voluntary organizations, of which professional associations are a subset, has increased. In a recent national survey of adult participation in voluntary organizations, Hyman and Wright (1971) found that membership in organizations in which individuals join for mutual interest and benefit increased 9% from 1955 to 1962, the same period during which membership in the A.N.A. declined 10%.

The A.N.A., with a membership penetration of one in five employed registered nurses, is a ship without a crew.* Although it both develops and attempts to implement policies for nursing, 79% of the registered nurses it ostensibly represents do not choose to hold membership in it. As the professional association for nursing, the A.N.A. has a number of important functions, including: setting standards; influencing legislation; providing formal means for communication among members; working to improve nursing service and nursing education; and advancing research in nursing, the conditions under which nurses work, and the economic and social welfare of nurses. These functions are undertaken by the association with negligible input from most of the 800,000[†] employed registered nurses who might be affected by the consequences of its actions.

Participation in voluntary organizations is believed by some to be associated with the interaction between the costs and benefits of such action (Rogers and others, 1972). The exchange theory contends that as the personal benefits from participation increase and as the costs to the individual decrease, participation increases. More specifically, a person's motivation to join and participate in an organization is thought to be "a function of the inducements provided by the organization (as valued by a person), the contribution exacted by the organization (as valued by a person) and the alternatives he perceives to be available to him (Rogers and others, 1972, p. 184). Thus costs and benefits need not be real or actual, only perceived. If an individual perceives an "imaginary" cost (benefit or alternative) to being a member, the imagined cost (benefit or alternative) is real in its essence because it influences the individual's participation mode.

The literature on membership and participation in voluntary associations suggests that those persons who participate the most are also the persons who receive (or believe they receive) the most benefits from participation at the least personal cost. Conversely, nonparticipants are persons who believe they have the least to gain from membership. Warner and Hefferman (1967) also point out that, as participation in voluntary associations increases, there is probably a concomitant increase in recognition of benefits. Similarly, the reverse is probably true; as recognition of benefits increase, participation tends to increase.

The purpose of this chapter is to provide a possible explanation for the low membership penetration of the A.N.A. among employed registered nurses by using the cost-benefit model and then to suggest ways by which A.N.A. membership

---

*It should also be noted that a substantially smaller portion of all the registered nurses, employed and unemployed, belong to the A.N.A.

†American Nurses' Association, 1974b.

might be increased. It is our contention that persons who join the A.N.A. have, in general, more to gain (with less cost) than persons who choose not to join. We will assess the validity of this contention by comparing and contrasting members and nonmembers of the A.N.A. in terms of costs and benefits of membership. Our findings, while more suggestive than conclusive, should nonetheless provide additional insight concerning nurses' relationship to the A.N.A.

The data used in this chapter have been published recently by the A.N.A. in a narrowly circulated, confidential report titled *A.N.A. in Profile* (American Nurses' Association, 1974a). This A.N.A. study incorporated data from 43 state nurses' associations. Data from *The Nation's Nurses: 1972 Inventory of Registered Nurses* (American Nurses' Association, 1974b) are also utilized for comparisons between A.N.A. members and all registered nurses.

These two data sets were used because they constitute the most recent surveys of A.N.A. members and all registered nurses in the United States. The data have two major limitations. First, it is clear that any comparison of the A.N.A. membership in 1974 to all registered nurses in 1972 does not provide for the most accurate analysis.* The data as presented, however, do reflect the relative differences between A.N.A. members and all nurses. Second, the A.N.A. membership data are compiled from only 43 of the 50 state nurses' associations (S.N.A.s).† The 43 S.N.A.s included are those that permitted the A.N.A. to process their membership applications and renewal forms through its automated computer accounting system.

FINDINGS

The major costs and benefits of membership in the A.N.A. are found in Table 7. More benefits than costs are listed; however, equal weight is not necessarily associated with each item. In fact, given the A.N.A.'s small membership penetration, it can be inferred that the vast majority of registered nurses perceive the costs of membership as outweighing the benefits. It is also quite possible that many registered nurses are cognizant only of the costs of A.N.A. membership, not the benefits. Moreover, some registered nurses may be entirely unfamiliar with the A.N.A. and its functions.

An examination of the characteristics of registered nurses who were or were not members of the A.N.A. indicated a number of important differences having implications for our cost-benefit thesis. Table 8 summarizes some of the most salient characteristics.

Table 9 provides an index of the likelihood that registered nurses in various categories belong to the A.N.A. The data provide a useful indicator of the relative

---

*The A.N.A. makes similar comparisons in *A.N.A. in Profile*.
†The missing S.N.A.s include New York, California, Florida, Colorado, Iowa, Kentucky, and Rhode Island. Although approximately 25% of the employed registered nurses reside in these seven states, it is not believed that their absence from this study will seriously reduce its validity.

Table 7. Costs and benefits to membership in the American Nurses' Association

Costs of membership	Benefits of membership
1. Financial (such as dues) 2. Participation (such as time for meetings, activities) 3. Identification with specific ideology (that is, unions, work stoppage)	1. Professional development (such as contacts with other career-oriented registered nurses; exchange of ideas, information, and experience) 2. Personal influence on policies and activities of local association 3. Identification (such as status, fellowship) 4. Job protection 5. Discounts (such as lower insurance rates, workshop fees, specially priced tours) 6. Newspaper

differences in A.N.A. membership penetration by type of position held, field of nursing, and education.

Membership in the A.N.A. among instructors (29) and administration (26) is approximately four times as great as among general duty nurses (7), three times as great as among head nurses (9), and twice as great as among supervisors (14). Nurses employed in schools of nursing, with membership penetration of 32, are almost twice as likely to belong to the A.N.A. as nurses in schools and public health (17), three times as likely as nurses in hospitals and other institutions (9), and more than five times as likely as nurses in private duty and office employment (6) and nurses in industrial settings (4).

Nurses with doctorate and master's degrees are more likely to belong to the A.N.A. (39 and 31, respectively) than nurses with diploma degrees (7). They are at least twice as likely to join as compared with baccalaureate and associate degree nurses (both 14).

Our data show that A.N.A. members are overrepresented among registered nurses with the following characteristics: 35 years of age or older; single; instructors, administrators, and supervisors; employed in schools of nursing, in public health, and as school nurses; with doctorates and master's degrees. Conversely, A.N.A. members are underrepresented among registered nurses in the largest numerical categories: under 35 years of age; married; staff and head nurses; employed in hospitals and other institutions; industrial, office, and private duty; and with diploma degrees. In other words, the membership of the A.N.A. is composed of nurses with considerable freedom from the demands of family responsibilities, because many of them are single and those who are married tend to be older. In addition, they are the educational and occupational elite.

DISCUSSION

The data presented suggest that only a small, homogenous, elite cohort of registered nurses believe membership in the A.N.A. offers more benefits than liabilities. A.N.A. members are nursing's elite because, compared with nonmembers,

Table 8. Demographic characteristics of A.N.A. members (1974)
and all registered nurses (1972)*

Characteristics	Percent of	
	ANA members	All registered nurses
Age		
Under 25	8	7
25-34	23	30
35-44	19	24
45-54	22	25
55-64	20	12
Over 65	6	6
Total	100	100
Marital status		
Single	26	15
Married	60	74
Widowed	7	6
Divorced/separated	7	5
Total	100	100
Type of position held		
General duty or staff nurse	36	56
Head nurse	14	15
Supervisor	14	10
Instructor	12	4
Administrator	9	4
Other	13	4
Not reported	4	7
Total	100	100
Field of nursing		
Hospital and other institutions	66	70
Private duty, other	6	12
School nurse, public health	11	9
Industrial	1	3
Nursing school	11	4
Other	5	—
Total	100	100
Education		
Doctorate	1	—†
Master's	12	3
Baccalaureate	23	15
Associate	7	5
Diploma	57	77
Total	100	100

*American Nurses' Association, 1974a.
†Less than 0.5%.

Table 9. Index of the likelihood of registered nurses to belong to the A.N.A.
by type of position held, field of nursing, and education*

Type of position held	
Instructor	29
Administrator	26
Supervisor	14
Head nurse	9
General duty or staff nurses	7
Field of nursing	
Nursing school	32
School nurse, public health	17
Hospital and other institutions	9
Private duty, office	6
Industrial	4
Education	
Doctorate	39
Master's	31
Baccalaureate	14
Associate	14
Diploma	7

*Based on all employed registered nurses in 1972 (American Nurses' Association, 1974b) and
A.N.A. members in only 46 S.N.A.s (American Nurses' Association, 1974a). This is calculated by dividing the total number of employed registered nurses in a category into the total
number of A.N.A. members in the same category. Since the calculations are derivative of
1972 and 1974 data, the proportion in each category is smaller than is actually the case; however, the relative proportions between categories should be reasonably accurate.

they are the best educated; they hold positions in nursing with the most status,
prestige, and authority; and they receive the greatest financial remuneration for
their work.

The type of employment position nurses have (or aspire to) appears to be the
major causal factor affecting whether or not they join the A.N.A. This contention is based on two interrelated conditions: (1) Nurses who obtain administrative, supervisory, or positions in nurse education (or are striving for such positions) have made the decision to commit themselves to a career in nursing; and
(2) nurses with positions of authority and status are encouraged to participate
in professional nursing activities by their employers, who may provide them with
the time and finances to facilitate their participation.

Membership in the A.N.A. also provides nurses with membership in the state
nurses' association (S.N.A.). Nurses who make a commitment to nursing as a
career find that membership in these associations offers numerous benefits. Participation provides these registered nurses with useful contacts with other career-
oriented nurses who may be sought out (1) when a job vacancy occurs, (2) when
they wish to change their employment situation, or (3) when, for example, a consultant is required. Moreover, A.N.A. membership can help nurses keep informed
about current technical, political, legal, economic, and educational developments

in nursing that may have implications for their work. Membership also allows these nurses to participate in the development of policy affecting the nursing profession.* For nurses in educational positions, active participation in S.N.A.- or A.N.A.-sponsored workshops, committees, conventions, and so forth can influence their tenure and promotion in academic rank. Active participation by these nurses allows them to become known at the state and national levels. Professional recognition may also assist in the nurses' upward career mobility.

Even if a nurse is career oriented and wants to belong to the A.N.A., her employment situation must allow for her participation in association activities. Nurses in positions of authority and status frequently are expected to participate in professional nursing activities in order to represent their employer. Some employers provide key administrative and supervisory nurses with compensatory time for participation in professional activities; others permit their registered nurses to participate during their working hours, especially if the activity is related to their work (such as a technical workshop or conference on communication skills); and many employers even pay the expenses of their participating nurses. However, the majority of staff nurses receive no support—financial, compensatory time, or morale—for their involvement in the A.N.A.

Nurse employers who facilitate the participation of some of their nurses in professional association activities probably do so out of vested interests. For example, an employer can benefit greatly by its nurses (1) advertising the advantages of their employment situation, (2) obtaining information regarding nurses who are looking for new employment opportunities, and (3) gaining information regarding technological and social advances in nursing. Perhaps more important, nurse-representatives provide a mechanism to keep their employer apprised of new political or economic developments in nursing (such as collective bargaining strategy and attitudes toward work stoppage) on both the local and national levels.

The so-called average registered nurse does not, as pointed out above, join the A.N.A. Apparently, she perceives that (1) the benefits of membership have little personal value, given her orientation to her work; (2) the cost of A.N.A. membership is too high; and (3) there are better alternatives to A.N.A. membership. We shall now discuss each one of these points in order to further explicate the relationship of staff nurses to the A.N.A.

The nursing literature characterizes the staff or general duty nurse as lacking professional commitment to her work. Typically, the staff nurse is a second wage earner who works out of necessity rather than as a result of her primary interest in or commitment to helping patients.† As might be expected, then, the nurse's

---

*It should be pointed out that the average A.N.A. member probably has only a limited amount of input into the development of A.N.A. policy. However, members have more input than nonmembers and can increase their input by increasing their participation.

†We do not mean to suggest that nurses are not interested in the well-being of their patients; in reality, they tend to have an intense clinical interest and strive to improve their clinical skills whenever possible.

focus of concern is not congruent with the goals of the A.N.A. For example, she does not identify easily with such A.N.A. goals as the advancement of nursing as a profession, the development of standards of nursing practice, influencing legislation, improving nursing education, and advancing research in nursing, because such goals have little immediate, direct impact upon her work situation, her ability to provide care, or her economic status. Furthermore, the lack of relevancy of the A.N.A.'s goals allows the nurse to rationalize nonparticipation as a result of the demands of her family, for instance; family responsibilities preclude her involvement in any extraemployment activities. Staff nurses belonging to the A.N.A. may feel powerless because the association tends to be directed by and oriented toward nurse employers, administrators, and educators.

Dues* and the amount of time required for association participation appear to be the most formidable costs of membership in the A.N.A. The staff nurse not only does not relate to the association's goals, but she receives few benefits of substance for her money and participation. A.N.A. dues are not exorbitant by other professional standards (neither are the salaries of registered nurses); however, the lack of obvious incentives or benefits of membership forces prospective members to consider very carefully what they will receive for their dues before investing in membership. Apparently, many new registered nurses who initially decide to join the association choose to drop their membership after 1 or 2 years rather than continue to pay dues without receiving any return.[†]

The majority of staff and general duty nurses are married and have young children who require a considerable amount of their time and considerable expense for child care while they work. Hospitals and other health agencies and institutions generally do not provide staff nurses with compensatory time for professional association activities. To participate in their professional association, staff nurses must sacrifice time with their families. In addition, they may have to lose time from work and, thus, income. Corwin and Taves (1963) point out that unmarried women are more likely to involve themselves in nursing activities than married women. They contend that unmarried women in nursing have traditionally been the most committed. For unmarried women, "a career is probably a second choice, a compensation for the absence of successful marriage. They are among the most dedicated of nurses and the leaders of the professional nursing movement" (p. 204).

Traditionally, staff nurse involvement in professional nursing activities has not received much employer support. A few select staff nurses may be permitted to attend professional meetings but, generally, are not financially reimbursed for their

---

*In 1974, American Nurses' Association yearly dues ranged from a low of $39 in Mississippi to a high of $159 in California. The variation between states is a function of state dues: A.N.A. national dues are $25.
†It should be pointed out that registered nurses also tend to become "unemployed registered nurses" after 1 or 2 years.

child care, travel, registration fees, and daily expenses. In fact, active participation has even engendered employer disapproval or censorship. Employers appear to believe that membership in the A.N.A. has no functional purpose for staff nurses and tend to interpret nurse involvement as potentially disruptive. Employers' concern with nurse participation in A.N.A. activities may stem from their suspicion that their nurses will become unionized and more militant in their efforts to achieve employment benefits.

Staff nurses have several viable alternatives to A.N.A. membership. They can, for instance, join a nurse special interest group (such as the American Association of Critical Care Nurses, Association of Operating Room Nurses, or American Association of Nurse Anesthetists) or choose not to obtain membership in any nursing organization. Since most staff and general duty nurses have a minimal commitment to nursing and the nursing profession, either of these options would appear acceptable. For nurses with a focused clinical interest, membership in a special interest group will further such an interest considerably more than membership in the A.N.A. will. Conversely, nurses lacking both a clinical focus and a concern for advancing the nursing profession, developing standards of practice, and so forth will not choose to join the A.N.A. or a nurse special interest group. As non-A.N.A. members, they can, as pointed out earlier, reap many of the same benefits as A.N.A. members, because the contributions of A.N.A. members influence the profession of nursing as a whole.

Given the benefits, both manifest and latent, provided to members of the American Nurses' Association, it appears that the leadership of the association may intentionally pursue a course designed to preclude large numbers of staff nurses from joining the association. This considerable indictment of the leadership of the A.N.A. is based on the preceding analysis, which shows that the A.N.A. provides few substantive benefits to staff nurse members. Those benefits made available, it has been noted, can be obtained only at considerable cost to the general duty or staff nurse. The A.N.A.'s leadership, while ostensibly concerned with the extremely low proportion of nurses in the association, appears to have taken little remedial action. Accordingly, one could interpret this omission of effective remedial activity as passive disregard for the low membership penetration. The position taken by the leadership seems, then, to be rhetorically designed to dispense with criticism of the association's obvious lack of legitimacy to represent all registered nurses.

The A.N.A., with a membership drawn very heavily from supervisors, administrators, and nurse educators, has a significant vested interest in the present configuration and distribution of membership. Any radical changes in the association's organization, orientation, and objectives would probably be challenged vehemently by the present membership. Surely this select group is aware that an increase in the benefits provided A.N.A. members would probably result in a large influx of new members, especially staff nurses. Although a larger proportion of registered nurses should be advantageous to the A.N.A. in terms of increased financial resources and political power, any increase in membership might seriously erode the power of the present association leadership. The dynamic nature of nursing, with new and exciting developments in collective bargaining, the extended role of the nurse, legal standards, and standards of nursing practice, requires more than ever before a unified effort by all nurses. This unified effort will create an environment that will ensure that decisions made and legislation proposed and nurtured will best serve the interests, present and future, of nursing. There is, however, little chance that the proper guidance can be obtained if the A.N.A. continues to follow a policy designed to ensure that only the elite of nursing join the American Nurses' Association.

The membership penetration problem of the A.N.A. described here must be attributed as much to local (district and state) nursing leadership as to the national nursing association leadership. State nurses' associations and district nurses' associations, although they have some independence of action, closely follow the policies advocated by the national association leadership.

CONCLUSION

The underrepresentation of staff and general duty nurses in the American Nurses' Association and the overrepresentation of administrators, supervisors, and nurse educators indicate that the association has evolved to the point where it is more attractive to nurses in elite employment positions or to nurses who aspire to such positions. We have argued that the staff or general duty nurse does not join the A.N.A. because the benefits to be derived by her from membership do not surpass the costs of membership. It was noted that nurses forego membership in the A.N.A. because there are other more viable alternatives to membership open to them that result from the imbalance between the costs and benefits in membership. These include the numerous nurse special interest groups and not joining any nursing professional association. Since nonmembers are not penalized for not joining, except to the extent that they may be hurt by policies adopted by the association that do not represent their preference, there is no real incentive for the staff nurse to join. We also have suggested rather forcefully that the cost/benefit policy adhered to by the A.N.A. is associated with the low A.N.A. membership penetration among staff nurses. This policy, intentionally subscribed to by A.N.A. leadership, has the purpose of maintaining the present membership status quo.

We believe a number of policy changes are in order if staff nurses are to be attracted to the A.N.A. First, more substantial benefits to the staff nurse must be provided so that the considerable costs in time and money of membership can be offset. New benefits might include journal subscriptions with membership, one for the association and one for a special interest group. Augmentation of membership benefits (without increasing the costs) will have the result of decreasing the benefits received by nonmembers. Second, nurse employers must be informed that the active involvement of their staff nurses in A.N.A. activities can benefit the nurses in their work. For example, A.N.A.-sponsored workshops and continuing education programs can increase nurse efficiency and overall quality of care. In other words, an industry in which the employees are highly organized into professional associations or unions may actually benefit an employer by reducing employee unrest. Third, policies should be adopted by the A.N.A. that are more popular with the staff nurses who it needs to attract. We do not mean that a professional association should adopt policies unpopular with the persons it represents, but only that there should be greater convergence between the needs of the nurses who constitute the profession of nursing (staff and general duty nurses) and the policies advocated by the A.N.A.

REFERENCES

Alutto, J.A.: The professional association and collective bargaining; the case of the American nurses. In Arnold, M. F., Blankenship, L. V., and Hess, J. M., editors: Administering health systems; issues and perspectives, Chicago, 1971, Aldine Publishing Co.

American Dental Association: Inventory of dentists—1973. J. Am. Den. Assoc. **87:** 1244, Nov., 1973.

American Nurses' Association: Facts about nursing, Kansas City, 1950-1974, The Association.

American Nurses' Association: A.N.A. in profile, Kansas City, 1974a, The Association.

American Nurses' Association: The nation's nurses; 1972 inventory of registered nurses, Kansas City, 1974b, The Association.

American Nurses' Association and National League for Nursing: The A.N.A.-N.L.N., a joint statement of functions and activities, Am. J. Nurs. **56:**69, April 1956.

Corwin, R. G., and Taves, M. J.: Nursing and other health professions. In Freeman, H. E., Levine, S., and Reeder, L. G., editors: Handbook of medical sociology, Englewood Cliffs, N.J., 1963, Prentice-Hall, Inc., pp. 187-212.

Hyman, H. H., and Wright, C.: Trends in voluntary association memberships of American adults; replication based on secondary analysis of natural sample survey, Am. Sociol. Rev. **36:**191, April 1971.

Lipset, S. M., Trow, M., and Coleman, J.: Union democracy; the inside politics of the International Typographical Union, Glencoe, Ill., 1956, The Free Press.

Merton, R. K.: The functions of the professional association, Am. J. Nurs. **58:**50, Jan. 1958.

Moore, W. E.: The professions; roles and rules, New York, 1970, Russell Sage Foundation.

Oshin, E. S.: How does the A.N.A. stack up as a professional organization? R.N. **25:**39, Feb. 1962.

Rogers, D. L., Hefferman, W. D., and Warner, W. K.: Benefits and role performance in voluntary organizations; an exploration of social exchange, Sociol. Q. **13:**183, Spring 1972.

Warner, W. K. and Hefferman, W. D.: The benefit-participation contingency in voluntary farm organizations, Rural Sociol. **32:** 139, June 1967

White, R. F.: Which nurses join professional organizations? Mod. Hosp. **97:**123, Sept. 1961.

12 Toward a theory of professional work stoppage

the case of nursing

MICHAEL H. MILLER
LEE DODSON

Industrial work stoppage* has been widely studied (Britt and Galle, 1972; Kerr and Siegel, 1954; Ross and Hartman, 1960). Professional[†] work stoppage, however, has not received much attention. While much of the research examining industrial work stoppage has been analytical and has generated numerous factors accounting for the nature, scope, and cause of strike actions in industry, the few studies of work stoppage among professionals (such as physicians, nurses, teachers, and social workers) (Thompkins, 1967) have generally been descriptive and relatively devoid of theoretical consideration. The dearth of information about professional work stoppages is associated with their past infrequent occurrence relative to industrial work stoppages. The lack of standardized national data about professional work stoppage also has contributed to this lack of understanding.

As professional workers show increased signs of unionization, an increase in their work stoppage can be expected. Accordingly, a theory of professional work stoppage behavior, empirically grounded in generalizations about the content and structure of such behavior, will permit a more comprehensive understanding of this action.

Clearly, nonprofessional work and professional work differ; similarly, persons employed in nonprofessional occupations differ in many ways from persons pursuing careers as professionals. Whereas it would appear that the causes of work stoppages among professional and nonprofessional workers differ, it is in fact not clear that the natures of their work stoppages are dissimilar.

Work stoppage among registered nurses[‡] has been chosen for examination

---

*In this research, work stoppage is defined as any action by employees to refuse to continue to work. Typically, professionals have declined, except under unusual circumstances, to define a work stoppage as a strike because of the stigma attached to the term. Synonyms for strikes are demonstrations, mass resignations, and so forth.
†Although professionals are employed in industrial settings and may strike, there are so few incidents of such behavior that it was decided to consider industrial work stoppage as occurring solely among nonprofessional workers.
‡Registered nurses include nurses trained in associate degree programs (2 years), diploma programs (3 years), and baccalaureate programs (4 years).

because registered nurses have exhibited an increased propensity over the last decade to strike; registered nurses constitute the largest group of professional health workers; and data on the incidence, cause, and scope of registered nurse work stoppages could be obtained. It is hoped that the propositions developed here can be applied to work stoppage among all professionals.

PROFESSIONALS AND WORK STOPPAGE

Professions have long been distinguished from nonprofessions by numerous characteristics (Moore, 1970; Jackson, 1970). For any study of work stoppage a key issue would appear to be the workers' attitude toward striking: Do the workers accept or reject the notion of work stoppage for gaining employment ends? It was deemed that the "service orientation" of professionals and nonprofessionals constitute a major area of consideration for differentiating their respective work stoppages. Service orientation refers to the image that the workers have concerning the place of their work in society. For example, Moore (1970) identifies professionals as having altruism in service and nonprofessionals as dominated by self-interests. However, Parsons (1939) and Jackson (1970) indicate that work motivation among these groups is not dissimilar.

Our concern is the degree to which work groups "emphasize the ideal of service to clients and public as their *primary* goal and as part of their ideology. Also important is the extent to which this claim is (at least tacitly) publicly acknowledged" (Pavalko, 1971, p. 20). Moore argues that the professional, having acquired a specialized body of knowledge, has a moral responsibility to make it available. This responsibility springs from the professional's commitment to a calling and its associated norm of service (Moore, 1970, p. 224).

Obviously, scrupulous adherence to the service ideal and its consequences as indicated would incline the professional to forego any action, collective or individual, that would deprive needy clients of his service. Thus, strikes or walkouts would be unthinkable. Moore implicitly makes such a primary service orientation the defining condition of true professionalism: "The failure of the normal presumption of primary service to the client puts in doubt the claims of professionalism by the groups involved. This harsh, objective judgement applies to any occupational group claiming professional status and failing to give service to clients a very high priority" (Moore, 1970, p. 206).

Nursing is a highly service-oriented profession. Surely, the services rendered by registered nurses are like medicine, of a basic, life-supporting nature. In many cases, the withdrawal of such services by registered nurses could mean the death, physical impairment, and, at the least, discomfort of the client. This consideration, in conjunction with the nature and implications of the general service ideal for professionals, makes it unlikely that registered nurses would engage in work stoppage.

Before 1968 the American Nurses' Association adhered to a no-strike policy. As a result of this policy registered nurses voluntarily relinquished their right to strike, a privilege ordinarily available to employees in their efforts to improve their working conditions. The A.N.A. adopted the no-strike policy in 1950 in a magnanimous attempt to help maintain and ensure continuous nursing care. During the 18-year tenure of the no-strike policy, nurses generally bargained with their employers from a position of extreme weakness (Kleingartner, 1967). What means, besides resigning, were available to them to gain concessions from their employers when they had minimal power and low status?

Collective bargaining did not help nurses because of the lack of binding arbitration, the unresponsive nature of employer negotiations, the total rejection of collective bargaining by some employers and, also, the unwillingness of most registered nurses to engage in collective bargaining. However, during the late 1950s and especially in the early 1960s, nurses began to reevaluate their position in relation to their employers. It became evident to many nurses that their restraint from using overt power in labor negotiations resulted in the benign neglect of their grievances by their employers. Accordingly, in 1968 the American Nurses' Association renounced its no-strike policy, and most state nurses' associations followed suit (Miller, 1975).

APPLICATIONS OF EXISTING THEORIES TO NURSE WORK STOPPAGE

To deal with worker protest in general and nurse work stoppage in particular, it is necessary to distinguish the behavioral alternatives consequent with worker dissatisfaction. Udy (1965) dichotomizes such alternatives into the categories of group protest and individual reaction. Hirschman (1970) adds to these the notions of "voice" and "exit" behavior. Voice behavior, a form of group protest action, occurs when groups of individuals protest the unsatisfactory aspects of their employment through such action as strikes and demonstrations. Exit behavior, on the other hand, represents an individual reaction to an unsatisfactory employment situation and is exemplified by a high turnover rate.*

The various findings and theories of industrial work stoppage applicable to nursing may be summarized as follows. Low wages (Ellis and James, 1974, p. 17), weak economic conditions (Stearn, 1974, p. 23), ecological conditions unsuited to group interaction (Udy, 1965, p. 705), middle-class values (Ross and Hartman, 1960, p. 46), the absence of unions or other structural alternatives (Kornhauser, 1954, p. 10), the availability of substitute work of equal or better quality (Hirschman, 1970, p. 51), a concern primarily with price or wages (Stearn, 1974, p. 11), and sex (female) (Kerr and Siegel, 1954, p. 195; Kassalow, 1966, p. 339) are associated with exit behavior. Insofar as any of these conditions and characteristics are prevalent, their presence will contribute to the exercise of the exit alternative. To the extent to which they are not present, their absence *may* contribute to voice

---

*Exit and voice behavior are not the only possible behaviors resulting from work dissatisfaction: The dissatisfied worker may endure the sources of his dissatisfaction for any of a variety of reasons, or he may engage in a more clandestine protest such as industrial sabotage.

behavior. In general, the choice of exit by some weakens the likelihood of voice behavior (Stearn, 1974, p. 26). Concern with the quality of work, loyalty to the work organization, and the presence of unions are associated with the exercise of the voice option. The absence of unions or other structural alternatives such as professional or collective bargaining associations, which by their presence could serve to reduce the costs of voice behavior, increase the likelihood of the choice of exit behavior.

If we conceive of these descriptive findings as indicative of the relative costs and benefits of the voice and exit behavioral alternatives, they may be applied to nurses as follows: To the extent that nurses earn a low wage in comparison to their co-workers with approximately the same or less training and to the extent that alternative employment is available with more benefits, better wages, better hours, and so forth, nurses will exercise an exit option. Insofar as nurses subscribe to middle-class values and mores, they will probably choose to leave an unsatisfactory work situation rather than risk the interruption of income entailed by a strike or other voice option.

The community context in which voice and exit alternatives are chosen may have a significant effect on this decision. For example, the research of Harbison and Coleman (1951), Bernstein (1965), and Tannenbaum (1965) suggests that community size is related to industrial conflict, with the largest communities having the greatest number of work stoppages. Harbison and Coleman contend that small and medium-sized communities are more conducive to industrial harmony than large urban centers because: "The mere fact that all kinds of relationships in a small community are closer and more informal probably promotes industrial peace" (p. 132). Thus, size of place may be a necessary, but not sufficient, condition for the exercise of voice alternatives.

THE DATA

In order to establish a theory of professional work stoppage, it was necessary to find data about its occurrence. Unfortunately, there are few published data in this area. Only recently has the Bureau of Labor Statistics published information about work stoppage of nurses employed by the government (U.S. Department of Labor, 1973). Data concerning nurse strike behavior was found, however, in *The American Journal of Nursing*. In the news column of this journal, considerable data are published about the frequency, scope, and character of nurse work stoppage.

In an effort to ascertain the completeness and accuracy of the Journal's coverage of nurse work stoppages, all state nurses' associations were surveyed concerning nurse work stoppage during the period under study (1960-1974). Of the 42 state associations (84%) that responded, there were only five incidents of work stoppage not reported by the Journal: No incidents of overreporting were discovered. Interestingly, the incidents reported by the state nurses' associations but unreported by the Journal occurred in 1973 and 1974. This may suggest that the newsworthiness of local collective action has declined or that the state associations no longer report such items to the Journal.

We have noted some reluctance on the part of nurses to label their collective activities according to the usual parlance of organized labor. In part, we can attribute this reluctance to nurses' concept of professionalism:

> There are those who still believe that professionalism and collective bargaining are incompatible in both concept and practice. It is for this reason that many professional associations advocate the employment of bargaining techniques under the guise of euphemisms such as "mass resignations" or "concerted sick calls" (i.e., strikes) (Alutto, 1971, p. 105).

Our cognizance of this labeling tactic has led us to classify demonstrations, mass resignations, and strikes as equal incidents of work stoppage.

During the 14-year period under study, a total of 103 incidents of nurse work stoppage was noted, and at least 60 incidents of threatened work stoppage were noted. The first recorded stoppage was in 1962; there were no work stoppage actions again until 1965, after which the number of incidents increased to a peak of 34 in 1967. In 1968 there was a 67% decrease in work stoppage incidents. The number leveled off in 1969 before declining further in 1971. A slight increase was observed in 1974.

If we consider demonstrations, mass resignations, and strikes separately, we find that demonstrations (40 incidents or 39%) constitute the largest type of nurse work stoppage action. There were 32 incidents of strikes (31%) and 31 incidents of mass resignations (30%). During the period under study, we find a greater incidence of demonstrations and mass resignations before 1969 and a higher proportion of strikes after 1969. Before this period, nurses apparently were inclined to use such work stoppage action as demonstrations and mass resignations (27 out of 40 and 26 out of 31, respectively); after 1969, however, over 52% of all work stoppage incidents were strikes. The increase in strikes may be associated with increased acceptance of these actions by nurses. Another possible interpretation of the data is that nurses have begun to label their work protest action "strikes" instead of using euphemisms such as demonstrations and mass resignations.

Relative to the number of registered nurses employed in the United States during the period from 1960 to 1974, few nurses actually engaged in work stoppage actions. The Journal indicated that more than 20,000 nurses were involved in the various actions during the period; the state nurses' associations were able to document a total of only 9,354 nurses. We believe that the Journal's figures are more accurate than the state nurses' associations', because they represent a tabulation made at the time of each work stoppage action. The state nurses' associations had to compile their data from records or memory, possibly making their figures less reliable. Considering that there was a yearly average total of 600,000 employed registered nurses during the period from 1960 to 1974, it is clear that the 9,000 to 20,000 registered nurses engaged in work stoppage actions constituted a very small portion of the total nurse population.

We were able to obtain data regarding the reasons given by the nurses for only 80 of the 103 work stoppages. In 41 of the 80 cases, nurses indicated that their decision to engage in a work stoppage action was directly related to wage inequities.

Less frequently cited by nurses as the primary reason for their work stoppage were working conditions (14%), representation (15%), quality of care (5%), staff shortage (5%), and other (3%).

Although wages were cited by nurses as the primary reason for their work stoppage action, there is no direct way to determine whether nurse work stoppage actions were successful in increasing wage benefits. The figures for median annual salaries of staff registered nurses in two different public health nursing services · during the period from 1963 to 1973 show a sharp rise in the percentage increase in annual salary for staff nurses after 1966. For the period before the occurrence of nurse work stoppage (1963-1965), there was an average annual percentage increase of 4% for nurses in local official health units and nonofficial agencies. But after 1965 and the initiation of numerous nurse work stoppage actions, the average annual percentage increase was 8% for both groups of nurses. When, however, the annual percentage increase is calculated for only the period from 1971 to 1973, the period during which work stoppage actions declined, we find that there was a marked drop in the salaries provided nurses. The annual percentage increase for nurses in local official health units declined from 9% in the period from 1966 to 1972 to 6% in the period from 1971 to 1973; for nurses in nonofficial agencies, annual percentage increase dropped from 11% to 4% between the two periods. Although these data are only for nurses employed in public health nursing service, they probably reflect the relative changes in salary increase of most registered nurses.

Nurse work stoppages occured in 27 of the 50 states and in the District of Columbia. By section of the country, it was found that the western region had a slightly higher work stoppage incidence (35 of 103) than the others. The second highest number of incidents was found in the central region with 27, followed by the Atlantic and southern regions with 22 and 19, respectively. Significantly, seven states and the District of Columbia accounted for almost three fourths of all the incidents. California had the largest number (18), followed by Illinois (15), New York (11), Pennsylvania, Washington, and the District of Columbia (6 each). Arizona and Ohio each had 5 incidents.

The vast majority of the work stoppages took place in large urban centers. Only 11 of the 103 incidents occurred in a county or city of less than 100,000 population. Furthermore, since 1969, work stoppage actions have occurred exclusively in large metropolitan areas. On the basis of these data, it appears that nurse work stoppages are highly correlated with community size. The data also suggest that nurse work stoppages do not occur randomly; 46% of the states had no incidents, while seven states plus the District of Columbia had a higher proportion than could be expected by chance.

DISCUSSION

The data of nurse work stoppage shows a dramatic change in the behavior of nurses toward engaging in work stoppage. In 1965, there was suddenly a rash of work stoppage incidents, but soon thereafter another change in behavior occurred as the number of nurse work stoppages decreased. Apparently, something happened in the mid-1960s that resulted in incidents of nurse work stoppage. But subsequent to 1967, it appears that those factors responsible for nurse work stoppage were brought under control.

Why did nurses engage in work stoppage actions in the first place, and why did they initiate this activity in the mid-1960s? In order to determine the validity of the various predictions based on the current theories of industrial work stoppage for nurses, consider first the profile of the "average" nurse. Alutto (1971, pp. 106-107) describes nurses as likely to be women, to receive a relatively low wage, to be in a situation unfavorable to after-work group interaction in nursing association meetings, to avail themselves of work substitutes of equal or better quality, to be concerned primarily with price and wages, and to lack or not avail themselves of their professional organization (union).* As previously noted, all these characteristics are associated with exit (quitting) behavior. From Alutto's description and its correspondence with many of the characteristics associated with exit behavior in the literature on industrial work stoppage, we would not expect a preponderance of strikes or voice behavior among nurses.

The characteristics of individuals who choose to pursue careers in nursing suggest other reasons registered nurses have not actively engaged in work stoppage actions. Mauksch (1972, p. 216), for example, contends that the lower middle class and Christian background of most registered nurses sets "the stage for an occupation group which is not likely to be characterized by assertiveness, risk-taking, and personal autonomy, and the (educational) socialization process further tends to reinforce these tendencies." Moreover, Mauksch asserts that nursing's domination by women with a "traditionally perceived female role . . . creates a woman who serves sacrificially, who supports and who protects a dominant male, and who identifies her success as a nurse with her success as a woman" (p. 217).

It has also been pointed out by Meyer (1960) that registered nurses prefer interacting with patients and physicians to associating with other registered nurses. Neither is the extensive spatial distribution of nurses in their practice settings conducive to drawing nurses together. These two points are particularly significant because they explain, at least in part, why registered nurses lack group cohesiveness or group consciousness. Specifically, the nurses' spatial distance and their seeming disdain for other members of their profession reduce the possibility of communication. Since communication acts as the major catalyst in the formation of social movements (McCarthy and Zald, 1973, p. 17), nurses may not be particularly cognizant of grievances they share with other nurses. Accordingly, group action, which is dependent on an effective communication network, is stifled.

---

*Since a major focus of this study was on the mid-1960s, when nurses work stoppage reached a peak, Alutto's "period" description was chosen as most illustrative of conditions of that time span.

One possible means to allow us to begin an explanation of the particular nature of nurse work stoppage is the application of the reference group model. This theory, used by Ross (1958, pp. 49-50) to explain industrial work stoppage, asserts that "comparison plays a large and often dominant role as a standard of equity in the determination of wages under collective bargaining." Belote (1967, p. 268) supports this position by stating that nurses were "tired of seeing the difference in results from ladylike communications to nurse employers of 'minimum employment standards' and the results of plumbers' or automobile workers' union activities." While Belote's comment is indicative of a process of comparison, it does not sufficiently explain why nurses became tired of these inequities in the mid-1960s instead of at some other time.

Ross (1958, pp. 49-50) argues that "in collective bargaining determination, the strongest equalizing tendencies emanate from the force of organization and the force of ideas." The American Nurses' Association, although relatively weak in terms of membership numbers (about 20% of all employed nurses belong) still possesses some force of organization. As for the force of ideas, the changes in the training of nurses during the 1960s may have provided the impetus for a comparison such as that suggested by Belote.

Beginning in the 1960s, registered nurses in increasing proportions were prepared in collegiate nursing programs instead of in the more traditional hospital schools of nursing. We contend that educational attainment is correlated positively with political activism and that the collegate nursing programs constituted an increase in the education of registered nurses. Campbell (1962, p. 20) supports the relationship between education and activism. McCarthy and Zald (1974, p. 4) add to this notion that "the more America becomes a middle-class society, the higher the societal rate of participation in sociopolitical concerns." To the extent that work stoppage constitutes a kind of sociopolitical activity, the increase in education of nurses would appear highly relevant in helping to explain the occurrence of nurse work stoppage. Thus, as more and more of these college-trained nurses entered the health care system, they found their income status and decision-making role substantially less than what they anticipated, or what they observed other professionals to have. That is, their high expectations were not fulfilled, and they became dissatisfied (Conta, 1972; Seidman, 1970).

The increased militancy of the American Nurses' Association in matters of salary and benefits appears to have been another significant factor contributing to the new behavior of the nurses. In 1966 the A.N.A. House of Delegates adopted a starting practitioner salary goal of $6,500. This national goal, which was subsequently adopted by most state nurses' associations, provided nurses with some basic level of comparison. Thus nurses, when offered a much lower base salary, had a basic referent with which to compare their own remuneration.

The juxtaposition of the annual percentage salary increase with the distribution of nurse work stoppage suggests that work stoppage frequency declined in response to large wage increases. It also appears that nurses may have initiated work stoppage actions in 1965 after having long experienced low wages. Although the first action by nurses in 1965 failed to bring about major wage increases (reflected in the percentage increases for 1966) or convince hospital administrators and public health agency officials that nurses would resort to collective means to achieve their goals, the large number of work stoppage actions in 1966 and 1967 succeeded both in bringing about higher wages and in changing nurse employers' attitudes toward engaging in collective bargaining with nurses. Once nurses' wage expectations and achievements were brought into line, their work stoppage actions declined. Interestingly, by 1971 there was also a decline in nurses' percentage increase in annual earnings. This decline suggests that the work stoppage actions in 1966 and 1967 acted only as a booster shot: Their effectiveness declined over the next 6-year period.

Still another possible explanation for the particular surge in nurse work stoppage is that this surge represents a manifestation of a trend that was occurring in society at large. As McCarthy and Zald point out, "The 1960's was a period of increased social movement activity" (1973, p. 12). There was, perhaps as a result of increased participation by Americans in various sociopolitical activities, a general feeling that changes could be effected in society.

Analysis of all work stoppage during this period shows a definite "7-year trend of annual increases in strike indexes, which began in 1964 and peaked in 1970" (U.S. Department of Labor, 1971, p. 2). In 1963 there were approximately 3,500 industrial work stoppages; their number increased to 4,000 in 1965, to 5,000 in 1968, and to 5,700 in both 1969 and 1970. In 1971 there was a drop of 10% to 5,100 incidents.

Government work stoppage showed a similar upsurge during this period. In 1963 there were only 29 incidents, increasing to 41 in 1964, to 42 in 1965, to 142 in 1966, to 181 in 1968, to 254 in 1969, and to 412 in 1970. A 20% decline occurred in 1971 to 239 work stoppages (U.S. Department of Labor, 1970, p. 9; 1971, p. 7).

Apparently the spread of increased social activity, particularly the success of the Civil Rights Movement, inclined workers in many sectors of the labor force to believe for the first time that they could and should initiate action to resolve their employment grievances. Included in this group were teachers, firemen, policemen, registered nurses, and even, in a few cases, physicians.

Contagion, "the rapid spread of an idea or pattern of conduct by spontaneous imitation" (Swanson, 1971, p. 96), may also help to account for the eruption of nurse work stoppage actions during this period. But contagion does not occur at random; apparently, the likelihood of its taking place increases among individuals "as pressure to do something [about a particular problem] increases" (Swanson, 1971, p. 96). Contagion occurs, then, when people wish to do something about a particular situation but require something to motivate or propel them into action. It does not evolve from the more prestigious members of the group but occurs when an individual "embodies what others [are] already prepared to do" (Swanson, 1971, p. 96). In other words, the initiation of traditional labor techniques (collective bargaining and striking) among groups such as teachers, policemen, and civil servants provided additional incentive for nurses to imitate similar actions. Thus, we observe a snowball or contagion effect: "Everybody's doing it."

As quickly as the onset of nurse work stoppage actions took place, their numbers declined. After 1967, there were only an average of 7 work stoppages per year; between 1965 and 1967, there occurred an average of 17 per year. The observed decline in work stoppages after 1967 may have resulted in part from the achievement of some of the nurses' demands.

The evidence presented seems to show that some nurses achieved, at least partially, their demands for increases in salary. As we have seen in the percentage increases in median annual salaries for public health staff nurses, the increases following the years of highest work stoppage activity were much higher than in the years before such actions. Although such achievements were at best temporary, they may have given nurses a false sense of success followed by a drop in demand. We note the subsequent deterioration of the annual increases during the period of declining work stoppage frequency.

CONCLUSION

We believe that changes in training (and therefore in reference groups), the A.N.A.'s salary goal of 1966, imitation or contagion, and a large community size all may have contributed to the emergence of work stoppage as a labor tactic among nurses. Only the last of these factors has received significant previous treatment in the literature on industrial work stoppage. Accordingly, we suggest that previous theories of industrial work stoppage or the conditions favorable to voice and exit alternatives are not necessarily germane for the explanation of nurse work stoppage. Insofar as the case of nursing may be more similar to that of other professionals than to that of occupations, we also suggest that such factors may not prove particularly relevant as a theoretical basis for explaining professional work stoppage in general. Consonant with our own study, we believe that a more fruitful basis for a theory of professional work stoppage may be provided by some combination of reference group theory with a conception of imitation, contagion, or "focal points" (on this last possibility, see Oberschall, 1973, p. 138). While our work suggests one such possible combination, we believe that a comprehensive theoretical synthesis must await studies of additional professions.

THE FUTURE

It is likely that the late 1970s will see an increased number of nurse work stoppages as the economic position of nurses continues to decline and as their importance to the success of the delivery of health care in hospitals increases. The passage of the Taft-Hartley amendment, which now includes nonprofit hospitals under collective bargaining regulation, will have some impact, at least initially, in reducing nurse-management strife. However, when nurses discover that collective bargaining without an ultimate force to support their demands, such as mandatory arbitration or striking, is without utilitarian value, work stoppage incidents will be implemented. If, on the other hand, the recent major strikes in Honolulu, San Francisco, and Youngstown, where nurses were extremely successful in achieving their professional and economic goals, serve as a signal to hospital administrators that nurses can no longer be disregarded, work stoppage may be offset by hospital administrator actions.

REFERENCES

Alutto, J. A.: The professional association and collective bargaining; the case of the American Nurses' Association. In Arnold, M. F., Blankenship, L. V., and Hess, J. M., editors: Administering health systems; issues and perspectives, Chicago, 1971, Aldine Publishing Co.

Belote, M.: Nurses are making it happen, Am. J. Nurs. **67:**285, Feb. 1967.

Bernstein, I.: Labor relations in Los Angeles, Industrial Relations **4:**8, Feb. 1965.

Bowman, R. A., and Culpepper, R. C.: Power; R$_x$ for change, Am. J. Nurs. **74:**1053, June 1974.

Britt, D., and Galle, O. R.: Industrial conflict and unionization, Am. Sociol. Rev. **37:**46, Feb. 1972.

Campbell, A.: The passive citizen, Acta Sociologica **6:**2, 1962.

Conta, A. L.: Bargaining by professionals, Am. J. Nurs. **72:**309, 1972.

Ellis, L., and James, P. L.: Alternative forms of worker protest; an exploratory study of industrial striking and quitting (paper presented at the Southern Sociological Society Annual Meeting, Atlanta, Georgia, April 18-20, 1974).

Etzioni, A., editor: The semi-professions and the organizations; teachers, nurses, social workers, New York, 1969, The Free Press.

Gurr, T.: Why men rebel, Princeton, N.J., 1970, Princeton University Press.

Harbison, F. H., and Coleman, J. R.: Goals and strategy in collective bargaining, New York, 1951, Harper & Row, Publishers.

Hirschman, A. O.: Exit, voice and loyalty; responses to decline in firms, organizations, and states, Cambridge, Mass., 1970, Harvard University Press.

Jackson, J. A.: Professions and professionalization, Cambridge, Eng., 1970, Cambridge University Press.

Kassalow, E. M.: White-collar unionism in the United States. In Sturmthal, A. F., editor: White-collar trade unions, Urbana, Ill., 1966, University of Illinois Press.

Kerr, C., and Siegel, A.: The interindustry propensity to strike; an international comparison. In Kornhauser, A., Dubin, R., and Ross, A. M., editors: Industrial conflict, New York, 1954, McGraw-Hill Book Co.

Kleingartner, A. N.: Nurses, collective bargaining and labor legislation, Labor Law J. **18:**244, April 1967.

Kornhauser, A., Dubin, R., and Ross, A., editors: Industrial conflict, New York, 1954, McGraw-Hill Book Co.

Lipset, S. M.: White-collar workers and professionals; their attitudes and behavior towards unions. In Faunce, W. A., editor: Readings in industrial sociology, New York, 1967, Appleton-Century-Crofts, pp. 527-548.

Lipset, S. M., and Trow, M.: Reference group theory and trade union policy. In Komarovsky, M., editor: Common frontiers of the social sciences, Glencoe, Ill., 1957, The Free Press, pp. 391-411.

Mauksch, H. O.: Nursing; churning for change. In Freeman, H. E., Levine, S., and Reeder, L. R., editors: Handbook of medical sociology, ed. 2, Englewood Cliffs, N.J., 1972, Prentice-Hall, Inc., pp. 206-230.

McCarthy, J. D., and Zald, M. N.: The trend of social movement in America; professionalization of resource mobilization, Morristown, N.J., 1973, General Learning Corporation.

McCloskey, J.: Influences of rewards and incentives in staff nurse turnover rate, Nurs. Res. **23:**239, May-June 1974.

Meyer, G. R.: Tenderness and technique; nursing values in transition, Monograph No. 6, Los Angeles, Calif., 1960, Institute of Industrial Relations, University of California.

Miller, M. H.: Nurses' right to strike, J. Nurs. Admin. **5:**35, Feb. 1975.

Moore, W. E., in collaboration with Rosenblum, G. W.: The professions; roles and rules, New York, 1970, Russell Sage Foundation.

National Labor Relations Board: National Labor Relations Act jurisdiction over health care institutions (pamphlet), Washington, D.C., 1975, U.S. Department of Labor.

Oberschall, A.: Social conflict and social movements, Englewood Cliffs, N.J., 1973, Prentice-Hall, Inc.

Parsons, T.: The professions and social structure, Social Forces **17:**457, 1939.

Pavalko, R. M.: Sociology of occupations and professions, Itasca, Ill., 1971, F. E. Peacock Publishers, Inc.

Rehmus, C. M.: Professional employees and the right to representation, Professional Engineer (American) **40:**48, Feb. 1970.

Ross, A. M.: Do we have a new industrial feudalism? Am. Econ. Rev. **48:**903, Dec. 1958.

Ross, A. M., and Hartman, P. T.: Changing patterns of industrial conflict, New York, 1960, John Wiley & Sons, Inc.

Seidman, J.: Nurses and collective bargaining, International Labor Relations Review **23:**335, 1970.

Stearn, R. N.: The community context of industrial conflict (unpublished dissertation, Vanderbilt University, Department of Sociology, 1974).

Swanson, G. E.: Social change, Glenview, Ill., 1971, Scott, Foresman and Co.

Tannenbaum, A.: Unions. In March, J. G., editor: Handbook of organizations, Chicago, 1965, Rand McNally & Co., pp. 710-763.

Tompkins, D. C., compiler: Strikes by public employees and professional personnel; a bibliography, Berkeley, Calif., 1967, University of California Institute of Government Studies.

Udy, S. H.: The comparative analysis of organizations. In March, J. G., editor: Handbook of organizations, Chicago, 1965, Rand McNally, pp. 678-709.

U.S. Department of Labor, Bureau of Labor Statistics: Work stoppages in government 1958-1968, Report 348, p. 13, 1970.

U.S. Department of Labor, Bureau of Labor Statistics: Government work stoppages 1960, 1969, and 1970, Summary Report, Nov. 1971.

U.S. Department of Labor, Bureau of Labor Statistics: Analysis of work stoppages 1971, Bulletin 1777, p. 39, 1973.

U.S. Department of Labor, Bureau of Labor Statistics: Work stoppages in government, 1972, Report 434, p. 5, 1974.

Yett, D. E.: The supply of nurses; an economist's view, Hosp. Prog. **46:**88, Feb. 1965.

part V
EDUCATIONAL ISSUES

Broadly speaking, education includes any process by which an individual or group transmits elements of culture to another person or group. All groups also provide education to a more limited extent by passing selected knowledge, skills, and values on to their members in order to prepare them for effective group membership. In this section, we are concerned with specific issues in the educational process through which nurses are prepared for their professional roles.

Nursing education is, doubtless, one of the most essential as well as controversial areas in nursing. Throughout the history of formal education in nursing—dating back to the Bellevue Hospital School in 1873—there have been periodic efforts to modify and improve both the educational institutions and their curricula. Accordingly, nursing education has progressed through cycles of unrest, ferment, and innovation. What should be taught? To whom? By whom? How? These are among the questions being asked of nursing education today.

The first of the three chapters of this section addresses various illusions that have remained unresolved for the past two decades about nurse educators in baccalaureate and graduate nursing degree programs. This chapter clearly points out that the mystique about nurse educators is replete with numerous paradoxes, half-truths, naive assumptions about normative behavior, incidents of failure in nursing education, and efforts to uphold vested interest. Dr. Passos classifies these myths into three categories: (1) scholarship motives, (2) credentials versus competencies, and (3) complexity and predictability of nursing phenomena. Although the chapter raises the same difficult questions again, it does not, however, make the problems easier for nursing by providing many viable solutions.

The chapter by Wood and Ohlson examines the knowledge, skills, values, and orientation being taught to graduate students in community (or public) health nursing. The authors take exception to the individualistic focus of baccalaureate nursing programs; instead, they contend, emphasis in these programs should be on the family as a functioning unit. Wood and Ohlson propose a three-dimensional model for preparation of graduate nursing students in community nursing practice. The model integrates groups (such as families, population groups, and communities), prevention (primary, secondary, and tertiary), and process (assessment, intervention, and evaluation). Although not included in the model, the authors see research as crucial to the education of community nurse practitioners.

Earlier in this text (Part III), various issues and trends related to the practice and role of the nurse practitioner were discussed in chapters by Henshaw (histori-

143

cal) and Gage (team approach to care). The final chapter in this section examines the impact of the educational process on behavioral and attitudinal changes among nurse practitioner students. Dr. Miller questions the extent to which nurses entering new primary care roles undergo a resocialization process as suggested by other researchers. His study assesses changes in stress, assertiveness, and sex role ideology of students in two primary care nursing programs: family nurse practitioner and family nurse clinician. The results of Miller's study show that the stress generally associated with entry into a new role can be controlled and that the didactic phase of the nurse practitioner program has less impact upon behavioral and attitudinal changes among nurse practitioner students than does the students' actual employment in the role.

13 The nurse educator

myths and mystique

JOYCE Y. PASSOS

If you think you understand the problem, you don't have
enough information.

Anonymous

Education has been viewed for centuries in our country as the key to the golden
door of opportunity. Mandatory public education laws have existed since the birth
of the nation, expressing our near-reverence for education, historically accompanied by profound respect for the educator. Our early faith in education and educators was quasimythical, held by a citizenry of whom the majority could scarcely
read and write; our forefathers believed, beyond their comprehension, in the intrinsic value of education.

In the two centuries since the founding of our nation, the average number of
years of schooling has risen steadily, as have the educational requirements for most
occupations. Nursing as an occupational field reflects this trend. In the midnine-
teenth century, preparation for nursing consisted primarily of hospital-based ap-
prenticeship. In 1975, we witnessed approval by the New York State Nurses' Association of the position that minimum preparation for practice as a registered nurse
be a baccalaureate degree in nursing. Evidence of changing patterns of preparation
for nursing suggests that it may soon be realistic to require a baccalaureate degree
as a minimum educational preparation for nursing. In the 12 years from 1962 to
1973, the percentage of graduates from hospital-based diploma programs decreased
from 84% to 36%, while graduates from baccalaureate programs increased from
14% to 22% (American Nurses' Association, 1974). However, as the general level
of education of nurses has been rising, the difference between the lowest and highest levels of educational preparation obtained by nurses has been steadily increasing. In the 5 years from 1969 to 1973, the number of nurses with earned doctorates
doubled from 504 to 1,020. Even at the 1973 level, nurses with earned doctorates
represented only 0.12% of all employed registered nurses ($N = 815,000$), the majority of whom possessed a diploma in nursing as their highest educational credential (Pitel and Vian, 1975). For the majority of nurses, who have had no
personal experience in colleges or universities, there is still a mystique about higher
education in general and about nurse educators with advanced preparation in par-

ticular. The mystique of the nurse educator is composed of a number of paradoxical notions. Some of these notions derive from half-truths about the nature of nursing; some are naive assumptions about the normative behavior of nurses; some reflect a failure to distinguish between educational credentials and competencies; and others are espoused by nurse and nonnurse administrators to defend empirically unsupportable staffing decisions.

This chapter will demonstrate the mythical nature of the following ten widely held notions about nurse educators employed to teach in baccalaureate and higher-degree programs. The myths are classified into three categories: (1) scholarship motives of educators and their resultant omniscience, (2) credentials in contrast to competencies, and (3) complexity and predictability of nursing phenomena. The paradoxical nature of the myths about the nurse educator becomes evident as one compares the myths that cast the educator as a member of an intellectual elite from whom much is expected and received (Myths 1-4) with those myths that appear to deny any connection between professional credentials and the competencies required for the educator to be effective in proposed roles (Myths 5-9).

MYTH 1

- Nurses who elect to qualify themselves for faculty positions do so primarily because of the intellectual challenge in the teacher role.

In examining the work values of nurses with stated preferences for teaching and clinical nursing practice careers, Heidgerken (1970) found that neither group ranked scholarship very high, as evidenced by low ratings given to those activities related to research, writing, and publishing. Among activities of the teaching preference group that outranked scholarly activities were independence in work assignments, flexible working hours, motivating others to learn, opportunity to increase their own fund of information in a specific subject, and opportunity to further the professionalization of nursing. Kramer (1974) documented the exodus from nursing of many nurses who had been unable to use professional nursing judgment and skills in hospitals and nursing homes. I believe that many more nurses who would otherwise leave nursing go to graduate school to prepare for faculty positions, a change of vocation that represents a back-door exit from nursing for some. Mereness (1975) supports this contention with her observations as a dean on the motivation of nurses for graduate study and teaching careers:

> The need to avoid obvious conflicts that exist in the world of work and the fear of being unable to meet employers' expectations are some of the motivations which propel some recent graduates of generic baccalaureate programs into graduate study (Mereness, 1975, p. 639).

Because of the acute manpower shortage of educationally prepared teachers of nursing, the majority of such graduates ultimately are propelled into faculty positions, thus escaping from the challenge to develop as competent practitioners, accountable to the consumer of nursing service.

MYTH 2

- Faculty in baccalaureate and higher-degree programs in nursing have a broader and deeper base of current knowledge than other nurses because of the opportunities and resources available in a community of scholars.

This myth assumes access by nurse educators to the scholarship of higher education, a qualitative benefit to their knowledge and skills from that access, and an ability to provide leadership to the profession because of their richer resources. However, as Pechiulis (1972) discovered, the climate within the nursing unit of the university can resemble that found in a fortress erected to protect the status quo more than it resembles a community of scholars. This may be due in part to the speed with which nursing has been catapulted into higher education. The first half of this decade has seen an accelerated shift from hospital- to university-based programs of nursing education in a period when qualified faculty are our scarcest nursing manpower resource. In 1972, almost 11% of full-time and 30% of part-time faculty in baccalaureate and higher-degree programs held less than a master's degree (National League for Nursing, 1972). It is reasonable to assume that many nurses who suddenly find themselves with a university faculty appointment have not had the opportunity to fully comprehend the responsibilities, rights, and privileges that accompany membership in a community of scholars.

When the collective wisdom of a faculty is freely accessible to each of its members, the programs tend to be more dynamic and more responsive to outside influences. Open communications are a necessary attribute for the development of a community of scholars and to the planning for change necessary to keep nursing education relevant to the rapidly evolving health care system. Schenk (1970) found a high correlation between faculty morale and amount of change planning taking place in baccalaureate nursing programs. There is some evidence that changes being planned are not in accord with trends well described in our society. To the extent that faculty in the nursing program contribute to policy decisions such as admission rates, there is evidence of failure to track current trends realistically and to alter practices accordingly. In 1973, we had nearly exceeded the level of total admissions to nursing programs predicted by Altman (1971) for 1980, and we are fast approaching his prediction of the proportional distribution of enrollments by type of program. The question arises as to whether or not faculty have the knowledge and skill necessary to lead in stemming the flow before we are inundated with graduates of uncertain competencies, to the detriment of both the consumer (erosion of the quality of care) and the profession (economic consequences for individual nurses). However, in one respect faculty in baccalaureate programs may be beginning to reap the benefits of the scholarly climate in institutions of higher education, as reflected in trends in the 1970s toward qualitative differences in baccalaureate curricula. These trends include movement toward greater community involvement, interdisciplinary participation, independent study, and specialization (Robischon, 1972).

For decades the educators in nursing have decided what nurses should learn and how they should be prepared (Lewis, 1973). Among faculty in baccalaureate and higher-degree programs are nurses who constitute a real reservoir of clinical knowledge and skills. As the trend toward mandatory continuing education for relicensure develops, these nurses are called on more and more to conduct workshops and courses for which continuing education units (C.E.U.s) are awarded. Faculty able to service this need because of their effectiveness in self-directed learning may find themselves in a paradoxical situation. This paradox was summed up with eloquent simplicity recently when a workshop participant asked me, "Where do *you* get *your* C.E.U.s?"

One area in which nurse educators have been unable to prepare themselves to meet a growing demand is that of instruction in extended assessment skills. A major obstacle encountered by the many nursing education programs that now aspire to prepare students for an expanded nurse practitioner role has been that available faculty lacked the necessary knowledge and skills to teach and serve as practitioner role models for students. One of the first steps in any major modification of curricula outcomes in these programs has been to ensure that faculty are competent in areas in which students will be expected to learn (Awtrey, 1974; Malkemes, 1974; McGivern, 1974). There are multiple means of maintaining competency, but "whatever the profession, it must be recognized that continuing education is only a means—and as yet an unvalidated means—to an end, and the end is the maintenance of competence, the improvement of competence, or the acquisition of additional competencies" (American Association of Colleges of Pharmacy and American Pharmaceutical Association Task Force on Continuing Competence in Pharmacy, 1974). Continuing competency as opposed to continuing education is an issue that pharmacy and some other professions have faced; nursing has not yet confronted it (Forni, 1975).

MYTH 3

- Nurse educators in baccalaureate and higher-degree programs consistently provide research-based instruction for students.

Research-based teaching requires creative thought. At this juncture in nursing education, there are innumerable internal and external constraints on faculty creativity and consequent involvement in nursing research. Among those constraints are pressure to conformity through group and committee decision making and through such teaching strategies as team teaching; lack of self-confidence and assertiveness among educators socialized to more passive roles; a tendency toward premature closure on ideas, intolerance for ambiguity, and a tendency toward inflexibility; lack of administrative support for innovation; and lack of blocks of uninterrupted time for reflection (Kalish, 1975). Some of the factors that prohibit faculty from having blocks of time for reflection and study, both of which are critical to research-based teaching, are crushing teaching loads, frequently heavy service loads as we move toward greater popularity of joint appointments, and the ever-burgeoning number of committee assignments. Cleland (1975) views the "excessive counseling of students and the excessive refinement of objectives as games some faculties play to avoid doing research." When faculty think in terms of "covering content," the result is the teaching of half-truths, and the long-term effect is premature closure of the mind, with no questions asked. If this is to be avoided, educators must find a way to integrate the methods and findings of research, and not continue to add them on as a senior-level luxury.

MYTH 4

■ Nurse educators have a clear conception of the distinctions between associate degree, diploma, and baccalaureate program curricula and the performance characteristics of their graduates.

Generations of nursing leaders have assumed that professional practice would follow professional education, and thus they devoted their energies almost exclusively to improving nursing education. The result has been the emergence of several levels of nursing education but the persistence of a single level of nursing practice (Sheahan, 1972). In deploring the present chaos of nursing education, Fagin (1976) states: "Our basically defensive position regarding the definition of the term 'nurse,' and particularly 'registered nurse,' poses considerable difficulty for any clear and consistent statement which the public can understand and support." The 1971 official statement of the Council of Diploma Programs of the National League for Nursing is illustrative of the blurring of performance characteristics of products of different levels of nursing education; the statement described the role, knowledge, and abilities of the diploma program graduate, but the description could just as well apply to the proposed characteristics of graduates of any preprofessional program, with the single exception that the diploma graduate was intended to use those abilities to function primarily "in hospitals and similar community institutions." Evidence that the lack of differentiation persists and is of concern to education is obvious in such projects as the curriculum proposal at the University of Nebraska College of Nursing for articulation of associate degree, through baccalaureate to master's degree. One of the anticipated outcomes of the curriculum project was that levels of practice be defined (Boyle, 1972).

Lack of identification of end-of-program nursing competencies has created a number of internal problems for education as well as for the employers of nurses. It has been difficult to develop criteria for admission to graduate study other than that the applicant be a "graduate of an accredited baccalaureate nursing program." It has also been difficult to individualize program and instructional design for students transferring into a baccalaureate program following graduation from a diploma or associate degree program (Lenburg and Yeaworth, 1975).

If there is to be a distinction among graduates of the three types of preprofessional nursing programs on the basis of their performance characteristics, qualitative distinctions should be identifiable in the various curricula. Bullough and Sparks (1975) found that students were identifiably different in their care or cure orientation to the nursing role by type of program and that this difference probably resulted from the socialization process in the type of program selected by the student. Reasons given by students for choosing a particular type of program were extremely practical, such as proximity of a program to their homes or selection of the schools that would accept them. Reasons for program selection failed to support the hypothesis that students with different orientations are recruited to or choose different types of generic nursing programs.

An interesting characteristic on which one might expect graduates of different types of programs to vary is their perception of physician leadership. Bates and Chamberlin (1970) found that nurses attributed a high degree of importance to the directiveness of physician behavior and that they accepted and even desired such directive leadership, independent of the amount or recentness of the individual nurse's education. Some encouraging differences are beginning to emerge, however. One recent examination of the characteristics of diploma and degree nurses found that as education increased, nurses showed greater preference for active (in contrast to bedfast) patients, were more interested in teaching and supportive care functions, and were less restricted in their preferences (Hover, 1975).

MYTHS 5-9

- Competence as a nurse practitioner qualifies an individual to take full responsibility for clinical instruction of nursing students.
- Faculty in preprofessional nursing programs do not need to meet the same rigorous qualifications as faculty in graduate programs and other courses of instruction that admit only registered nurses.
- Possession of an earned doctorate is a sufficient qualification for a person to teach research courses and to direct clinical studies of both undergraduate and graduate nursing students.
- The most experienced, knowledgeable, and successful teachers of clinical nursing are the best candidates or choices for promotion to administrative positions.
- The only faculty member in a baccalaureate nursing program who needs to have an earned doctorate is the director of the program.

These five myths are all related in some way to the competencies required to meet present needs in nursing and to the credentials of persons available for and selected to fill positions related to present needs. Therefore, these five myths will be discussed as a single entity.

At a time when the greatest manpower need in nursing is for teachers prepared to interpret, use, and conduct research, the trend in enrollments in master's-degree programs is toward an increase in preparation for advanced clinical practice and a decline in enrollments in teaching in the various content areas. Ten years ago, only about 17% of full-time master's-degree candidates were preparing for advanced clinical practice, and the majority of enrollments were in teaching. Among graduates of master's-degree programs in 1972-1973, the largest number among all functional areas of study was in advanced clinical practice—55.2% of all graduates (National League for Nursing 1975). Even in medical-surgical nursing, the clinical area in which the majority of students in teaching were enrolled, more advanced practitioners than teachers were prepared.

Elements of both the cause and effect of the current critical shortage of faculty can be seen by examining the distribution of basic and registered nurse student enrollments in baccalaureate programs in nursing in 1973. Nearly 35% (about 16,000) of the 96,867 students registered in baccalaureate programs were enrolled in programs not accredited by the National League for Nursing. Although many factors may contribute to the nonaccredited status of a program, an insufficient number of appropriately prepared faculty is frequently a contributing factor. It is only from the pool of graduates of baccalaureate programs that master's and doctoral degree programs can recruit applicants. Fortunately, there is an increase in both the number and percentage of basic nursing graduates from baccalaureate programs. But despite the enlargement of the pool from which graduate education draws, there is a slight but distressing decrease in the ratio of master's-degree to baccalaureate graduations: in 1965, the ratio was 1 to 4; in 1973, the ratio was 1 to 5. (National League for Nursing, 1975).

Because of the critical need for master's degree–prepared nurses in teaching roles, there has been a tendency to justify appointments to teaching positions of nurses with graduate degrees earned in almost any discipline, on the basis that the real contribution of graduate study is the intellectual discipline acquired by the graduate. For those whose master's degrees are in advanced clinical practice, there may be considerable congruence between some practice and teaching skills if their practice has had as a major focus the helping of others to make their own decisions. A most important role of a faculty member is to serve as a "process consultant" (Sedgwick, 1973) to both students and nursing service personnel, helping the consultees to make their own immediate and long-range decisions. At Case Western Reserve University, where the concept of joint appointment between education and service was tested in a 5-year demonstration project, individuals being considered for joint appointments must be approved by both systems. The possession of clinical expertise is not considered *prima facie* evidence of ability to take full responsibility for clinical instruction of students. One university program surveyed the nurses who completed advanced clinical practice majors in its master's-degree program from 1968 to 1971 and found that over half the group would have preferred that the program include preparation for both teaching and administration as well as advanced preparation in clinical nursing (Donley, 1973).

When one examines the teaching assignments of faculty in university programs in relation to the strength of credentials and teaching experience of faculty, there appears to be a consistent ordering: Those faculty who rank highest on credentials and teaching experience teach graduate students; those who rank lowest on credentials and teaching experience teach basic undergraduate students; and faculty in the middle range of credentials and teaching experience teach registered nurse undergraduate students. There is some evidence to support this pattern of assignment for graduate and undergraduate students. In a study of the characteristics of the effective teacher in nursing education, Kiker (1973) found that graduate students consistently ranked as most important the characteristic of professional competence, whereas undergraduate students more often gave highest priority to quality of relationship with students. However, in comparing registered nursing students and basic senior students, Gortner (1968) found evidence to both support and discourage continuance of separate programs for registered nursing students. In some respects, Gortner's data suggested that the registered nursing student is more like the graduate student than the basic student; her findings distinctly differentiated the registered nursing student from the basic student on the basis of stronger professional motivations, theoretical inclinations, and postbaccalaureate career plans.

Relatively little attention has been given to the impact of persons holding advanced educational credentials on the areas of need in nursing. An outstanding exception to this was the survey of 1,576 nurses by Verhonick and associates (1968), which demonstrated that advanced educational preparation has significance for refinement of clinical judgment. Performance in the conduct of research does not seem to fare as well. In reviewing the research literature on issues in nursing manpower for the 13 years from 1956 to 1968, Flint and Spensley (1969) concluded that nurse researchers seemed rarely to have formulated questions carefully and that those questions that had been asked had frequently been researched inappropriately or inadequately. They suggested that if nursing is to establish itself as a discipline with a research emphasis, it must demonstrate the ability both to pose meaningful questions and to execute well-designed studies that have problem-solving utility. Many practices in graduate education in nursing, justified on the basis of special and acute need, tend to slow progress toward the goal of increased sophistication in research. Practices such as removing graduate programs in nursing from the school of graduate studies of a university, in order to make it possible for all faculty in the nursing program, with or without earned doctorates or research experience, to teach and advise master's-degree students (Moxley and White, 1975), may be acceptable as interim strategies, but they will ultimately weaken the quality of the product of such programs and of the talent pool nationally. Such strategies are classic examples of means to win the battle and lose the war.

As indicated previously, the available nurses with doctoral preparation are woefully inadequate in regard to the needs of the profession for research competencies. Of the 915 nurses with doctoral preparation who are currently employed, only about 4% describe themselves as "researchers" (Pitel and Vian, 1975), while 80% are employed as faculty; only about one third of the responsibilities of those in faculty positions relate to research. A major drain on the availability to nursing research of the research training of doctorally prepared nurses is the tendency to push these people "up" to positions with heavy administrative responsibility. Many deans appear to believe that the interests of nursing are best served in the university community when represented by those few faculty whose doctoral degrees give them equal status with colleagues in other fields. That effect may or may not be achieved, but the frequent involvement of such appointees in the maze of university governance results inevitably in a "brain drain" from research-related activities. Carlisle (1975) observed that universities, in handling their academic administrative affairs through representative bodies and committees, tend to force all academicians to be administrators. Many academicians have neither the inclination nor the ability and training to assume such roles.

Another almost irresistible force that diminishes or eliminates the research productivity of doctorally prepared nurses by moving them into administrative positions is the lure of benefits; in most institutions of higher education, top administrators receive higher salaries and greater benefits than do full professors. In many instances, the result of such a promotion is another example of the triumph of the Peter Principle: "In a hierarchy every employee tends to rise to his level of incompetence" (Peter, 1972). It is axiomatic that the dean of a nursing program in higher education should possess an earned doctorate, and ideally others in positions of major responsibility should also possess that credential. But there must be judicious use of the scarce commodity of research-trained nurses; greater care must be given to reserving larger numbers of them for positions in which they can combine teaching and research activities at both the undergraduate and graduate levels of nursing education. Otherwise, we will find in the very near future that we have lost our only hope to build nursing knowledge based on research.

MYTH 10

- Clinical instruction of nursing students can be equated with laboratory sections of physical and biological sciences in establishing standards for faculty work loads.

This myth is by far the most dangerous: first, because it is based on gross oversimplification of the nature and complexity of nursing phenomena encountered in nonsimulated clinical nursing laboratories; second, because it is believed by many educators rather than by the rank and file of nurses. The statement equating science and nursing laboratories may be partially true when instruction takes place in a simulated clinical situation, where a discrete number of variables can be isolated and controlled to maximize learning and minimize student anxiety. But when instruction takes place in the presence of real people facing health-related problems, there are at least five characteristics of the clinical nursing laboratory that differentiate it from laboratory sections of physical and biological sciences.

The whole-part problem

A dominant feature of human adaptation is that "the behavior of a person is affected by and affects all persons and events with which he is involved" (Beland

and Passos, 1975). Whatever objectives the clinical laboratory is designed to help students achieve and however skillful the faculty member is in selecting experiences to meet those objectives, the variables of concern to the learner cannot be isolated for observation, study, or practice from the total response of the person or persons whose situation the student enters.

Predictability of phenomena

In conducting and interpreting the results of laboratory experiments in the physical and biological sciences, the student usually works with a limited number of factors whose nature and relationships are known in the discipline. In the clinical nursing laboratory, many of the factors operating in the situation have not yet been identified; some are known but their influence is poorly understood. Only a few, such as some physiological parameters of an individual's status, are sufficiently well understood to allow prediction, with any degree of certainty, of either problems of or responses to selected therapeutic interventions.

Situational stability

As suggested in the first characteristic of the clinical nursing laboratory, the presence of the student or teacher or both, serves as a stimulus to produce a new situation for the person or persons selected for experience. Encounter settings vary in the amount of control that can be exerted by the teacher and student over the situational context. Their control is probably lowest in community and family groups and highest in institutional settings. But even when the encounter is with an incapacitated geriatric patient in a long-term care facility, control and stability of the situational context often prove to be illusions shattered by sudden changes in patient response or in availability of expected nursing personnel or equipment and materials. A major outcome of the clinical nursing laboratory is the student's awareness of the unexpected and his or her ability to respond appropriately to it. This characteristic of low situational stability may help to explain why so few faculty who express belief in the laboratory concept of clinical experience in nursing education as defined by Infante (1975) are able to practice or apply that concept in their clinical teaching.

Faculty-student ratio

No college or university could long afford undergraduate science courses that required a faculty-student ratio of 1 to 10 for each laboratory section. Yet Merrill (1974) found in a national survey of 286 baccalaureate programs accredited by the National League for Nursing that the average faculty-student ratio for clinical courses was 1 to 9.3 (mode = 1:8). Anyone who has taught in the clinical nursing laboratory knows that the three characteristics previously cited can interact in such a way that even a faculty-student ratio of 1 to 8 becomes totally unmanageable for the teacher. It has been demonstrated that in some settings, such as the intensive care unit, a faculty-student ratio of 1 to 2 is the permissible maximum to ensure effective clinical instruction (Geels and others, 1974).

Faculty work load and the time cost of the clinical nursing laboratory

The proponents and opponents of existing practices in the conduct of the clinical nursing laboratory are legion. Cleland (1975) has urged examination and evaluation of the number of "clinical supervision hours" provided by faculty in relation to the number of credit hours obtained by the student for the laboratory experience. A widely used formula for determining the number of clock hours allocated to the laboratory portion of clinical nursing courses in baccalaureate programs is 3 clock hours to 1 credit hour. Classroom instruction is usually allotted 1 clock hour to 1 credit hour. An assumption that appears to underlie the difference in these credit hour to clock hour ratios is that the student requires about one third as much time to prepare for clinical laboratory as for classroom learning activities. One of the tragic consequences of the application of this ratio to the design and scheduling of clinical nursing courses is its contribution to the calculation of deceptively low faculty work loads.

An example illustrates the magnitude of the deception. Instructor A is teaching two laboratory sections in an eight-credit junior-level nursing course of which four credits are allocated to clinical laboratory experience. Most institutions of higher education would consider this assignment an 8–credit hour work load, well within accepted standards for an optimum undergraduate teaching load. Guidelines established by the American Association of University Professors (Committee C on Teaching, Research, and Publication, 1970) for faculty teaching undergraduate students state that 12 hours per week of formal class meetings constitute a maximum teaching load and 9 hours per week constitute an optimum teaching load. In addition to taking full responsibility for the two laboratory sections, Instructor A also participates in curriculum and course planning and teaches 6 hours in the general assembly section of the course during the semester, in the area of her clinical specialty. Each week she averages 24 to 28 scheduled student contact hours, which include neither the time required for planning and selecting experiences before each laboratory nor the time required to evaluate or grade student progress. If one added only 5 hours per week per section for necessary pre- and postlaboratory activities, Instructor A would be committed to 34 to 38 hours per week. Even at this presumably "optimum" work load, the amount of involvement in scheduled activities prohibits the reflection and study necessary for consistent use of a scholarly approach to teaching. Even if Instructor A is willing and able to devote most of her waking hours to her teacher role, the resulting overextension of effort and unbalanced living cannot be sustained indefinitely; eventually, the point of diminishing returns is reached, and mediocre education results.

The baccalaureate nursing program at Boston State College will graduate its first class in June 1977. In January 1975, when the first class was enrolled in a sophomore-level, four-credit clinical nursing course, we began collecting data to identify the nature and clock-hour cost of various critical elements of clinical instruction. We are now halfway through the first year of offering junior-level instruction, and our preliminary data suggest that the nature of critical elements will be stable across levels of the program, clinical settings, and clinical faculty. However, it appears that there will be great variation in the clock-hour cost of those elements across program levels and clinical faculty. Variation may also emerge along other dimensions as well.

In planning the four-credit sophomore-level nursing course, we allotted two credits (6 clock hours per week) to clinical instruction. We realized that faculty would spend more than 6 hours per week in teaching a laboratory section, but, lacking data on actual clock-hour cost to faculty, we estimated 10 hours per week per faculty for each section of eight students. A 25% sample of the semester's clinical instruction activities revealed that clinical faculty spent an average of 16.8 hours each week in activities essential to providing 6 hours of clinical instruction to one laboratory section of eight students. A portion of this high time cost may have been attributable to such factors as the newness of the program, the readiness of students, the variable teaching experience of the clinical faculty, or their high enthusiasm for their teaching responsibility.* Analysis of data in subsequent years will seek to determine the influence of these and other factors on the time cost of clinical instruction.

But whatever the possible circumstances operating to explain our findings, it is apparent that on the basis of time, clinical instruction of nursing students *cannot* be equated with laboratory sections of physical and biological sciences in establishing standards for faculty work loads. It is clearly the responsibility of nursing faculty to develop research-based work-load standards for nursing faculty that can be comprehended and supported by administrators in higher education.

SUMMARY

Some of the myths supporting the mystique of the nurse educator have been described and criticized. Some of the myths are believed primarily by the rank and file of nurses, some primarily by nurse educators themselves, and others are shared by all nurses and the larger society of which they are an integral part. All of the myths presented relate in some way to the definition of nursing as an intellectual discipline, obligated to use scientific inquiry to expand its knowledge base as the most effective means by which to improve the quality of its service to the health needs of society. The profession should work diligently to make some of the myths a reality and to dispel others with all possible haste.

---

*All eight of the clinical faculty involved in sophomore-level clinical instruction were joint appointments with agencies in which they also carried service responsibility; all were master's degree prepared in a clinical specialty; and all but one had more experience in practice than in education.

REFERENCES

Altman, S. H.: Present and future supply of registered nurses, Pub. No. (N.I.H.) 72-134, Washington, D.C., 1971, Department of Health, Education, and Welfare.

American Association of Colleges of Phar-

macy and American Pharmaceutical Association Task Force on Continuing Competence in Pharmacy: The continuing competence of pharmacists, final report, Washington, D.C., Sept. 1974, The Association, pp. 3-14.

American Nurses' Association: Facts about nursing, Kansas City, 1974, The Association, pp. 72-73.

Awtrey, J. S.: Teaching the expanded role, Nurs. Outlook **22:**98, 1974.

Bates, B., and Chamberlin, R. W.: Physician leadership as perceived by nurses, Nurs. Res. **19:**534, 1970.

Beland, I. L., and Passos, J. Y.: Clinical nursing, ed. 3, New York, 1975, Macmillan, Inc.

Boyle, R. A.: Articulation; from associate degree through masters, Nurs. Outlook **20:**67, 1972.

Bullough, B., and Sparks, C.: Baccalaureate vs. associate degree nurses; the care-cure dichotomy, Nurs. Outlook **23:**688, 1975.

Carlisle, H. M.: University administration and the change process, Phi Kappa Phi J. **55:** 26, 1975.

Cleland, V.: Nursing research and graduate education, Nurs. Outlook **23:**642, 1975.

Committee C on Teaching, Research, and Publication: Statement on faculty workload, A.A.U.P. Bull. **56:**30, March 1970.

Council of Diploma Programs, National League for Nursing: Roles, knowledge, and abilities of the graduate of the diploma program in nursing, Nurs. Outlook **19:**463, 1971.

Donley, R., Sr., and others: Graduate education for practice realities, Nurs. Outlook **21:**646, 1973.

Fagin, C., and others: Can we bring order out of the chaos of nursing education? Am. J. Nurs. **75:**98, 1976.

Flint, R. T., and Spensley, K. C.: Recent issues in nursing manpower; a review, Nurs. Res. **18:**217, 1969.

Forni, P. R.: Continuing education vs. continuing competence, J. Nurs. Admin. **5:**34, 1975.

Geels, W. J., Brand, L. M., and Passos, J. Y.: The I.C.U. and collegiate nursing education, J. Nurs. Educ. **13:**15, 1974.

Gortner, S. R.: Nursing majors in 12 western universities; a comparison of registered nurse students and basic senior students, Nurs. Res. **17:**121, 1968.

Heidgerken, L. E.: Work values and career preferences of nurses for teaching and clinical nursing practice, Nurs. Res. **19:**219, 1970.

Hover, J.: Diploma vs. degree nurses; are they alike? Nurs. Outlook **23:**684, 1975.

Infante, M. S.: The clinical laboratory in nursing education, New York, 1975, John Wiley & Sons, Inc.

Kalish, B.: Creativity and nursing research. Nurs. Outlook **23:**314, 1975.

Kiker, M.: Characteristics of the effective teacher, Nurs. Outlook **21:**721, 1973.

Kramer, M.: Reality shock, St. Louis, 1974, The C. V. Mosby Co.

Lenburg, C. G., and Yeaworth, R. C.: Who shall be admitted to graduate study? Nurs. Outlook **23:**633, 1975.

Lewis, E. P.: Continuing education; the form and the substance, Nurs. Outlook **21:**499, 1973.

Malkemes, L. C.: Resocialization; a model for nurse practitioner preparation, Nurs. Outlook **22:**90, 1974.

McGivern, D.: Baccalaureate preparation of the nurse practitioner, Nurs. Outlook **22:** 94, 1974.

Mereness, D. A.: Graduate education, as one dean sees it, Nurs. Outlook **23:**638, 1975.

Merrill, L. J.: The faculty-student ratio, Nurs. Outlook **22:**452, 1974.

Moxley, P. A., and White, D. T.: Fitting the graduate program to the student, Nurs. Outlook **23:**625, 1975.

National League for Nursing: 1972 nurse-faculty census, Pub. No. 19-1442, New York, 1972, The League.

National League for Nursing: Some statistics on baccalaureate and higher degree programs in nursing, 1973-74, New York, 1975, The League Division of Research.

Pechiulis, D.: The academic honeymoon is over, Nurs. Outlook **20:**180, 1972.

Peter, L. J.: The Peter prescription, New York, 1972, William Morrow & Co., Inc.

Pierik, M. M.: Joint appointments; collaboration for better patient care, Nurs. Outlook **21:**576, 1973.

Pitel, M., and Vian, J.: Analysis of nurse-doctorates; data collected for the international directory of nurses with doctoral degrees, Nurs. Res. **24:**340, 1975.

Robischon, P.: Trends in baccalaureate nursing education, Nurs. Outlook **20:**273, 1972.

Schenk, K. N.: A measure of faculty morale, Nurs. Res. **19:**135, 1970.

Sedgwick, R.: The role of the process consultant, Nurs. Outlook **21:**773, 1973.

Sheahan, D., Sr.: The game of the name; nurse professional and nurse technician, Nurs. Outlook **20:**440, 1972.

Verhonick, P. J., and others: I came, I saw, I responded; nursing observation and action survey, Nurs. Res. **17:**38, 1968.

14 Graduate preparation for community health nursing practice

JEAN WOOD
VIRGINIA OHLSON

> But minute enquires into conditions enable us to know that in such a district,
> nay, in such a street, in such a particular house
> or even on one floor of that particular house,
> will be an excess of mortality, that is, the person will die
> who ought not to have died before old age.
>
> *Florence Nightingale*

It appears important to begin to consider the specialty content for graduate preparation in community nursing practice by approaching the subject from a broad perspective aimed at identifying the relationship between public health nursing and general nursing education. Nursing, like all other professions, has developed out of societal need, and over time needs and values of society change. As these needs and values change, the profession must change accordingly, and the profession's educational system, to be relevant, must be involved in effecting, as well as transmitting, this change.

Society has both health and illness care needs. The general focus of nursing education is directed toward moving the patient from a state of illness to a state of health. This focus is documented by the fact that approximately two thirds of all practicing nurses are employed by hospitals. The remaining one third is distributed among private medical practice, community health agencies, schools and occupational settings, and nursing education programs (Scott, 1974). This inequitable distribution by setting of practicing nurses is confounded further by the fact that only about 15% of all health and illness care problems are evidenced in the institutional population (National Commission for the Study of Nursing and Nursing Education, 1973).

The union of education for public health nursing and baccalaureate nursing education has brought compromises, as well as benefits, for public health nursing education. The benefits accrued from this union are seen clearly in the development of clinical nursing skills by students, while compromises have resulted in a lessening of the knowledge base in the public health sciences.

Baccalaureate nursing programs focus predominantly on nursing care for individuals, while nursing care for community or population groups may be overlooked.

In this chapter community health nursing and public health nursing are used interchangeably.

In most instances, the focus on the uniqueness of individuals and their diseases has precluded attention to the "common characteristics" associated with health or illness of individuals or groups and thus has limited the potential for providing nursing service to community groups, be those groups families, communities, or subgroups of communities. The concept of family care in the baccalaureate program is most frequently centered on one or more individuals who have a health or illness need. Although the illness of an individual member may be addressed within the framework of the family, the impingement of the individual member's health on other family members or on the family as a functioning unit is frequently not considered. Seldom is the family cared for as a biological, physical, and social unit capable of producing illness or disease and promoting health.

Regardless of the fact that health is broadly defined (verbally), it is commonly perceived only as the positive counterpart of disease and frequently denotes only the physiological component of health to the neglect of social and psychological components. Prevention is most frequently taught in relation to limiting disease progress or limiting disability rather than circumventing the occurrence of disease or illness.

Perhaps the most neglected of all public health nursing concepts is the community. Identification of broad community health needs and participation in community development as it relates to the health needs and wants of the community may be totally neglected in the preparation of nurses for entry-level positions in community health.

Since the union of public health nursing education and baccalaureate nursing education, curricula have undergone considerable changes, and the preparation for beginning-level practice in public health nursing has varied among schools. The medical model, at one time a universal model used for organizing the content of baccalaureate curricula, has been replaced in part or whole by a variety of behavioral, sociological, and nursing models. The extent to which the previously cited public health nursing concepts are integral parts of these models is unknown.

Opportunities for student learning in baccalaureate programs are based primarily in hospitals and other institutions whose primary goal is to care for the sick (acute and long-term). Such settings bring to the student's repertoire of experience a population that is representative neither of disease and illness nor of health of people in general. Little attention is directed to those segments of the population who have health conditions but do not avail themselves of care or for whom care is not accessible. Thus, the base on which graduate preparation in public health nursing is built is tenuous at best.

The identification of content for specialty preparation in community health is complicated further if one begins to approach content through definitions. In practice, the term is defined in relation to place and population, while the knowledge and skill for practice remains undefined. No other specialty field in nursing differentiates its field of specialty by place.

More recently, there has been a trend in the field to equate community health practice with distributive care. The placement of community health nursing in the context of distributive care has prompted the development of a variety of programs that prepare nurses for "extended roles" in personal health care services. Some of these educational programs have developed in association with, or as an integral part of, graduate programs in public health nursing, that is, nurse practitioner programs. In some cases, this is the whole of specialization in graduate education in departments of community health nursing of schools and colleges of nursing. The major focus of these programs is on the preparation of nurses as providers of direct, personal health care for individuals and their families with the purpose of monitoring health conditions and disease states. The programs are primarily clinical, emphasizing early detection of disease and the management of stabilized chronic health conditions. Many of these programs report that the intent of preparation is family nursing practice, while the curricula give clear indication that the graduates of the programs are prepared to give care to individuals of all ages.

From this brief review of the current relationship between nursing education and community health nursing education, it is clear that little direction for developing the specialty content in community health nursing education can be ascertained from the content of educational programs or definitions. It is also unlikely that this direction will come from service settings, since current practice is, in part, a reflection of our educational programs and definitions and the increasing demand for medical care service. We suggest that the major portion of the content formulation will be derived from the level of the people's health and our knowledge about health and prevention.

Distinguishing health promotion and disease prevention from detection, treatment, and cure of disease is important in view of current health problems and the history of prevention. Cardiovascular disease, cancer, diabetes, arthritis, mental disorders, failure to thrive, and respiratory tract infections are but a few examples, among many, of illness states for which no evidence exists to indicate a substantial decline in incidence (Cassel, 1973). The current decline in cerebrovascular disease mortality cannot be attributed to drug therapy for hypertensive disease, since this decline in mortality antedates the use of drug therapy (Paffenbarger and others, 1966).

McGavern (1959) noted that few instances have been reported that indicate that treatment of disease has an effect on disease in society. The greatest impact on disease has been made when efforts have been directed toward altering the environment of well people. For example, the decline of infectious disease in infancy was accomplished by altering the environment of well infants. Public health nurses participated in this endeavor by identifying well infants and helping mothers provide a safe food supply for their children. The identification of well infants was not accomplished by waiting for mothers to bring their infants to a health care unit but by actively seeking out the well, vulnerable infants.

In recent years the body of evidence from both animal and human studies that points to a relationship between the social environment and disease has grown.

Studies indicate that one third of all illness is related to man's interaction with his social environment; disruptive events in an individual's life seem to occur just before the onset or exacerbation of disease (Brown and Birley, 1968; Hinkle and others, 1958; Holmes and others, 1957). Cultural conflict, acculturation, cultural ambiguity, and mobility have been implicated in hypertension and heart disease and other functional disabilities (Cassel and Tyroler, 1961; Jackson, 1962; Kaplan and others, 1971). Families tend to share a similar quality of life (Downs, 1942). If one spouse dies, a greater-than-chance possibility exists that death of the other spouse will soon follow (Ciocco, 1940; Shurtleff, 1955). This accumulation of evidence from human studies does not permit us to ignore the potential of the social environment for the implementation of preventive practices. These studies have given us information about the time when illness and disease may occur and the situations under which they may occur. If primary prevention is to occur through nursing practice, community health nurses must use this information to actively seek out the vulnerable, well people. For example, the use of death certificates may be the means of identifying the well spouse, or census data may identify the family or families in cultural conflict and vulnerable to disease or illness. With this kind of information, the community health nursing program may intervene by identifying or developing the necessary social support system required so that individuals and families might reduce their risk potential. Numerous examples can be cited which indicate that data are available that could put the community nurse in touch with the vulnerable, well individual or family. These data await the appropriate applications to health and the appropriate interventions by the specialist in community health nursing.

This concept of prevention as it is related to health, communities, families, and nursing practice encouraged our faculty at the University of Illinois—Chicago, College of Nursing to consider the graduate preparation for community nursing practice in relation to primary prevention and population groups. For the purpose of our program the community health nurse practitioner is defined as follows.

The community nurse is a practitioner with specialty preparation in the sciences of public health and nursing. This practice derives its base of knowledge from the integration of the behavioral, social, biological, and physical sciences. The practitioner designs practice in relation to health and illness of communities, populations, and family groups. The practitioner has special skills in:

1. Assessing community health status through systematic methods.
2. Identifying families and population groups at risk to health conditions and illnesses.
3. Planning community health nursing programs for the health of communities, populations, and family groups during various stages of the health-illness continuum
4. Evaluating the effectiveness of community nursing programs through health outcomes.
5. Formulating research questions in the areas of community nursing practice.

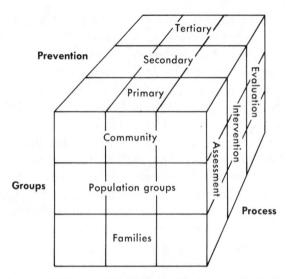

Fig. 3. Curriculum model for specialty preparation in community nursing practice.

The organizing framework for curriculum development is three-dimensional—groups, prevention, and process. The curriculum model is presented in Fig. 3.

This educational program has three components: (1) a common core that includes the sciences of public health and community health nursing, (2) an elective option, and (3) research. The sciences of public health that make up a part of the common core are biometrics, epidemiology, and theories for health programming. The community health nursing aspect of the core is community assessment, nursing intervention for groups, and program evaluation. The sciences of public health are an integral part of the community nursing content. Epidemiology as taught in our program is primarily analytical rather than descriptive. Therefore, the emphasis is on methods, rather than on disease, and on health problems as they are distributed in the population. Epidemiology and selected theories of social and behavioral sciences related to disease and illness prevention and nursing science are applied to the assessment of the community, intervention through nursing programs, and the evaluation of those programs.

For each of the nursing courses, a concurrent laboratory practice is required. During the laboratory practice, students have the opportunity to work in one community with professionals and consumers over 1 academic year. The nature of the practice permits students to work toward the solution of community health problems through experimentation. The specific health problems selected by the students for study may be identified by agency personnel, the student's assessment of the community, or a consumer group. The health problems selected for study must be placed in the framework of the community or population at risk and must be relevant to both the health needs and wants of the people. The expected outcome for the student is the design of a nursing intervention program that includes an evaluation plan. Throughout the laboratory practice, students are able to experiment with various aspects of the proposed nursing intervention program.

The elective option in the program is designed to provide in-depth study in a specific area of community health in relation to the student's career goal. The elective option has an underlying theme and is planned by the student in consultation with the faculty adviser. Laboratory practice is also a major part of the elective option. Thus far, we have identified several elective options available through the resources of the university and the communities with which we have an association. These options may be adult health, child health, epidemiology, family health, population planning, occupational health, international health, or primary care. The last two options require at least one additional quarter of study for most students in order to provide the essential laboratory practice.

The research component of our program is perceived as a crucial element, and perhaps this component will have the greatest impact for community health nursing. For some time now, our community health nursing practice has been carried out without an underlying data base. Practitioners entering into leadership positions must be prepared to generate practice-related research questions in order to establish a necessary data base. This research need requires continuous effort on the part of faculty to incorporate research aspects throughout the program.

As one begins to prepare community nurse practitioners, consideration must be given to the potential role for these persons in the service setting. We do not believe the service setting role has been defined, since roles are primarily developed out of expectations of others, and at present there are few indications that nurses are functioning or expected to function in the manner described. Furthermore, with the exception of infants, few agencies actively seek out the well person. More and more community health nursing agencies seek their cases through professional or self-referral that occurs after disease onset. Therefore, the faculty and service personnel must work together to bring about a change in current health programming if the fullest potential for prevention is to be achieved through nursing services.

Possibly the greatest potential for practice described for community nurse practitioners, at present, is in supervisory and administrative positions. However, if this is where community nurse practitioners will function, many of the current managerial responsibilities that supervisors and administrators hold must be assigned to other personnel, who might be designated assistant administrators or supervisors. Only then can the supervisor or administrator focus his or her attention and skill on: (1) the assessment of the community health needs, wants, and resources; (2) the planning for and implementation of nursing services in the community based on assessment; and (3) the continued evaluation of nursing service to communities or population groups based on health outcomes.

The educational institution must be prepared to help its graduates negotiate their community nurse practitioner role.

REFERENCES

Brown, W., and Birley, J. L.: Crisis and life changes and the onset of schizophrenia, J. Health Soc. Behav. **9:**203, 1968.

Cassel, J. C.: Planning for public health; the case for prevention. In Redesigning nursing education for public health, Bethesda, Md., 1973, U.S. Department of Health, Education, and Welfare.

Cassel, J. C., and Tyroler, H. A.: Epidemiology of cultural change, Arch. Environ. Health **3:**25, 1961.

Ciocco, A.: On the mortality in husbands and wives, Hum. Biol. **12:**509, 1940.

Downes, J.: Illness in the chronic disease family, Am. J. Public Health, **32:**591, 1942.

Hinkle, L., and others: Studies in human ecology; the distribution of sickness disability in a homogeneous group of healthy men, Am. J. Hyg. **64:**220, 1958.

Holmes, R. T., and others: Psychosocial and psychophysiological studies of tuberculosis, Psychosom. Med. **19:**134, 1957.

Jackson, E. F.: Status consistency and symptoms of stress, Am. Sociol. Rev. **27:**469, 1962.

Kaplan, B. H., and others: Occupational mobility and coronary heart disease, Arch. Intern. Med. **128:**938, 1971.

McGavern, E.: The promise of public health, Can. J. Public Health **50:**197, 1959.

National Commission for the Study of Nursing and Nursing Education: Distributive nursing practice, development and fusion of the roles, Rochester, N.Y., 1973, The Commission.

Nightingale, F.: Notes on nursing, what it is and what it is not, London, 1970, Gerald Duckworth and Co. Ltd.

Paffenbarger, R. S., and others: Trends in death rates from hypertensive disease in Memphis, Tennessee, 1920-1960, J. Chronic Dis. **19:**847, 1966.

Scott, J. M.: The changing health care environment; its implications for nursing, Am. J. Public Health **64:**364, 1974.

Shurtleff, D.: Mortality and marital status, Public Health Rep. **70:**248, 1955.

15 Changes in self-perception of nurse practitioners

stress, assertiveness, and sex role ideology

MICHAEL H. MILLER

The nurse practitioner role entails much more than the registered nurse's gaining of new nursing and medical skills; it requires a reorientation by the nurse to her career, her abilities, and herself as she assumes greater independence and responsibility (Malkemes, 1974). The term nurse practitioner refers to the ambulatory care nurse with "advanced skills in the assessment of the physical and psychosocial health-illness status of individuals, families or groups in a variety of settings through health and development history-taking and physical examination" (American Nurses' Association, 1975).

According to reference group theory (Merton and Kitt, 1950; Shibutani, 1967), the transition from registered nurse to nurse practitioner will result not only in an increase in the nurse's skills but also in modifications of her social and professional norms, attitudes, and values in accordance with her perception (real or imagined) of the role of the nurse practitioner. In other words, registered nurses who aspire to be nurse practitioners generally use that group as their frame of reference (Shibutani, 1967, p. 161), that is, as the group through which they perceive the world. Reference groups are important because people respond to situations as a result of their past, present, and future beliefs and experiences. Unless the nurse's perception of the nurse practitioner role is accurate, she may prepare herself, socially and psychologically, for a role that does not exist.

Mauksch (1975) writes that the nurse practitioner role requires accountability, risk taking, initiative, and collegiality beyond that normally exhibited by the registered nurse. Accordingly, successful training of nurse practitioners involves a resocialization of the students into the new role through either formal education (degree or nondegree) or continuing education. Students undergo a change in self-concept through the formal process by which they learn the beliefs, attitudes, and

The author is indebted to Nancy Elsenbrandt, Kathy Morgan, Beverly Burch, and Judy Eron for their assistance in this research. Thanks are also in order to Virginia George, Project Director of the Primex and Family Nurse Clinician Projects and Dean Sara Archer for their ideas and support. My appreciation is also extended to Kenneth A. Wallston, whose advice on an earlier draft of this chapter was invaluable.

165

values of the nurse practitioner role. Malkemes (1974, p. 90) writes: "If [nurse practitioners] are to behave differently, then basic changes in their nurse identity must take place." Moreover, the transition from the role of the registered nurse to that of nurse practitioner requires considerable personal and social changes that, according to Linn (1975), are accompanied by prevalent social, psychological, and physical stress among the nurse practitioner students involved in the transition.

There is a plethora of behavioral research documenting the existence of high levels of stress and anxiety among individuals who are directly affected by rapid social changes. It is believed that nurse practitioner students will exhibit abnormally high levels of personal stress and anxiety during their training for their new nursing roles. They undergo rapid role augmentation over a period of 1 year or less as they make the substantial transition from the traditional nursing role to a role for which no established role model exists. Moreover, nurse practitioner students cannot even be certain of the outcome of their training; in other words, there is ambiguity concerning the response their role will receive from other members of the health care team, particularly physicians. It is not unreasonable to expect that nurse practitioner students will report higher levels of anxiety and stress than employed registered nurses or nursing students pursuing a traditional registered nursing curriculum.

Nurse practitioners generally are faced with the dual burden of establishing a place in their setting for their new nursing role and developing viable relationships with their medical co-workers who are not aware of the nurse practitioner's functions. The difficulties encountered by nurse practitioners in their adjustment to their new role are compounded by the fact that they are primarily women and physicians are primarily men. Contrary to convention, nurse practitioners are capable of working as colleagues with physicians rather than as subordinates (that is, their traditional nursing role); however, physicians "are unaccustomed to collegial relationships with women." The traditional superior-inferior relationship of men to women pervades all of society, including the health care system (Brown, 1974, p. 110). This same point is echoed by Mauksch and Young (1974). They point out that the superordinate-subordinate relationship of physicians to nurses with concomitant dominance and submissiveness negatively sanctions interaction between the two groups. In the case of nurse practitioners, the conflict between physicians and nurses over professional control is particularly relevant because the two groups come into conflict "when nurses insist upon using their knowledge and competencies in mature and responsible decision-making" (Shetland, 1971, p. 1961).

To undertake such a difficult role change, it seems clear that nurse practitioner students will need to develop or expand certain personality characteristics as well as medical skills. Their self-confidence may need to be strengthened; their ability to be assertive should grow; and the extent to which they identify with a traditional "feminine" role (passive, yielding) may need altering so that they can comfortably act in ways that are considered "masculine" (assertive, self-reliant). The degree to which changes such as these are necessary will vary, of course, among individuals, depending on the degree to which they have already developed such qualities. However, the extent to which they fail to develop these qualities could be reflected in how much of the expanded role they actually fill. The new skills that students acquire in both the didactic and clinical phases of their training will hopefully increase their level of self-confidence, ego strength, and feeling of importance and will elevate their self-concept. Simultaneously, nurses in this role should undergo some neutralization of their female passivity (Linn, 1975, p. 18).

There is a scarcity of data regarding the degree to which nurse practitioner curricula alone provide necessary preparation for this role change. Accordingly, I initiated this study to determine what changes, if any, were occurring in the student enrolled in Vanderbilt University School of Nursing's two nurse practitioner programs.

In light of the information presented (some better supported than others) on changes in stress, assertiveness, and sex-role ideology of nurse practitioners, three questions were formulated to guide our investigation: (1) Are nurse practitioner students assertive, under great stress, profeminist, and masculine oriented? (2) Do nurse practitioner students, as a result of their primary care training, become over time more assertive, more profeminist, and more masculine oriented? (3) Does the stress associated with the innovative, nontraditional role of the nurse practitioner decrease as the nurse practitioner students proceed through their training and into practice?

METHODOLOGY
Instruments

Assertiveness was measured by the Rathus Assertiveness Scale (Rathus, 1973), a self-reporting, 30-item inventory for assessing assertive behavior. The items tap self-perceived outspokenness, aggressiveness, social boldness or assertiveness, and confidence in various social and interpersonal situations. Each item has six response alternatives, ranging from "very characteristic of me, extremely descriptive of me," to "very uncharacteristic of me, extremely nondescriptive."

The Spielberger State-Trait Anxiety Scale (Spielberger, 1966) was employed to measure the nurse's level of stress. This instrument is designed to measure two distinctive anxiety or stress concepts: trait and state anxiety. The state subscale measures how the respondent feels at the particular time she is completing the questionnaire; the trait subscale measures how the respondent generally feels. Thus state stress is conceptualized as a transitory emotional condition that varies in intensity and fluctuates over time. Trait stress or anxiety, on the other hand, measures variations "among people in the disposition or tendence to perceive a wide range of situations as threatening and to respond to these situations with differential elevations" in anxiety (Spielberger, 1975, p. 137).

The amount of agreement or disagreement that an individual has with societal attitudes toward the role of women was measured by the Spence-Helmreich Attitude Toward Women Scale (Spence and others, 1973). The version of the scale used in this research included 25 statements* pertaining to the roles and rights of women in such areas as etiquette, sexual behavior, marital relationships, and educational, intellectual, and occupational activities. Each statement had four response choices, ranging from "agree strongly" to "disagree strongly." Responses are scored from 0 to 3, with 0 representing the most traditional response and 3 the most contemporary, profeminist response.

The Bem Sex Role Inventory (Bem, 1974, 1975) was included in this research in order to measure the extent to which an individual identifies with a male role, a female role, or an "androgynous" role. This inventory contains both a masculinity and femininity scale, each of which includes 20 personality characteristics selected on the basis of sex-typed social desirability. Examples of traits characterized as masculine include: self-reliant, aggressive, competitive, and athletic. Feminine personality characteristics include: yielding, compassionate, warm, and gentle. Respondents receive an "androgyne score" that characterizes them as masculine, feminine, or androgynous, based on the difference between their endorsement of masculine and feminine personality characteristics. A person is sex typed either feminine, with a high positive score, masculine, with a high negative score, or androgyne, with a score that approaches zero.

Sample

Responses from 25 nurse practitioner students (15 family nurse clinician students [F.N.C.] and 10 family nurse practitioner students [F.N.P.]) and 39 controls (23 senior baccalaureate nursing students and 16 hospital staff nurses†) are reported in this chapter. The nurse practitioner sample includes both F.N.P.s and and F.N.C.s for several reasons. Both are primary care roles; students in both groups undergo a similar role change; the length of their curriculum is identical; and the content of their course work is similar. The basic difference between the two programs is that the F.N.C. program is a graduate program leading to a master's degree (M.S.N.) while the F.N.P. program is a continuing education program for registered nurses.‡ The nurse practitioner students began their programs at Vanderbilt University School of Nursing in September 1974.

The controls volunteered to participate in a study of attitudes about nursing conducted by the School of Nursing. The baccalaureate nursing students were chosen in order to provide data on changes that a traditional group of senior nursing students go through during the academic school year. It was anticipated that these students would undergo some role changes as a result of their curriculum, but not to the same extent as students undertaking an expanded role.

---

*The longer version of this scale was not used, because the respondents had to complete four other questionnaires. Moreover, the short version correlates highly (0.95) with the long version (Spence and others, 1973).
†Twenty-five persons were included in the original testing of each of these two groups; however, through attrition only 39 controls were available after 9 months for the second testing.
‡The exception to this last point is that 3 of the 10 family nurse practitioner students were senior baccalaureate nursing students who were taking this program as an elective.

The second control group consisted of Vanderbilt University Hospital staff nurses who were chosen (from the volunteers) to approximate the training, age, and experience of the nurse practitioner students. The data from this group were used as a control for changes that nurses might be going through over the same period of time without the stimulus of a curriculum. This group would also be the control for any changes that might occur as a result of the influence of larger societal changes, particularly in respect to the roles of women.

Table 10 provides a comparison between the nurse practitioners and the control group for selected demographic variables. Clearly, the two groups were quite similar; approximately half of each group was single; the median age of the nurse practitioner students was 27.5 years compared with 25.4 years for the control group; both had about 4 years of work experience as registered nurses; and all the respondents, except one male nurse practitioner student, were female.

Table 11 shows that the study group, composed of F.N.C. and F.N.P. students, had considerable demographic intragroup similarity. Conversely, the senior nursing students and the hospital nurses, who together constituted the control group, had several demographic differences. These differences were: More of the senior nursing students than the hospital nurses were single (87% to 25%); the hospital nurses were, on the average, older than the senior nursing students (26.4 years to 23.1 years); and the hospital nurses had more years of nursing work-experience than the senior nursing students (4.5 years to 1.7 years).

Procedure

Both the experimental and control groups were given the four scales described above. The experimental group completed the instruments five times over an 18-month period. The first administration was in September 1974, at the beginning of the nurse practitioner programs; the second was in January 1975, at the midpoint in the didactic phase of the curriculum; the third was in May 1975, at the end of the didactic phase of the curriculum; the fourth was in August 1975, at the end of the preceptorships; and the final administration was in February 1976,

Table 10. Selected demographic characteristics of nurse practitioner students and control group

Demographic characteristics	Nurse practitioner students	Control group
Marital status		
Single	52% (13)	57% (24)
Married	41% (11)	33% (13)
Divorced, widowed, and so forth	7% (1)	5% (2)
Median age (years)	27.5	25.4
Mean years experience as registered nurse	4.1	3.7
Sex		
Female	96% (24)	100% (39)
Male	4% (1)	

Table 11. Selected demographic characteristics for the family nurse clinician and family nurse practitioner students (study group) and senior baccalaureate nursing students and hospital staff nurses (control group)

Demographic characteristics	Study group		Control group	
	F.N.C. (15)	F.N.P. (10)	Senior nursing students (23)	Hospital staff nurses (16)
Marital status				
Single	47%	60%	87%	25%
Married	47%	40%	13%	63%
Divorced	6%	—	—	12%
Median age (years)	26.5	29.1	23.1	26.4
Mean years experience as registered nurse	4.9	3.7	1.7	4.5
Sex				
Female	93%	100%	100%	100%
Male	7%	—	—	—

after the graduates had been employed for 6 months. The control group, on the other hand, was given the four instruments only twice: in September 1974 and in May 1975. The control group was tested only twice because of our interest in controlling for the impact of the curriculum on the experimental groups. In retrospect, we recognize this as problematic, because it reduces our certainty regarding the significance of the responses of the study group for its third, fourth, and fifth testings.

Question 1

- Are nurse practitioner students assertive, under great stress, profeminist, and masculine oriented?

Table 12 shows significant differences between the study and control groups,* but only for stress attitude toward women. The nurse practitioner students exhibited a significantly higher mean level of stress than the controls on the Speilberger scale for state (39.36 to 33.92) and trait (37.04 to 34.44) stress. On the Spence-Helmreich Attitude Toward Women Scale, the nurse practitioner students' mean score was significantly higher (and thus more profeminist) than the control group (61.72 to 54.05). Interestingly, the mean score of both groups was highly profeminist since the highest (and most profeminist) score is 75.00.

No significant differences were found between the study and control groups for assertiveness and androgyny. Both the nurse practitioner students' and the control group's mean assertiveness scores of 15.90 and 12.49, respectively, were in the neutral range since the least assertive score is −90 and the most assertive score

---

*No significant differences were found between the two separate groups that constituted the controls on this or any of the subsequent testing.

Table 12. Mean scores of nurse practitioners and control group on attitude and perception scales by time of testing*

	Sept. 1974	Jan. 1975	May 1975	Aug. 1975	Feb. 1976
Rathus Assertiveness Scale					
Nurse practitioners (25)	15.90	17.72	19.67†	20.03	30.67‡
Controls (39)	12.49	—	11.84	—	—
Speilberger (State)					
Nurse practitioners (25)	39.36†	38.26	38.73	33.94‡	29.01‡
Controls (39)	33.92	—	34.85	—	—
Speilberger (Trait)					
Nurse practitioners (25)	37.04†	36.17	33.88‡	32.87‡	28.67‡
Controls (39)	34.44	—	32.87	—	—
Bem Sex Role Inventory					
Nurse practitioners (25)	0.25	0.20	0.05‡	−0.03‡	−0.16‡
Controls (39)	0.18	—	0.15	—	—
Spence-Helmreich Attitude					
Toward Women Scale					
Nurse practitioners (25)	61.72†	62.43	63.85†	64.38	65.36
Controls (39)	54.05	—	54.69	—	—

*The controls were only tested twice: September 1974 and May 1975.
†Indicates a significant difference of $p < 0.05$ using the t test between the nurse practitioner students and the control group on this testing.
‡Shows significant difference at the 0.01 level using Newman Keuls between this testing and the first testing.

is +90. The mean scores of the study and control groups on the Bem Sex Role Inventory indicated the existence of androgynous personality characteristics (0.25 and 0.18). In other words, their personalities were not dominated by either masculine or feminine characteristics.

Question 2

■ Do nurse practitioner students, as a result of their expanded role training, become over time more assertive, more profeminist, and more masculine oriented?

Table 12 shows that the control group showed no significant changes in their mean scores on the Rathus Assertiveness Scale, the Bem Sex Role Inventory, or the Spence-Helmreich Attitude Toward Women Scale. The nurse practitioner students, on the other hand, became significantly more assertive and masculine oriented.* The nurse practitioner students did not, however, experience any significant alteration in profeminism (Spence-Helmreich Attitude Toward Women Scale).

---

*Although the nurse practitioner students describe themselves as significantly more masculine after their preceptorships (mean, —0.03) than at the beginning of their program, the level at which they are responding is, according to Bem's (1974) normative standards, in the neutral or androgynous range rather than at the masculine level. In other words, because the mean scores are ≥ 1.0 and ≥ -1.0, they represent a state of androgyny. If they were > 2.025 or < -2.025, we could classify them as feminine or masculine. However, Bem does indicate that these cut-off points need not be rigidly adhered to under all conditions.

The data show that the first significant change in androgyny (less femininity) occurred by the end of the didactic phase of the students' training. They continued to become even less feminine and more masculine through their preceptorship and into the first 6 months of their employment. The nurse practitioner students became significantly more assertive only after having been employed for 6 months. Before this point they showed a gradual increase in assertiveness, but the largest jump occurred after their primary care role training was completed. Finally, the nurse practitioner students were found to be significantly more assertive than the controls by the completion of the nurse practitioner students' didactic phase. As was the case at the first testing on the Spence-Helmreich Attitude Toward Women Scale, the nurse practitioner students were significantly more profeminist than the controls after 9 months of didactic training.

Question 3

■ Does the stress associated with the innovative, nontraditional role of the nurse practitioner decrease as the nurse practitioner students proceed through their training and into practice?

Table 12 shows that stress, both state and trait, was significantly higher at the beginning of the nurse practitioners' training and that it decreased significantly through the completion of their didactic phase (trait), the conclusion of their preceptorship, and after 6 months of employment. The control group's stress was significantly lower than that of the nurse practitioner students at the beginning of the study; their stress level remained constant through the second testing.

DISCUSSION AND CONCLUSION

The data from the 25 nurse practitioner students and the 39 controls, whose responses formed the basis of this research, answer only in part the three questions formulated. The findings of this research compel a reevaluation of the initial assumptions on which the questions addressed here are based.

It generally has been assumed that nurse practitioner students must belong to a special breed of nurse to want to pursue a new, innovative nursing role. That is, students entering a nurse practitioner program will be more aggressive, more profeminine, and under more stress than persons not embarking upon such an educational experience. It also has been assumed that because of the new nursing demands of the nurse practitioner role, nurse practitioner students will undergo various attitudinal and behavioral changes through both their educational training and their employment as nurse practitioners. Finally, it has been assumed that the new nursing theories and skills taught during the didactic phase of nurse practitioner training will increase student stress; however, after the students have had an opportunity to use their new skills and become comfortable in their use, student stress will decrease.

Specifically, the data only agree in part with the question based on the first assumption. The nurse practitioner students were significantly different from hospital staff nurses and senior baccalaureate nursing students only as far as stress and attitudes positive to women's rights and roles; they were not, however, significantly more assertive or more masculine oriented. This finding is relevant to Malkemes' (1974) contention that nurse practitioner students must undergo some basic changes in self-concept during the course of their training if any fundamental alterations are to occur in their nursing identity. Surely assertiveness and such masculine traits as self-reliance, aggressiveness, and competitiveness are linked with the nurse practitioner role, where greater independence of action (compared with the role of the registered nurse) is required if the functions of the nurse practitioner role are to be fulfilled.

Substantial data are presented in this chapter in support of most of the assumptions that underlie Question 2. The nurse practitioner students did become more assertive and more masculine oriented over the 18-month period of the study. However, curriculum does not appear to have had much immediate impact upon assertiveness, since the first significant increase was found only after the nurse practitioner students had been employed for 6 months. In other words, the nurse practitioner students' level of assertiveness was found to have increased significantly after they had been practicing in their new role for a period of 6 months. In regard to androgynous behavior, the nurse practitioner students first exhibited a significantly more masculine orientation at the completion of their didactic training. Beyond this point, the nurse practitioner students continued to show even higher masculine scores in their responses. Thus Linn's (1975) contention that nurse practitioners actually experience an alteration in androgyny (that is, from female passivity to male aggressiveness) appears to be supported by these findings. Nonetheless, the nurse practitioner did not show any significant change in their attitudes toward women. Although they were significantly more profeminist than the control group, their training and subsequent practice did not result in any significant alteration in their perspective about women. This lack of significant change may be due in part to the nurse practitioner students' initial high level of profeminism. For them to have become significantly more profeminist, they would have had to respond profeminist on at least 23 of the 25 items of the Spence-Helmreich Attitude Toward Women Scale.

The data relating to Question 3 suggest a basic weakness in the assumption that nurse practitioner students' level of stress would increase during the didactic phase of their training (Linn, 1975). The data in this study clearly contradict this contention. The nurse practitioner students studied showed no significant change in their level of stress until the end of their didactic phase (trait stress); by the conclusion of the preceptorship, both state and trait stress had declined significantly, and both continued to decline through 6 months of employment. It appears that either the nurse practitioner students in this study were prepared for the stress associated with a new nursing role and thus able to keep their anxiety level under check, or the faculty of the nurse practitioner programs were cognizant of the existence of stress among their students and, accordingly, were able to help the students contain it. The second alternative would appear to be most likely. The faculty, having had considerable experience with nurse practitioner students' anxiety and stress, has routinely employed various stress-reducing programs (such as rap sessions and conferences) to deal with stress and anxiety.

The above findings seem to indicate that the didactic phase of the nurse practitioner program has less impact upon behavioral and attitudinal changes among nurse practitioner students than does the students' actual working in the nurse practitioner role (either in a preceptorship situation or as fully employed nurse practitioner). Apparently, the nurse practitioner student must first work as a nurse practitioner before becoming cognizant that the new role actually requires assertiveness, self-reliance, aggressiveness, and competitiveness. Moreover, the stress generally associated with training of nurse practitioners need not occur if the faculty is able and willing to deal effectively with it.

The nurse practitioner students experienced significantly more stress and were significantly more profeminist than the control group; over the 18 months of this study, the nurse practitioner students became significantly more assertive, more masculine oriented, and exhibited a significant decline in their level of stress.

REFERENCES

American Nurses' Association: Pediatric nurse practitioners; the practice today, Kansas City, 1975, The Association.

Bem, S. L.: The measurement of psychological androgyny, J. Consult. Clin. Psychol. 42(2):155, 1974.

Bem, S. L.: Sex role adaptability; one consequence of psychological androgyny, J. Pers. Soc. Psychol. 31(4):634, 1975.

Brown, K. C.: The nurse practitioner in a private group practice, Nurs. Outlook 22:110, Feb. 1974.

Linn, L. S.: Primex trainees under stress, J. Nurs. Educ. 14:10, April 1975.

Malkemes, L. C.: Resocialization; a model for nurse practitioner preparation, Nurs. Outlook 22:90, Feb. 1974.

Mauksch, I. G.: Nursing is coming of age; through the practitioner movement, Am. J. Nurs. 75:1834, Oct. 1975.

Mauksch, I. G., and Young, P. R.: Nurse-physician interaction in a family medical care center, Nurs. Outlook 22:114, Feb. 1974.

Merton, R. K., and Kitt, A.: Contributions to the theory of reference group behavior. In Merton, R. K., and Lazarsfeld, P. F., editors: Studies in the scope and method of

The American soldier, Glencoe, Ill., 1950, The Free Press, pp. 42-53.

Rathus, S. A.: A 30-item schedule for assessing assertive behavior, Behav. Ther. 4:398, 1973.

Shetland, M. L.: An approach to role expansion; the elaborate network, Am. J. Public Health 61:1961, Oct. 1971.

Shibutani, T.: Reference groups as perspectives. In Manis, J. G., and Meltzer, B. N., editors: Symbolic interaction; a reader in social psychology, Boston, 1967, Allyn & Bacon, Inc., pp. 159-170.

Spence, J. T., Helmreich, R., and Stapp, J.: A short version of the attitudes toward women scale (A.W.S.), Bull. Psychol. Sociol. 2(4):219, 1973.

Spielberger, C. D.: The effects of anxiety on complex learning and academic achievement. In Spielberger, C. D., editor: Anxiety and behavior, New York, 1966, Academic Press, Inc.

Spielberger, C. D.: Anxiety; state-trait process. In Spielberger, C. D., and Sarason, I. G., editors: Stress and anxiety, vol. 1, Washington, D.C., 1975, Hemisphere Publishing Corporation, pp. 115-144.